THE

American Heritage

Series

UNDER THE GENERAL EDITORSHIP OF

LEONARD W. LEVY AND ALFRED YOUNG

The English Libertarian Heritage

From the Writings of

JOHN TRENCHARD AND THOMAS GORDON

in *The Independent Whig* and *Cato's Letters*

EDITED BY

DAVID L. JACOBSON

University of California, Davis

THE BOBBS-MERRILL COMPANY, INC.

A Subsidiary of Howard W. Sams & Co., Inc.

PUBLISHERS • INDIANAPOLIS • NEW YORK • KANSAS CITY

The English Libertarian Heritage

THE AMERICAN HERITAGE SERIES

Foreword

In the past decade or so there has been a rediscovery of the works of John Trenchard and Thomas Gordon, authors of *The Independent Whig* and *Cato's Letters: Essays on Liberty, Civil and Religious*. Excepting rare and fugitive references to these books, they had been not only neglected by scholars of American history; they had been unread, even by specialists in the history of American political and constitutional theory, intellectual history, or the history of the colonial and Revolutionary periods. Their unavailability, until now, except in a few of the oldest and largest libraries, may account in part for the shroud of oblivion that cloaked our knowledge of these stanch advocates of constitutional government and personal freedom.

"Cato," remarked an anonymous English contemporary, in his *Historical View of the Political Writers of Great Britain* (1740), was a "Man of severe Principles with regard to Liberty . . . the only Man in his Time who on political Subjects wrote what he thought, and wrote it for no other Reason but because he thought it, and that it would be of Service to his Country to know it. These Letters however had a great Character by their being more free from Party-Zeal and Personal Reflections than any other publick Writing that ever appeared." The writings on political theory by the great John Locke were pre-eminent, of course, and the basis too of much of Trenchard and Gordon. But the common people or newspaper public did not read formal political theory. Trenchard and Gordon, who were political journalists, popularized Locke and radical Whig ideas for readers on both sides of the Atlantic.

Clinton Rossiter probably deserves credit for the recent rediscovery of Trenchard and Gordon. In a striking display of scholarly one-man-upmanship, he commented, in his *Seedtime of the Republic* (1953), "No man can spend any time in the newspapers, library inventories, and pamphlets of colonial America without realizing that *Cato's Letters* rather than Locke's *Civil Government* was the most popular, quotable, esteemed source of political ideas in the colonial period." Professor Rossiter was right, and Professor Jacobson musters the evidence of proof.

American newspapers of the eighteenth century, composed as much with scissors and pastepot as with the pen, conscripted Trenchard and Gordon for a variety of American causes. Pirated essays from *The Independent Whig* served in the battles fought by rationalists, dissenters, and anticlericals in every phase of the struggle for religious liberty. As late as 1817 Connecticut republicans used it as a battering-ram against the crumbling alliance of church and state. As early as 1721, shortly after their initial publication in London, several of Cato's essays on political liberty were republished in the *New-England Courant*. When its editor was imprisoned a year later for criticizing the local authorities, his young brother, Ben Franklin, ran one of Cato's letters on freedom of the press. Cato gained American popularity during the time of the Zenger prosecution; by the time of the American Revolution, reliance on him was commonplace. In 1771, when the American constitutional position was being sharpened, his letters, according to a Boston newspaper, *The Massachusetts Spy*, were "now busily parceling out in almost every essay with which of late we are pretty plentifully served up; and Cato I assure you, Sir, gives us a shocking image of despotism."

The reasons for the appeal of Trenchard and Gordon to Americans of the eighteenth century are explained by Professor Jacobson. His judicious abridgment of *The Independent Whig* and *Cato's Letters* makes conveniently available to scholars and students, for the first time, these sources of great influence on American thought during its formative period. This is not only the first American edition of *Cato's Letters* ever published in book form; it is the first reprinting on either side of the Atlantic since 1755. If the neglect of Trenchard and Gordon is at all attributable to the fact that copies of their writings have been exceptionally rare, the deficiency has at last been remedied in this service to scholarship by Professor Jacobson.

This book is part of a series whose aim is to provide the essential primary sources of the American experience, especially of American thought, from the colonial period to the present. The series when completed will constitute a documentary library of our history. Many of these volumes will fill a need among scholars, students, libraries, and even general readers for authoritative collections of original materials that illuminate the thought of significant individuals, such as James Madison or Louis Brandeis; or of groups, such as Puritan political theorists or American Catholic leaders on social policy; or of movements, such as the Antifederalists or the Populists. There are a surprising number of subjects traditionally studied in American history for which there are no documentary anthologies. This series will be by far the most comprehensive and authoritative of its kind. It will also have the distinction of presenting representative pieces of substantial length, which have not been butchered into snippets and snatches.

Leonard W. Levy

Alfred Young

Contents

The Independent Whig

Cato's Letters

Introduction

Late in his life, John Adams reflected upon the events preceding American Independence and wrote that in the early
1770's "Cato's Letters and the Independent Whig, and all the
writings of Trenchard and Gordon, Mrs. Macaulay's History,
Burgh's Political Disquisitions, Clarendon's History . . . all the
writings relative to the revolutions in England became fashionable reading."[1] The importance attributed to the work of the
two Englishmen, John Trenchard and Thomas Gordon, by
John Adams has been recently affirmed by the American historian, Clinton Rossiter: "No one can spend any time in the
newspapers, library inventories, and pamphlets of colonial
America without realizing that *Cato's Letters* rather than
Locke's *Civil Government* was the most popular, quotable,
esteemed source of political ideas in the colonial period."[2] To
these comments of John Adams and Clinton Rossiter only two
qualifications need be added. The 1770's did not mark the
beginning of the popularity of the writings of Trenchard and
Gordon; these works had been well known for half a century
before the American decision for Independence. And secondly,
the general respect accorded to *Cato's Letters* was matched by
the popular esteem for Trenchard and Gordon's other great

---

[1] John Adams to Dr. J. Morse, January 5, 1816, in *The Life and Works
of John Adams,* ed. Charles Francis Adams (Boston: Little, Brown, 1850–
1856), X, 202.

[2] Clinton Rossiter, *Seedtime of the Republic* (New York: Harcourt,
Brace, 1953), p. 141.

work, *The Independent Whig*, with its vigorous anti-Catholicism and anticlericalism. In short, Adams, Rossiter, and a great part of the eighteenth-century American public could agree on the general significance of the "Divine English Cato" and "The Independent Whig"; to a large, if not precisely measurable extent, John Trenchard and Thomas Gordon helped shape political thought and institutions in the thirteen colonies.

The transmission of the radical Whiggery of Trenchard and Gordon from the home country to America followed a natural and relatively easy path. *The Independent Whig* and *Cato's Letters* were written in a period of political confusion, when the ideals of Whiggery, the Revolution of 1688-1689, and the new Hanoverian dynasty still had to be defended against the remnants of old-style Toryism, a variety of Jacobite conspiracies, and the claims of High-Churchmen. Trenchard and Gordon wrote expressly to justify the Glorious Revolution and to reject such doctrines as passive obedience to tyrannical government or the divine right of hereditary monarchs. To a limited extent, they wished to go beyond the accomplishments of the preceding decades, to increase toleration for and to extend greater rights to Protestant dissenters. But with a few such exceptions, they were happy with a Revolution which had already occurred but whose benefits seemed not yet to be fully secured against internal and external dangers. To a degree equaling that of the English population of the early eighteenth century, the American colonists accepted and enshrined a legend of 1688-1689 and even of their own supposed part in overthrowing Stuart tyranny. Thus, the old-style Tory was even less frequently found in the New than in the Old World, and Americans all could glory in their Whiggery and accept the statements and ideals of its English spokesmen. And they could apply the doctrines of Trenchard and Gordon in their own ways to new situations throughout the eighteenth century. In the anticlerical arguments of *The Independent Whig*, the colonists could find reasonings to resist the spread of the

Anglican Establishment or the imposition of bishops. In "Cato's" praise of tyrannicide and justification of resistance to the usurpation of power, they could find rationales for their own continuing opposition to British authority. From Trenchard and Gordon's attacks upon the doctrine of divine right might be drawn arguments finally for rejecting the authority of George III. The after-the-fact defense of one revolution thus easily provided arguments in support of another and later revolution by a people who, in 1776, believed they had kept the Whig tradition purer than the old country and that they were, to a large extent, simply maintaining and continuing that heritage of ideals and liberties.

I. THE CAREERS OF JOHN TRENCHARD

AND THOMAS GORDON

Of the two authors, John Trenchard was originally the more important contributor of ideas and arguments. And he was personally the more prominent and distinguished.[3] He came from a good and locally respected family: his father was a distant relation of Sir John Trenchard, a secretary of state under William III, and his mother, the daughter of a Sir George Norton. He received an appropriate education at Trinity Col-

---

[3] Scattered biographical information on John Trenchard may be found in John Burke, *History of the Commoners of Great Britain and Ireland* (London: H. Colbourn, 1833–1838), IV, 79; *Biographia Britannica* (London: W. Innys, 1766), VI, part 2, Supplement, 175–177; *Dictionary of National Biography* (Oxford: Oxford University Press, 1921–1922), XIX, 1125–1126; and in Gordon's "Prefaces" to later editions of their joint works.

lege, Dublin, attended the Inns of Court, and briefly entered upon the barrister's profession. A profitable opportunity to serve as a commissioner of forfeited estates in Ireland interrupted his legal career in 1690. Shortly thereafter he inherited an uncle's estate and then married Anne, daughter of Sir William Blackett. The net result of these events was to place him in what one biographer aptly terms "easy circumstances." And additional large properties were to become his after his father's death and through an inheritance from his mother's family. He became prominent enough so that, late in his career, he was to serve briefly in the House of Commons, though apparently without greatly distinguishing himself. He was, in short, a man of fair birth, good education, considerable wealth, and some small political importance.

Much less definite information is available concerning the early life of Thomas Gordon.[4] The date of his birth cannot be determined. He may have attended a Scottish university, but probably he did not do so. Although a Thomas Gordon was at King's College in 1713 and a Thomas Gordon submitted a law thesis at Edinburgh in 1716, there is no clear indication that either of these names refers to activities of the future pamphleteer. And there is some evidence that in the period from about 1713, the Thomas Gordon of this narrative was living in England in Wiltshire. Probably late in 1718 he moved to London and there, according to all accounts, survived by teaching languages. Whatever his earlier politics, about which later slander was directed at him, he now firmly committed himself to the Whig cause. In the latter part of the second decade of the eighteenth century, he began his long literary career.

[4] The primary sources for information on Gordon are the *Dictionary of National Biography*, VIII, 230, and J. M. Bulloch, "Thomas Gordon, The Independent Whig," University of Aberdeen Library *Bulletin*, III (1918), 598–612, 733–749. The Bulloch bibliography contains some errors in the dating of Gordon's works. For a few personal letters from Gordon, see *Eighth Report of the Royal Commission on Historical Manuscripts* (London: Her Majesty's Stationery Office, 1881), Appendix I, 314–315.

Well before meeting each other, Trenchard and Gordon each embarked upon journalistic activities. Trenchard, much the older of the two, contributed to the controversy over a standing army in the 1690's and was continuingly interested in this topic. In 1697 and again in 1698 he vigorously attacked plans for increasing the regular size of English forces and for garrisoning Continental mercenaries in England itself.[5] A decade later he wrote *The Natural History of Superstition,* a work which appeared anonymously in 1709. Gordon's first literary ventures were more lighthearted. In 1718 he wrote *A Dedication to a Great Man Concerning Dedications* and followed this with a series of ironic essays, issued singly and then published together as *The Humorist* in 1720 and dedicated appropriately enough to "the Man in the Moon." Gordon then turned to the more serious task of stating his position on the developing "Bangorian" controversy which erupted in 1717 over the statements of Benjamin Hoadly, then Bishop of Bangor.

The Bangorian Controversy

The Bangorian dispute was doubly important for Thomas Gordon: his contributions revealed that determined anticlericalism that marked his later works, and his pamphlets first brought him to the attention of John Trenchard and thus led to the celebrated collaboration of the two writers. Moreover, the dispute suggested some of the complexities of the religious and political questions on which *The Independent Whig* and *Cato's Letters* later focused their attention. The Bangorian controversy developed largely around two works of Benjamin Hoadly: his *Preservative Against the Principles and Practices of the Nonjurors* (1716) and a sermon on the "Nature of the

---

[5] John Trenchard and Walter Moyle, *An Argument Showing . . . a Standing Army Inconsistent with a Free Government* (London, 1697) and John Trenchard, *A Short History of Standing Armies in England* (London: A. Baldwin, 1698).

Kingdom of Christ" delivered before the royal family on March 31, 1717.[6] The place of the delivery of this latter work indicated Hoadly's strength and general position. Yet in succeeding months and years, at least two hundred works appeared in criticism or in support of the views of this sometime Bishop of Bangor. And very promptly after the appearance of Hoadly's sermon, the Lower House of Convocation of the clergy, assembled at Canterbury, received and put on record a committee report that was highly critical of his extreme latitudinarian views. Where the Bishop had condemned the exercise of church authority over the individual's conscience, the Lower House of Convocation pointedly defended the church's power and the right of the state to enforce conformity. Given the high Tory views of many of Hoadly's detractors and his own defenses of the Hanoverian succession, the Bishop had a position that was politically unimpeachable. The Convocation was prorogued by royal order, lest the Upper House join in the attack on Hoadly. And in succeeding years the Bishop of Bangor, who, incidentally, never visited that diocese during his tenure, successively advanced to more lucrative and eminent positions.

The issues of the Bangorian controversy naturally attracted the attention of both Gordon and Trenchard. Gordon's several pamphlets were in his typical early ironic style. Thus, he wrote *A Modest Apology for Parson Alberoni,* the Cardinal Alberoni who was the chief minister of Spain's King Philip V in 1717, and subtitled it "a short but unanswerable Defence of Priestcraft." Or in his *Apology for the Danger of the Church,* Gordon offered a long series of defenses of the High-Churchman along such lines as "A plain Proof that Laymen may lawfully commit Sin, if they will pay for it, and kneel for Pardon to the

---

[6] Benjamin Hoadly, *A Preservative Against the Principles and Practices of the Nonjurors both in Church and State* (London: Knapton and Childe, 1716) and *A Sermon on the Nature of the Kingdom of Christ* (London: Knapton, 1717).

Clergy."[7] By and large, these works of Gordon on the Bangorian affair did not include any notable or eloquent statements of
his own ideals. Rather, they were bitterly polemical, addressed
to the issues of the moment, direct and sarcastic attacks upon
High-Churchmen, upon clerical pretensions to wisdom or
power, and against political Jacobitism. In a positive way, they
included only a few statements of praise for Hoadly and in
support of toleration and latitudinarianism. Yet their style and
their decidedly Whiggish point of view attracted the attention
of John Trenchard and brought the two men together as
coauthors.

The Independent Whig

In 1719, at the Grecian Coffee House in Devereux Court,
London, Trenchard and Gordon met and joined their efforts.
Their first product was probably *The Character of an Independent Whig*.[8] It was a forthright statement of their general
position: their anticlericalism, their fear of standing armies, and
their pleas for the rights of Protestant dissenters. The theme
most emphasized was the last: the need for a fuller recognition
of the contributions of all Protestants to the continuing success
of the Whig traditions and patterns of government. *The Character* ends with the notice of a forthcoming pamphlet on "the
Affair of a Northern War." That work finally appeared in a
somewhat different form than promised as *Considerations
Offered Upon the Approaching Peace*. It was a demand that the
ministry *not* relinquish Gibraltar to Spain as part of a general

---

[7] *A Modest Apology for Parson Alberoni* (London: J. Roberts, 1717)
and *An Apology for the Danger of the Church* (London: J. Roberts, 1719).

[8] Bulloch, "Thomas Gordon," *loc. cit.*, p. 605, and some other writers assume the existence of an "Independent Whig" prior to *The Character* and
the *Considerations*. *The Character*, p. 31, includes the promise of a sequel;
Considerations notes the existence of a preceding pamphlet containing such
a promise. Thus, it seems certain that *The Character* was the first part of
that series by the "Independent Whig" of which *Considerations* was labeled "the second part."

European peace settlement. More important than its specific argument was the statement that the *Independent Whig* would now begin to appear regularly "in a Half Sheet," each Wednesday, beginning January 20, 1720. The first works by the "Independent Whig" had obviously been successful enough to warrant such a continuing collaboration.

Through the succeeding year, *The Independent Whig* appeared weekly. Its style was always vigorous, but it was at least slightly less bitter and more ably argued than some of Gordon's own earlier works. And as its style seemed to owe much to Trenchard's tempering of the words of his coauthor, so its contents owed much to his thinking. He took Gordon on at first as a kind of junior partner, even, according to some accounts, simply as an amanuensis. And, according to Gordon's own words, he was greatly affected by Trenchard's "strong way of thinking." But gradually Gordon began to play a more important and individual role. When *The Independent Whig* discontinued with its fifty-third number on December 31, 1720, Gordon had written twenty-two parts, Trenchard eighteen, the two collaborators jointly three, and an unidentified "C" (perhaps Anthony Collins) the remaining ten.[9] Gordon's earlier contributions in the Bangorian controversy, his own strong bias against the pretensions of the High-Churchmen, his gradual emergence as a full, or perhaps even dominant, partner with Trenchard, account for his public image as "The Independent Whig."

Cato's Letters

The concern of the authors of *The Independent Whig* was largely with problems of religion, particularly of church-state

---

[9] Anthony Collins (1676–1729) was a friend and disciple of John Locke and a well-known deistic writer. He used an advanced form of historical criticism in his religious arguments. His principal publications include *Priestcraft in Perfection* (1709), *Discourse on Free Thinking* (1713), and his celebrated (or notorious) *Discourse on Grounds and Reasons of the Christian Religion* (1724).

relationships, the role of the clergy, the problems of dissenters, and so on. But Trenchard and Gordon's interests were far broader. And to give expression to their more general views and perhaps to reach a larger audience through the regular weekly press, they began, in the latter part of 1720, their remarkable series of letters in *The London Journal* over the signature of "Cato." The authors aptly chose this signature both as an expression of their interest in the lessons of the history of the later Roman republic and as an indication of their devotion to the virtues and notions of liberty associated with the name of the "Great Cato," the opponent of Julius Caesar and uncle of the latter's chief assassin, Marcus Brutus.[10] Although the letters from "Cato" began with questions of immediate concern such as the fate of Gibraltar or the South Sea Bubble, they rapidly passed on to such broad issues as the nature of virtue, the values of liberty, and the justice of tyrannicide. By the end of the long series, Trenchard and Gordon had amply justified the subtitle used in some later editions of their work; the *Letters* were *Essays on Liberty, Civil and Religious, and Other Important Subjects.* The principal issues examined by the *Letters* included the following: the South Sea Scheme and the public corruption it involved (at least thirteen numbers), tyranny and other evils of government (fifteen essays), the wonders of liberty and its products (fourteen *Letters*), the particular question of freedom of speech (four essays), the dangers of the Jacobites, High-Churchmen, and their Papist allies (at least ten numbers), general questions relating to public morality and manners (approximately twenty-five numbers). Of the 138 items, Gordon wrote more than half. The exact number con-

---

[10] While Gordon paid tribute to Trenchard by comparing him to Cato the Elder, Gordon and Trenchard derived their signature name from Cato the Younger, the "Great Cato" in their own terminology. Their choice of the name of this Republican "martyr," who committed suicide rather than accept the rule of Julius Caesar, was undoubtedly influenced by the popularity of Joseph Addison's play *Cato.* The play, dating from 1713, gave Cato a heroic and virtuous character.

tributed by each author cannot be exactly determined; attributions varied slightly from edition to edition and an examination of styles indicates that there were probably more jointly written numbers than the use of the signature letters "T" or "G" would suggest. Although not an exact measure, a count of the sixth edition does give an approximation of each writer's contributions. In that edition, seventy-six essays were assigned to Gordon, fifty-six to Trenchard, and six to the two authors jointly.

The controversy raised by "Cato" seems to have been great and immediate.[11] Answers, attacks, defenses of "Cato" were widely prepared and published. Because the letters in the *London Journal* dealt forcefully and caustically with ministerial policy on many issues, that paper became a particular source of annoyance to the King's ministers. Various efforts to suppress the paper or to curb its criticism of the government followed. Parliament began an investigation. One writer, Benjamin Norton Defoe, an illegitimate son of Daniel Defoe, was briefly committed for "scandalous and seditious Libel," for a piece inspired, but not written, by Gordon. But these ministerial attacks bogged down in procedural confusion and hardly hindered the work of "Cato." As "Cato" would have argued himself, these attempts at censorship may simply have spread the fame of the *London Journal* and its noted writers. In spite of the ministry, the circulation and renown of the *London Journal* rose rapidly, and for two years the pieces by "Cato,"

---

[11] The tangled history of the *London Journal* is detailed in several accounts, each of which contains some minor errors of fact. See Charles B. Realey, "The London Journal and Its Authors," University of Kansas *Humanistic Studies* (Lawrence: University of Kansas Press, 1935), pp. 236–274; Laurence Hanson, *Government and the Press, 1695–1763* (Oxford: Oxford University Press, 1936); and K. L. Joshi, "The London Journal, 1719–1738," *Journal* of the University of Bombay, IX (1940), 33–66. For the story of the conversion of the *Journal's* owner to Walpole's side, see particularly E. Dobrée to Charles De La Faye, [no date], in Hanson, *Government and the Press*, pp. 144–145.

which appeared frequently but somewhat irregularly, were its great attention-gaining feature.

A more subtle and successful method to suppress the *Journal* and "Cato" was subsequently followed by the government, in which Robert Walpole was becoming increasingly dominant. The muzzling of this paper was fairly typical of the process by which Walpole for so many years in the future was to control and silence criticism and opposition. He used the funds and honors at his disposal to buy over the doubting and the hostile. The owner of the *London Journal* not only accepted Walpole's largess, but he apparently even suggested the idea of a subsidy in the first instance. After some tedious negotiations, the *London Journal* suddenly became a supporter of government policy and discontinued the letters by "Cato" in September of 1722. Soon the *London Journal* appeared with attacks on its former chief attraction, the arguments of "Cato," while Trenchard and Gordon themselves managed to continue their work, probably with much less influence, in the new and relatively weak *British Journal*. If Walpole had not yet completely silenced his critics, he had certainly muted the voice of "Cato."

The End of a Collaboration

The end of "Cato's" career involved two sets of events: first, the sickness and death of Trenchard; and, second, the seeming conversion of Gordon from some of his critical views on contemporary politics. The principal series of Letters in the *British Journal* was completed with a "Farewell" by "Cato" on July 27, 1723. Only a few additional, and not very inspired, letters by "Criton," that is, Gordon, appeared in the latter half of that year. Trenchard and Gordon had planned some additional works, but they were prevented from this by Trenchard's lingering illness and death in December. Though a later account implied that Trenchard died a suicide, Gordon testified that death came from an "ulcer of the kidneys" after several weeks of illness.[12] After the demise of his collaborator, Gordon reputedly underwent a strange transformation and became a supporter of Robert Walpole. His open political activities ceased for a time; he accepted a minor sinecure from the ministry; and his next writing of note, a translation and commentary on Tacitus, appeared five years later and was dedicated to the Prince of Wales and to that sometime foe, Walpole.[13]

The appearance of conversion led to contemporary cynicism about Gordon's motives, but such views should not be accepted without qualifications. Alexander Pope did jibe at Gordon and ask what use there was in opposing the ministry when

> *'twill only be thought*
> *The Great man [Walpole] never offered*
> * you a Groat.*
> *There's honest Tacitus once talked as big*
> *But is he now an Independent Whig?*[14]

Yet several factors should be noted in interpreting this latter phase of Gordon's career. He no longer had the inspiration of Trenchard to spur on his work. He no longer needed to work so furiously to support himself. He enjoyed his patronage job; his writings proved profitable; he inherited some property bequeathed to him in tribute to *The Independent Whig;* and, eventually, he married the widow of his sometime colleague and enjoyed, during his lifetime, her extensive wealth. (The date of the marriage is not known. Gordon suggests it occurred shortly after Trenchard's death and at the latter's suggestion,

---

[12] Gordon, "Preface," *Cato's Letters* (London: Walthoe, 1755), I, lix; William Cole, "Account of Conyers Middleton," in *Horace Walpole's Correspondence,* ed. W. S. Lewis (New Haven: Yale University Press, 1951), XV, 311.

[13] *The Works of Tacitus* (London: Woodward and Peale, 1728 and 1731), 2 volumes.

[14] Alexander Pope, "Epilogue to the Satires," Dialogue I.

but a contemporary account describes the widow's action as happening "very strangely," that is, unwisely, twenty years later.)[15] Furthermore, the anti-Jacobite activities of Robert Walpole and his attacks upon such High-Churchmen as Bishop Atterbury may have attracted some sympathy on the part of Gordon. In fact, several of Gordon's later writings, including some whose authorship he publicly disavowed but privately admitted, represented a return to the strident anticlericalism of the days of the Bangorian controversy.[16] And Gordon himself argued, somewhat after the fact, that even Trenchard "was more partial to this administration [i.e., Walpole's] than any other." [17]

Whatever the explanations, Gordon's later career was far less tempestuous. He seems to have become personally acquainted with Robert Walpole and other important men. He edited government pamphlets. He continued to write on his own. Numerous later works, largely on religious questions, appeared from his hand. These included some anonymous polemics and some, notably *A Sermon Preached before the Learned Society of Lincoln's-Inn*, which attracted considerable public attention.[18] But his most important publications after *Cato's Letters* were two translations from the Latin. A first volume of Tacitus was published in 1728, a second in 1731, and an edition of

---

[15] William Cole, "Account of Middleton," *loc. cit.*, p. 311.

[16] See, for example, Thomas Gordon to Patrick Lindsay, July 4, 1732, in *Eighth Report of the Royal Commission on Historical Manuscripts*, Appendix I, pp. 314–315. There Gordon admits writing *Facts and Reasonings of the Bishop of Chichester's Sermon Examined*, but adds "It is what I do not own to everybody, tho' many have guessed." The pamphlet was an answer to a sermon preached by Francis Hare, Bishop of Chichester, on January 31, 1731, the anniversary of the "martyrdom of King Charles the First." Gordon's work, with slight variations in the title, went through at least five London editions before the end of 1732.

[17] Gordon, "Preface," *Cato's Letters*, p. xliv.

[18] [Thomas Gordon], *A Sermon Preached before the Learned Society of Lincoln's-Inn* . . . (London: J. Peele, 1733). Printed anonymously.

Sallust in 1744. The *Tacitus* was especially popular and widely
praised. The great importance of these works, though, was not
in their classical scholarship, but in the lengthy and elaborate
political discourses they contained. Gordon used the vehicles
provided by these Roman authors to write of the dangers of
factions and parties, of corruption and vice, of trusting churchmen with civil power. In short, he commented on Roman
history with a view toward those same evils he had attacked in
The Independent Whig and *Cato's Letters.* While these discourses on Tacitus and Sallust were undeniably less polemical
and controversial, they were an echo from the early efforts of
Trenchard and Gordon.

Gordon lived on, affluent and increasingly plump, or "corpu-
lent," until 1751. Contemporary critics were not complimentary
to him. Gibbon thought him "commonplace." Pope satirized
him as noted earlier and as the snoring "Silenus" of the
Dunciad. William Cole described him brutally as "the author
of many infidel books . . . , a man of no address and of a most
ungain and awkward large person, with a monstrous belly and
red face." Bolingbroke, hearing of the death of the now for-
gotten Conyers Middleton on the same day as Gordon, harshly
commented: "Then there is the best writer in England gone and
the worst." [19] But if the "worst" writer in England, Gordon was
unusual. He gained an affluence and influence beyond that of
the ordinary political pamphleteers. And if high critics did not
appreciate *The Independent Whig* and *Cato's Letters,* there is
ample evidence, in the frequent reprinting and quoting of these
works, that the political public was greatly interested in these
writings of Trenchard and Gordon.

Popularity of Their Works

Trenchard and Gordon's collaborative works did enjoy wide-
spread circulation in the English-speaking world. Collections of

---

[19] Alexander Pope, *The Dunciad,* IV, 492; *Dictionary of National Biography,* VIII, 230; William Cole, "Account of Middleton," *loc. cit.,* p. 311.

the *Independent Whig* appeared in 1721, 1722, 1726, 1728, 1732, 1735, 1743, and 1747.[20] Two sets of selections from the *Whig* were also published before Gordon's death, one in 1748, the other in 1750. There were two American editions, one a partial serialization in New York in 1724 and the other a Philadelphia imprint of 1740. *Cato's Letters* were equally popular. They enjoyed wider circulation in their original form in the *London Journal*, perhaps eight thousand copies a week, than had probably been the case with the *Whig*. Two partial collections in 1721 were followed by complete, and then by expanded editions in 1724, 1731, 1733, 1737, and 1748, and by a final "corrected" edition in 1754–1755, the text on which the selections here are based. Even Gordon's translations from the Latin sold well: his *Tacitus* appeared in a first edition in London and Dublin, in at least six later editions in English, and became a standard, widely read work for its Whiggish discourses as much as for its text proper. Moreover, the writings of Trenchard and Gordon attained even wider distribution in the New World than the two editions of the *Whig* would suggest. English copies were to be found widely in the colonies and were, as will be suggested below, read, admired, and frequently copied or reprinted in part.

Although popular appreciation for *Cato's Letters* and *The Independent Whig* in Great Britain and America was of greater importance, the reception of the writings of Trenchard and Gordon on the continent of Europe was notable. *Cato's Letters*, which assumed the existence of a limited amount of public freedom as a prerequisite for their criticism of government policies, were less well received than *The Independent Whig*. The various numbers of the latter attacking Catholicism and clericalism provided a basis for attacks on the established church as found in most European monarchies, particularly in

---

[20] See the publishing history of the writings of Trenchard and Gordon on pp. lxi-lxiv.

France. Thus, Baron d'Holbach, the materialist philosopher, became interested in the writings of the two Englishmen.[21] In 1767 he translated and published portions of *The Independent Whig*, under the title of *L'Esprit du clergé*. Moreover, in the rather casual manner in which he often borrowed signatures to disguise those of his writings which contemporaries might regard as blasphemous or otherwise outrageous, d'Holbach borrowed the name of Trenchard and attached it to his own work, *La contagion sacrée* (1768). Thus, d'Holbach supplemented his own clear-cut materialism and hostility to all religion with the anticlerical arguments of Trenchard and Gordon. Far more popular than the *Whig* were Gordon's discourses. At least five editions of Tacitus appeared in French between 1742 and 1762. A French translation of Gordon's *Sallust* reached the public in 1759. And a translation of both Tacitus and Sallust was published during the French Revolution. This process of Continental borrowing reached a kind of illogical climax in 1840, when the first discourse on Sallust appeared in Madrid "traducido de Inglés al Francés, y de este al Español." [22] The choice of Gordon's discourses over · *Cato's Letters* may perhaps be explained by the fact that it was relatively safer to publish works concerning ancient tyrants rather than those dealing directly with European affairs. In any case, the Whiggery of the discourses and the anticlerical arguments of Trenchard and Gordon both secured a wide Continental audience in the eighteenth century.

[21] See William H. Wickwar, *Baron D'Holbach, A Prelude to the French Revolution* (London: Allen and Unwin, 1935), pp. 74, 77, 241, 242. The full titles of his works mentioned were *L'Esprit du clergé, ou le Christianisme primitif vengé des enterprises et des excès de nos prêtres modernes* (2 vols., London [Amsterdam]: Weller, 1767) and *La contagion sacrée, ou Histoire naturelle de la superstition* (2 vols., London [Amsterdam?], 1768).

[22] The French translations of Gordon's works are included in the publishing history on pp. lxi—lxiv. The scarcity of copies in this country and the sketchiness of descriptions in library catalogues has resulted in some uncertainty as to the exact number of European editions. The figures cited in the text are minimal estimates.

II. THE POLITICAL AND MORAL

PHILOSOPHY OF

TRENCHARD AND GORDON

Radical Whiggery

What in particular gave the writings of Trenchard and Gordon their wide appeal? What was the substance of their thinking? First, the views of the two authors were obviously rooted in the developing Whig tradition, with its anti-Catholic and anti-Stuart convictions. Yet Trenchard and Gordon represented a more radical brand of Whiggery than that of the comfortable establishment which emerged after the securing of the Hanoverian succession to the English throne. The greater part of the arguments of Trenchard and Gordon were common property among radical English Whigs, particularly among those whose thought had been heavily influenced by the writings and the example of the Whig martyr, Algernon Sidney.[23] Sidney's impact upon the authors of *Cato's Letters* was obviously great. Trenchard and Gordon not only quoted extensively from Sidney, but they used arguments and ideas which closely paralleled those of his *Discourses Concerning Government*. Sometimes reliance upon Sidney was shown in direct and open ways; for example, letters on the dangers of general corruption and on the characters of good and evil magistrates were simply long passages drawn from the *Discourses* with the briefest of editorial comments by Trenchard or Gordon. More frequently the influence of Sidney was not so openly shown or acknowl-

---

[23] On Algernon Sidney, see Caroline Robbins, "Algernon Sidney's Discourses Concerning Government," *William and Mary Quarterly,* 3rd series, IV (1947), 267–296, and her *Eighteenth Century Commonwealthman* (Cambridge: Harvard University Press, 1959), pp. 41–47, and on Trenchard and Gordon, pp. 115–125.

edged, but none the less it was present. Thus, the country-by-country tours taken by Trenchard and Gordon in *Cato's Letters* were derived in part from the pattern of historical examples found in the *Discourses*. Sidney was a martyr to all English Whigs, but he had supported ideas congenial specifically to the more radical supporters of that mixture of political ideas that was Whiggery. For example, Sidney had written an elaborate rejection of any notion of divine right on the part of rulers and a learned exposition of the rights of resistance and rebellion. He provided a fuller and more candid justification of revolution and of the process of social change by peaceful and by forcible means than was to be found in John Locke. And the Whiggery of *Cato's Letters* still had these ultimate radical implications. This more radical thought was the brand that took root in America, transplanted both by Sidney and by the more popular if less learned Trenchard and Gordon.

If Trenchard and Gordon were sometimes more radical than many of their contemporaries, they were yet close to the popular temper in their understanding of the recent English past and in their strong anti-Catholicism and anti-Jacobitism. The two authors shared the feeling of the overwhelming majority of their fellow subjects that Catholicism was a perverted and benighted form of religion and the worst of spiritual tyrannies. Pictures of the horrors to be found where "Popery" held sway abounded in *The Independent Whig* and *Cato's Letters*. And Trenchard and Gordon moved on from anti-Catholicism to a kind of general anticlericalism. Their defense of Hoadly, the previously mentioned Bishop of Bangor, was simply one instance of their general dislike of clerical pretensions to any kind of civil power or any form of special privilege or position. They viewed churchmen as the most ordinary of people at best and as men who had often perverted their role in society. Churchmen should, therefore, in the thinking of Trenchard and Gordon, be watched carefully and checked in their every effort to exceed their proper and very limited functions. Anti-Catholic and anti-Stuart prejudices were obviously entwined in the Whig tradition, the common mind, and the writings of Trenchard and Gordon. In *Cato's Letters,* the two authors thoroughly enjoyed describing the terrors of Stuart times and the various methods of subverting liberty used by the seventeenth-century kings. Not only did attacks upon the Stuarts provide a link between Trenchard and Gordon and the popular temper, but they provided a safely patriotic method for disguised attacks upon the objectionable policies of contemporary ministers. Thus, to avoid any possible difficulty under the English libel laws, Trenchard and Gordon often attacked acts which they ascribed to previous ministries as a subtle and not openly offensive or libelous way of denouncing the conduct of the existing government.

Not only did Trenchard and Gordon promote a radical variant of Whiggery, they also insisted upon the "Independence" of their beliefs on questions other than those of anti-Catholicism and anti-Jacobitism. Thus, their anti-Papist views did not lead them to accept without question the pretensions of the established Protestant church. Thus, fear of Jacobitism and its French and Irish supporters did not lead them to accept the necessity for expanding the power of the monarchy, particularly through the proposed establishment of a permanent army of great strength in England itself. This would simply have meant the same evils as in Stuart times. And their dislike for the Stuarts did not lead them to admire the figure of Oliver Cromwell; he had been simply a tyrant who took advantage of public confusion and antipathy toward Charles I to establish his own kind of arbitrary rule. These various hatreds and this attempt to avoid the risks of one extreme in hasty flight from another ran consistently through the writings of Trenchard and Gordon. Their anti-Catholic and anti-Stuart views were often stated in the most heated of language; against this, they tried to make a temperate and reasonable evaluation of the dangers that come of extreme political emotions.

The Nature of Human Liberty and Equality

Hatred of the Papacy and hatred of the Stuarts was, for Trenchard and Gordon, simply hatred for various kinds of tyranny; and the opposite of tyranny was the state in which man ought to live, the condition of liberty and all that it implied for the welfare of mankind. In one notable letter of "Cato," Number 59 of the series, Trenchard embarked upon the project of proving that "Liberty is the unalienable Right of all Mankind." In a later letter, Gordon suggested his own definition of that liberty. It was "the Power which every Man has over his own Actions, and his Right to enjoy the Fruit of his Labour, Art, and Industry, as far as by it he hurts not the Society, or any Members of it, by taking from any Member, or by hindering him from enjoying what he himself enjoys" (No. 62).[24] Whether stated in the precise words of one author or the other, the notion of the unalienable right to liberty and of the broad meaning and content of that liberty was at the heart of the writings of "Cato." Not only did the two authors try to prove the right to liberty, they also explained at length their notion of the fruits of liberty and argued that it alone was the root, the necessary source for the benefits of civilization. Liberty was "the Parent of all the Virtues" (No. 62). Liberty produced all civil blessings, "a due Distribution of Property and an equal Distribution of Justice" (No. 63). Only liberty would lead to the growth of trade and naval power; it was the source of true military virtue and valor; it alone could tolerate true religion. Arts, science, learning, property, commerce, all these could prosper only when man lived in a state of liberty. Thus, the whole thought of "Cato" was based upon a broad conception of the meaning of human liberty; it was an inalienable

---

[24] In this and the following paragraphs of section II, the numerals in parentheses indicate the numbers of *Cato's Letters* in which the quotations immediately above may be found. In general, the quotations are included in the selections herein.

right without which man could not grow or learn or act well in any of these vast areas of human endeavor. It was the essential right of man and the essential condition for the development of all that was good in his nature.

"Cato" argued not only for the unalienable rights of mankind but for the innate equality of all men. In their forty-fifth letter, Trenchard and Gordon boldly stated, "Men are naturally equal, and none ever rose above the rest but by Force or Consent: No Man was ever born above all the rest, nor below them all." This natural equality did not, of course, imply that all men enjoyed equal circumstances: the "glaring Effects of Fortune" and "of Contrivance or Chance" made for great distinctions among men. Yet this natural equality should lead to suspicion of pretensions to social position: "Those that think themselves furthest above the rest, are generally by their Education below them all. They are debased by a Conceit of their Greatness: they trust to their Blood; which, speaking naturally, gives them no Advantage; and neglect their Mind, which alone, by proper Improvements, sets one Man above another." The assertion of natural equality and the according distrust of the significance of "Blood" had another implication of importance; it led to a rejection of overstated claims to hereditary right and position. Trenchard and Gordon noted that the founders of great fortunes and families were often not men of notable virtue and for their descendants to claim greatness by inheritance, "by Proxy," was both absurd and evil. In one of the best examples of their ironic style, in this case primarily from the pen of Trenchard, they discussed the whole doctrine of hereditary right in Number 132 of *Cato's Letters* and noted the frequent national disasters which resulted from it. In another letter, the two authors summed up their views on the subject: "It is evident to common Sense, that there ought to be no Inequality in Society, but for the Sake of Society," and the claims to hereditary position ought to be judged by how they served or did not serve the "Sake of Society" (No. 45).

The Origins and Functions of Government

Governments were instituted by men, according to their powers and to serve their purposes. They did not owe their existence "to the immediate Revelation of God." Rather, the origins of all states were "within the Memory of Men or of Histories" and were to be found in "the Wisdom and Force of mere Men." So every government was derived "from the Laws and Constitutions of the Society, of which the Governors themselves are but Members" (No. 60). And as governments were humanly constituted, so they were limited to serving the good of mankind; if they failed in this function, they were but "Usurpation" (No. 59). Moreover, they could not properly be absolute; no man had the power or right to concede all of his liberties to the state. As no man had the ability to concede his own freedom, so most certainly he could not concede the "Lives and Liberties, Religion or acquired Property of his Posterity, who will be born as free as he himself was born." In short, there could be no binding of the future, no fixed, unalterable pact among generations as to the form of governments. To be sure, many governments obviously did not serve the good of society but ruled by force and fraud. But this kind of rule did not gain rightfulness from its existence or even from the passage of such time as might seem to indicate its acceptance and stability; rather, "Force can give no Title but to Revenge, and to the Use of Force again."

Who was to say whether government was fulfilling its purposes? "Who shall be Judge whether the Magistrate acts justly, and pursues his Trust?" For "Cato," the answer was clear and simple. The magistrate obviously could not be the final judge of his own actions. Rather, each subject must judge by his own conscience whether the magistrate be good or evil. There was an undoubted right to make such determinations; the people would surely be entitled to decide that a lunatic or an idiot was an unfit public official, and as surely they should judge whether "their Prince be good or bad, whether a Father or an Enemy" (No. 59). The doctrine of passive obedience to authority, without questioning the ways of the governors, was a doctrine utterly rejected by Trenchard and Gordon. The right to resist was good Whiggery and contrasted sharply with a Tory or High-Church acceptance of the misuse of power. The actions of the government were not to be accepted where they exceeded its authority just as if they were proper and constitutional. Rather, they were to be resisted; not to object to "any Man's Wickedness [was] to encourage it" (No. 62). And it was "Upon this Principle of People's judging for themselves, and resisting lawless Force" that had occurred the "late happy *Revolution*," which had established the Hanoverian dynasty in place of the Stuarts (No. 59). Lest readers worry that this Whig principle of resistance might be carried too far, Trenchard and Gordon stressed that the people were so accustomed to respect authority, so desirous of living in their settled ways, that they would not resist until their grievance became very great, and that there was greater danger of their waiting too long before acting than of their moving too quickly.

Freedom of Religion and of Speech

In their statements on religious toleration, Trenchard and Gordon expressed the most liberal of Whig viewpoints. With regard to belief, the greatest freedom ought always to be allowed: "In Matters of Conscience, he who does his best does well, though he is mistaken. . . . He who follows another in this case, without Enquiry, is Man's Votary, and not God's" (*Character*, 8). On the basis of this general ideal, a person who believed in natural religion or who had no religion ought to be accepted and accorded the freedoms of a loyal subject. As long as the individual's judgment was reached in good faith, the state had no right or affair to interfere with him. Yet, on the practical level, Trenchard and Gordon hinted at limitations on the actual application of this general principle of freedom of belief. Clearly, they wanted to extend the rights of those Protestants who did not belong to the Established Church. But on the problem of how far freedom should be extended, the two authors were not entirely candid. Sometimes, they seemed to speak of all men of good will and honest belief; at others, they seemed simply to be arguing the case of Protestant dissenters. While they sometimes obscured their meanings on the question of the rights of Catholics, Trenchard and Gordon did stress certain consistent themes in *The Independent Whig* and *Cato's Letters*. They frequently argued that religious freedom and rights should be extended more broadly than they were in the England of the 1720's, and they repeatedly attacked High-Churchmen and other advocates of special privileges for members of the Established Church. In short, within the context of English thought of the early eighteenth century, Trenchard and Gordon advocated the widest freedom of conscience and belief, arguing that any limitations on such freedom were immoral and also self-defeating, and hedging their argument slightly only when it came near to foundering on their intellectual heritage of anti-Popery.

If, on the question of religious beliefs, Trenchard and Gordon reached the limits of the Whig tradition, they went well beyond popular understanding of that tradition on the issue of freedom of expression. The fifteenth letter of "Cato," which appeared in February, 1720, contained perhaps their most eloquent statement on the subject: "Without Freedom of Thought, there can be no such Thing as Wisdom; and no such Thing as publick Liberty, without Freedom of Speech. . . . This sacred Privilege is so essential to free Government, that the Security of Property; and the Freedom of Speech, always go together." But Trenchard and Gordon were not content with mere rhetorical statements of general principles; they carefully analyzed the subject and advocated a far broader freedom of speech, and of the press in particular, than other political writers of their time. With a face-saving gesture in the way of accepting laws that served to punish false slanders, Trenchard and Gordon indicated a basic belief that lies were self-defeating and libel laws were not really necessary to defend government against untruthful charges. The best way to meet falsity was with truthful arguments or with the laughter and scorn it deserved. Moreover, in an analysis of the application of libel laws, "Cato" anticipated the later view that the truthfulness of the charges against government officials should be a defense in court, that the public interest was far better served by protecting the expression of the truth than by saving the dignity of an office filled by a corrupt individual. Only tyrants or others against whom accusations were actually truthful need have any fear of freedom of expression. They alone could be injured by free speech. Thus, Trenchard and Gordon upheld a somewhat optimistic view that truth would prevail over falsehood in the free competition of ideas and arguments.

Trenchard and Gordon's views on freedom of speech were intimately connected with their notion of human nature, with their optimistic view of the mass of mankind. The seeming democratic tendencies of some of "Cato's" statements should not be exaggerated; after all, Trenchard and Gordon did not advocate any extension of participation beyond the restricted political public of England. Yet "Cato's" statements on the people, their inherent rights, and their innate incorruptibility were broad and forthright enough: "the People, when they are not misled or corrupted, generally make a sound Judgment of Things." The two authors argued: "The People have no Biass to be Knaves. . . . No Ambition prompts them. . . . No aspiring or unsociable Passions incite them; they have no Rivals for Place, no Competitor to pull down . . . they can serve no End by Faction; they have no Interest, but the general Interest" (No. 24). The people's honesty, the general reasonableness of their requests from their governments, their affinity to the general interest of all, these tendencies were in marked contrast to the interests of "great men," of leaders of faction, of ministers of state, all of whom had dangerous ways that required constant public surveillance over their actions. In free governments, such as that of Great Britain, the people's own qualities and interests would lead them to support the state and its prince. In England, the public was given a share in government and exercised its powers with caution and prudence. The representatives in the House of Commons, whose election by an exceedingly small group of voters was not explicitly mentioned by "Cato," served the popular interest because their own interests were "so interwoven with the People's Happiness, that they must stand and fall together."

The Dangers to Liberty

With eloquence, Gordon contrasted free government, the system of rule under which liberty and the public prospered, with its opposite, tyranny: "So . . . Civil Government is only a partial Restraint put by the Laws of Agreement and Society upon natural and absolute Liberty, which might otherwise grow licentious: And Tyranny is an unlimited Restraint put upon natural Liberty, by the Will of one or a few" (No. 62). In a free society, the magistrates exercised their charges for the sake of the public, while "Tyrants abuse the People, for the Sake of Power. Free Government is the protecting the People in their Liberties by stated Rules: Tyranny is a brutish Struggle for unlimited Liberty to one or a few, who would rob all others of their Liberty, and act by no Rule but lawless Lust." In short, free government was rule by and according to well-defined law, while tyranny was rule by arbitrary and personal whim.

As Trenchard and Gordon stated the consequences of liberty with certainty, so they were sure of the results of tyranny. Under tyrannies, "Life grows precarious, always miserable, often intolerable" (No. 62). Such governments must inevitably produce a host of evils, evils which they could not and would not correct. They depended ultimately upon force, armed power exercised at the discretion of the ruler. Under such conditions, there could be no certainty or hope in the prosecution of business or the search for knowledge, the rewards for such activities being determined purely by the wishes of the tyrant, and therefore these, like all other human endeavors, must languish. Learning, the arts, commerce, all would sicken under arbitrary governments. Not only would the positive accomplishments of man decline, but vice and falsity would actually be encouraged by the state. Tyranny must depend upon a horde of informers. It must depend upon armies, and upon spies to keep those armies under constant check. It must try to corrupt all men and fear and destroy the few honest ones who would resist its corruption. It must, in Trenchard and Gordon's view, establish and encourage a false religion, which would inculcate in the public a habit of obedience and acceptance of whatever outrage was committed by the ruler. And a tyrant could not afford himself of the services of honest and capable ministers, out of his fear that that very capability might make the ministers too powerful for his security and out of his inability to trust the honesty of any in the midst of a system dependent upon force and corruption. In sum, almost every evil could be expected as a natural, inevitable product of tyranny stemming from the very essence of such government as arbitrary and personal power.

Yet, however strong man's desire for liberty, tyrannies existed and actually abounded in the world as seen by "Cato." How did such governments establish their power and perpetuate it in spite of their manifest evils and of man's natural inclinations? The processes which resulted in bad government were various and were discussed at length and repeatedly by Trenchard and Gordon. One source of infection might be the spirit of faction or party. The people might easily be led to support factions or parties, whose leaders were men of personal ambition, blinded to the public interest and carried along by excessive spirit. In the introductory description of his *Discourses on Sallust*, Gordon amply summed up the views of

Trenchard and himself on the dangers of faction and parties: "How apt Parties are to err in the Choice of their Leaders: How little they regard Truth and Morality, when in Competition with Party. The terrible Consequences of all this; worthy Men decried and persecuted; worthless and wicked Men popular and preferred; Liberty oppressed and expiring." As with parties in general, so it was with Whig and Tory in the 1720's. When in power, one party behaved much like the other, whatever its past declarations, and neither was to be trusted very much. Thus, even the title *The Independent Whig* stressed a distrust of the regular party man.

Factions and parties were, in a sense, only a first indication of the path to tyranny on which a state was traveling. Party and faction produced discord and weakened the fabric of the state; the dominant faction would come to rely upon force to destroy its opposition, or the public might turn to some armed deliverer who promised to restore order. In either case, the result would be the same; authority would come to depend upon force and liberty would be ended. The political dangers of armed force led Trenchard and Gordon to express great opposition to every proposal for strengthening the army of England. Such force might too easily be misused as it had been misused so many times in the past. In the thinking of "Cato," standing armies were not necessary to maintain order or protect against foreign powers; what was necessary was popular support for government, support that could be rallied to defeat any external enemy. On the other hand, such standing forces provided an easy access to power on the part of any potential tyrant.

Factional enthusiasm and force were not the only enemies of liberty. There was the dread evil of corruption in public places whereby the corrupt might gain power and then resort to further misdeeds in order to escape punishment. The discussions of public corruption by Trenchard and Gordon revealed two of the major themes of their work: an emphasis upon the history of the later Roman Republic and a cautioning for vigilance as to the present state of English politics. Rome provided the text for sermons on the great dangers of public corruption or the other insidious means by which tyranny might be slowly established. The public corruption of that city was stressed. One of *Cato's Letters*, for example, took as its initial theme the famous line addressed by King Jugurtha to Rome: "Mercenary City, ripe for Destruction, and just ready to deliver up thyself, and all thy Liberties, to the first Bidder, who is able to buy thee" (No. 18). Gordon's continuing interest in this same story of the decline of the Republic was, of course, expressed in his later career, in his editing of Tacitus and of Sallust's "The War against Jugurtha." Moreover, examples of Roman corruption had an immediate relevance to the situation in England as it was seen by Trenchard and Gordon. Indeed, the greater part of the early letters by "Cato" were directed toward one particular spectacle of public immorality, the South Sea scandal. While carefully assuring their readers of their devotion to the present monarch, of their personal belief in his incorruptibility and in the honesty of Parliament, Trenchard and Gordon made clear their belief in the existence of much public corruption. They trod a very careful line, often asserting that the evils they attacked had been experienced during the last reign, and that they simply hoped to avoid a repetition in this. Yet their point of view, that much unpunished and real misconduct persisted, was forcefully enough stated: "Publick Corruptions and Abuses have grown upon us: Fees in most, if not in all, Offices, are immensely increased: Places and Employments, which ought not to be sold at all, are sold for treble Values . . . the Public has run very much in Debt; and as those Debts have been encreasing, and the People growing poor, Salaries have been augmented, and Pensions multiplied." And, just because it was unpunished, such corruption was increasing: "Our common Rogues now scorn little Pilferings, and in the

Dark; 'tis all publick Robbery, and at Noon-day; nor is it, as formerly, for small Sums, but for the Ransom of Kings, and the Pay of Armies" (No. 20).

Another prop for bad governments was false religion. Trenchard and Gordon argued that no true religion, neither "the Christian Religion, nor Natural Religion, nor any Thing else that ought to be called Religion," could exist under tyranny (No. 66). Rather, evil rulers would depend upon various kinds of superstition to fetter men, "to make Mankind the ready Dupes of gloomy Imposters, and the tame Slaves of raging Tyrants." Superstition and fear were a necessary part of a system of tyranny, "For, Servitude established in the Mind, is best established." Most religious establishments had been founded upon "Ambition and Pride," by "Enthusiasts" or "designing and unpreferred Churchmen." Again the traditional English fears and points of view were expressed in part by "Cato." The Moslem Sultan of Turkey and the Pope of Rome were equated as evil rulers and spreaders of superstition. The Catholic Church was described as perfectly suited to the needs of the absolute rulers on the Continent. On the other hand, the Protestant Reformation had thrived among the free states. While some of the states which had joined in the Reformation were no longer free, they were now no more than nominally Protestant and the homes of "miserable Ignorance, and much bitter and implacable Bigotry." In England itself, the Protestant religion had been preserved only because the people were free and had the courage to resist the plans of James II. Here, too, Trenchard and Gordon clearly rejected some High-Church doctrines and particularly that of passive obedience to authority. And *The Independent Whig* and *Cato's Letters* both expressed the pious wish that the people of England would continue to understand the close connections between liberty and true religion.

In their discussion of tyranny and of all the problems of

government, Trenchard and Gordon gave voice to another idea commonly held among Englishmen: that their land was the freest in the world and one of the few which enjoyed any notable degree of liberty. Repeatedly, Trenchard and Gordon referred to the tyrannies of other parts of the world. Turkey was the most frequently used example of the horrors of an Oriental despotism. Russia still suffered under arbitrary rule, whatever the modernizing proclivities of Peter the Great. France continued to bear the burden of Bourbon authority, even though the late Louis XIV had ruled so wickedly that "he lived and died the Plague and Curse of Christendom" (No. 73). Moreover, tyranny was gradually extending its sway. The free states of Italy no longer flourished. Denmark was regarded as the most recent instance of the destruction of free institutions and the establishment of arbitrary rule. In short, Trenchard and Gordon believed that "Power encroaches daily upon Liberty, with a Success too evident; and the Balance between them is almost lost. Tyranny has engrossed almost the whole Earth, and striking at Mankind Root and Branch, makes the World a Slaughter-house; and will certainly go on to destroy, till it is either destroyed itself, or, which, is most likely, has left nothing else to destroy." Thus, England and a few other states stood out as great exceptions to the growing and almost all-pervasive force of evil government. This belief gave an extra edge to warnings in *Cato's Letters* about subversion, corruption, or armed force in England. A free people could not imagine "a Calamity which they do not feel," such as tyranny, and thus needed extra warnings of the dangers before them. A belief in an extraordinarily free Great Britain surrounded by arbitrary and evil states was, of course, one part of the message of Trenchard and Gordon particularly appealing to colonial Americans who increasingly came to think of themselves as preserving these patterns of freedom in purer form even than the British at home.

III.   TRENCHARD AND GORDON'S

IMPORTANCE IN AMERICA

Perhaps of longer duration and greater importance than Trenchard and Gordon's influence in Great Britain was their impact upon that country's colonies in the New World. In England itself, as the threats to the Hanoverian succession and the whole Revolutionary settlement declined, Whiggery tended to become a comfortable orthodoxy, whose supporters were content with things as they existed and were increasingly hostile to any advocacy of change. But in America the radical Whiggery of Trenchard and Gordon, popular from their very first writings, had a deeper significance as the colonies matured, their governmental institutions became more popular, and their political controversies more bitter. The timeliness of Trenchard and Gordon was one reason for their continuing popularity in the colonies. The authors had addressed themselves to some of the very same issues that aroused the Americans in the eighteenth century. They had considered the nature of the British Empire and presented arguments very close to the colonial views of the 1760's. But even more than this, Trenchard and Gordon provided fine, clear, concise statements of a brand of radical Whiggery which provided a philosophical basis for the whole American argument and not just for stands on specific issues. So the polemics and the more rational arguments of Trenchard and Gordon were often read and many times copied by the great colonial leaders. They provided a handy justification of popular actions and influenced the thinking and statements of the Revolutionary generation in America.

Trenchard and Gordon rarely dealt directly with the nature

and problems of the British Empire, but they did so in a manner very similar to later colonial viewpoints in Number 106 of *Cato's Letters*.[25] Written in 1722, this article was a somewhat prophetic statement about the problems of later relations between Great Britain and America. It argued that while colonies were founded in the first instance on a country's self-interest, they would remain loyal in the long run only if that country's policies served the interests of the settlers as well. Great Britain, as a free country, had so far been successful in its efforts to settle in the New World. Danger for the Empire could arise only from a failure on the part of the home government to sense and to aid the interests of the Americans. The proper method of keeping the loyalty of the colonists would be to encourage their growth and prosperity through wise trade regulations, regulations designed to increase their production of items needed in England, "Timber, Hemp, Iron, and other Metals, and indeed . . . most or all the Materials of Navigation." As the colonies grew, only a realistic policy could keep them tied to Great Britain; neither force nor sentiment would suffice if the needs of the settlements were ignored. Force might keep the colonies temporarily subordinate, but would either destroy their substance and profitability or make for such discontent as to lead to their separation. In fact, reliance on force was regarded by Trenchard and Gordon as the reason for the failure of "arbitrary countries" in colonizing. Sentiment might bind the Empire together for a time, but, in the long run, it would not be enough; colonies would not "continue their Subjection to another, only because their Great-Grandmothers were acquainted." Restraints or restrictions, or reliance purely on traditional attachments would finally lead to the "Independency" of the Americans. "Liberty and Encouragement," freedom plus positive acts by Britain in favor of its colonial subjects were both necessary to preserve the Empire.

---

[25] Number 106 of *Cato's Letters* is printed in its entirety in this volume.

Thus, Trenchard and Gordon supported a moderate and considerate colonial policy and provided material of use to later American pamphleteers protesting against British policies. John Dickinson, for example, echoed some of the phrases of Cato's Letters in his own Letters from a Pennsylvania Farmer in 1767–1768.[26]

Far more important in attracting early colonial interest than their arguments on the nature of the Empire were Trenchard and Gordon's views on religion and politics. For example, very early in his career and well before the great debates of the 1760's over the imperial constitution, Benjamin Franklin developed an admiration for the two English radical Whigs and expressed his agreement with many of their opinions. In July, 1722, he quoted, as part of his "Silence Dogood" letters in the New England Courant, from "Cato" on "Freedom of the Press" and the "Weaknesses and Inconsistencies of human Nature."[27] This Boston newspaper also reprinted portions of Cato's Letters on such subjects as libel and the necessity for restraints on the power of magistrates.[28] A decade later Franklin was still keeping up with the writings of Gordon. The American then borrowed from Gordon's Sermon Preached before the Learned Society of Lincoln's-Inn. That so-called Sermon was one of Gordon's more notable attacks upon persecution for conscience' sake. It compared the New World opposition to the Anglican Establishment with the old English

[26] See John Dickinson's "Letters from a Pennsylvania Farmer" in The Writings of John Dickinson, ed. Paul Leicester Ford (Philadelphia: Historical Society of Pennsylvania, 1895), and for his quoting from Cato's Letters, p. 343.

[27] The borrowings of "Silence Dogood" from "Cato" may be found in The Papers of Benjamin Franklin, ed. Leonard Labaree (New Haven: Yale University Press, 1959—), I, 27–32.

[28] See, for example, the New England Courant (Boston) for September 11, 1721, October 9, 16, 23, and 30, 1721. For these and many other newspaper references cited in subsequent footnotes, the editor is indebted to Professor Leonard W. Levy of Brandeis University.

hatred for ecclesiastical tyranny, in particular with the opposition to the policies of the Archbishop Laud in the 1640's.[29]
Thus, Franklin borrowed some of the ideas of Trenchard and
Gordon to bolster his own arguments. He also advised the
general reading of *The Independent Whig* and *Cato's Letters*.
In 1749, in his *Proposals Relating to the Education of Youth
in Pennsylvania*, he indicated his continued liking for the two
Englishmen, for their style, and, at least implicitly, for their
opinions. The Pennsylvanian suggested that "the English language might be taught by grammar; in which some of our best
writers as Tillotson, Addison, Pope, Algernon Sidney, *Cato's
Letters*, etc. should be classics; the styles principally to be cul-
tivated being the clear and the concise."[30]

Uses in Early Controversies

While the works of Trenchard and Gordon first attracted attention in America as fine, general statements of Whig beliefs,
they soon came to serve a more practical function as sources
for ideas and quotations in colonial disputes. Thus, the two
writers were frequently used during the prolonged "Zenger"
controversy in New York in the 1730's.[31] The jury's acquittal

---

[29] On Gordon's *Sermon*, see Carl Bridenbaugh, *Mitre and Sceptre* (New
York: Oxford University Press, 1962), p. 175. Bridenbaugh stresses the
issue of the Anglican episcopate in North America as a factor in the coming of the Revolution. For Franklin's use of the *Sermon*, see Labaree,
Papers of Franklin, II, 64–65.

[30] *The Works of Benjamin Franklin*, ed. Jared Sparks (Boston: Hilliard,
Gray, 1840–1847), I, 572.

[31] On the Zenger case and its aftermath, the following are helpful:
James Alexander, *A Brief Narrative of the Case and Trial of John Peter
Zenger*, ed. Stanley Nider Katz (Cambridge: Harvard University Press,
1963); Vincent Buranelli, *The Trial of Peter Zenger* (New York: New
York University Press, 1957); and Leonard W. Levy, *Legacy of Suppression* (Cambridge: Harvard University Press, 1960), pp. 126–175, and
his "Did the Zenger Case Really Matter?" *William and Mary Quarterly*,
3rd series, XVII (1960), 35–50.

of John Peter Zenger on charges of libel has long been cited as evidence of the early development in America of a broad conception of the freedom of the press. In fact, the immediate consequences of the Zenger case were much more limited. They amounted to the triumph of one side in a local political dispute and not to the establishment of a legal precedent of broad significance for the rest of the eighteenth century. Nonetheless, Zenger or, more accurately, his principal sponsor, James Alexander, appealed to "Cato," popularized his beliefs, and helped influence public opinion, if not legal authorities, in the colony of New York. In late 1733 the Zenger newspaper, the *New York Weekly Journal,* began printing excerpts from *Cato's Letters.*[32] It also used Gordon as an authority to back its arguments and quoted from the same passages of Tacitus as had provided the texts for some of his writings. In early 1734, when Zenger was under attack by the royal authorities, his paper quoted in full two numbers by "Cato" on freedom of the press and of speech.[33] And, when the government moved determinedly to prosecute Zenger, the *Journal* broadened the scope of its citations from Trenchard and Gordon; it began to quote them extensively on the dangers of tyranny or arbitrary government.[34] The *Journal* did not present a consistent line of argument on the problems of libel law and freedom of speech; it did find in *Cato's Letters* a series of immensely useful ideas on the powers of government and their proper limits. And when Zenger was acquitted, while his acquittal did not establish a legal precedent of immediate value, it did indicate some popular acceptance of an advanced notion of the people's freedom to criticize their government.

[32] *New York Weekly Journal,* November 19, December 10 and 31, 1733, and January 28, February 2 and 11, 1733/34.

[33] *New York Weekly Journal,* February 18 and 25, and March 4, 1733/34.

[34] Among other issues, see the *New York Weekly Journal* for July 7, 14, and 21, August 25, September 1, 8, 15, and 22, 1735.

Trenchard and Gordon were used in another celebrated controversy in the colony of New York. There, in the early 1750's, the control of the proposed King's College and the nature of its charter were issues furiously contended by the Anglicans on the one side and a variety of dissenters, principally Presbyterians, on the other. The controversy led to the publication of one of the more notable of pre-Revolutionary periodicals, *The Independent Reflector*.[35] *The Reflector* was chiefly the work of William Livingston and was consciously patterned after English periodical essays of an earlier day, particularly after *The Independent Whig*.[36] Livingston paid homage to Trenchard and Gordon in several ways. He quoted directly from "Cato" on the "vanity of birth and titles." The first number of *The Reflector* was patterned after the first two parts of *The Whig*. Eight other numbers closely followed other sections of the earlier work. And numerous scattered passages by Livingston paraphrased Trenchard and Gordon. Finally, the American sponsored the republication of Gordon's own *The Craftsmen* and added a preface attacking the Anglican Church in New York.[37] These various activities of Livingston were of considerable importance for the anti-Anglican faction and of vast annoyance to the opposition. The leader of that opposition, the American Samuel Johnson, staunch supporter of the Church of England and future President of King's College, denounced *The Reflector* and its obvious source

---

[35] On the background of the dispute and *The Independent Reflector*, see *The Independent Reflector*, ed. Milton Klein (Cambridge: Harvard University Press, 1963), pp. 1–50.

[36] For parallels between *The Independent Whig* and *The Reflector*, see *ibid.*, particularly Appendix III, 450–452.

[37] *The Craftsmen: A Sermon from the Independent Whig* (New York: Parker and Weyman, 1753), with an introduction by William Livingston and William Smith. Gordon's *The Craftsmen* should not be confused with the more famous *The Craftsman*, the anti-Walpole series of essays written by Henry St. John, Viscount Bolingbroke, and others in the late 1720's.

of ideas, the writings of Trenchard and Gordon.[38] In Johnson's view, *The Independent Reflector* grew so "outrageous as to reprint all *The Independent Whig's* trite reflections, only in other words." As for *The Whig* itself, Johnson regarded it as "pernicious," its writers as "famous infidel authors," and summed up his opinions by lamenting that while the enthusiasm of the revivalists had ebbed, "free thinking . . . which is worse, takes place of it, and now Chubb, Tindal, and *The Independent Whig* grow much in vogue, who do more mischief than the others, so that we have now these fatal principles chiefly to oppose and guard against." While Johnson and the Anglicans won on the immediate issue of the control and chartering of their college, they clearly foresaw and feared the continuing strength of these "fatal principles" supported by the works of Trenchard and Gordon.

The American Revolution

As they contributed to American thought in earlier controversies, so the writings of Trenchard and Gordon affected the beliefs of the leaders of the Revolutionary generation. Men of such different persuasions and from such different areas as John Adams of Massachusetts and Thomas Jefferson of Virginia were familiar with and admired *Cato's Letters* and *The Independent Whig*. Adams did not derive his thought from a few sources but rather from the wide range of his own experiences, his extensive reading, and his understanding of English and American political traditions. Yet he found in the

---

[38] The quotations from Samuel Johnson may be found in *Samuel Johnson, His Career and Writings*, eds. Herbert and Carol Schneider (New York: Columbia University Press, 1929); Johnson, "A Brief Vindication of the Proceedings of the Trustees Relating to the College" (originally published, New York: H. Gaine, 1754), IV, 194; Johnson to the Archbishop of Canterbury, June, 25, 1753, IV, 3; Johnson, "A Letter to the Reverend Jonathan Dickinson" (Boston: Rogers and Fowle, 1747), III, 191–192; and Johnson to Dr. Bearcroft, April 2, 1753, III, 247.

works of Trenchard and Gordon an anticlerical viewpoint with which he agreed, and he noted the considerable popularity of their writings, particularly in the years after the Boston Massacre, on the subject of standing armies and the dangers they represented in time of peace.[39] In Virginia, Jefferson knew well the writings of the ancient authors and of the political theorists of the seventeenth century. He possessed *Cato's Letters* and *The Whig*, but, in so far as the works of the two Englishmen were concerned, he left a record only of his considerable liking for Gordon's *Tacitus* and *Sallust*. Jefferson believed that the English translator had preserved the "spirit" of Tacitus in his works and added that Gordon's "selection of Tacitus & Sallust for translation seems to have been dictated by the similar causticity of his own genius."[40]

On the popular level, Trenchard and Gordon's writings were well-known and frequently cited before and during the 1760's and 1770's. Copies of *Cato's Letters* and *The Independent Whig* were commonly found in college and subscription libraries. Where records were kept and are extant as to library subscribers' interests, the reading of Trenchard and Gordon matched and perhaps exceeded that of the political works of John Locke.[41] Private libraries also frequently included the works of Trenchard and Gordon. In the homes of Virginia planters, for example, *Cato's Letters* and *The Whig* were as

---

[39] *Works of John Adams*, ed. C. F. Adams (Boston, 1850–1856), "Diary," II, 5; and John Adams to Dr. J. Morse, January 5, 1816, X, 202. See also *Catalogue of the John Adams Library in the Public Library of the City of Boston* (Boston: the Public Library, 1917), pp. 46, 106, 221, 240–241, and 247.

[40] E. Millicent Sowerby, *Catalogue of the Library of Thomas Jefferson* (Washington: Library of Congress, 1952—), I, 37–39 and III, 133. The quotation comes from Jefferson to Charles Clay, May 1, 1813, I, 37–38.

[41] For an example, see Chester T. Hallenbeck, "A Colonial Reading List, from the Union Library of Hatboro, Pennsylvania," *Pennsylvania Magazine of History and Biography*, LVI (1932), 289–340.

common as Locke's essentially political writings.[42] The probable extent of the influence of these English radical writings in the years preceding the American Revolution was noted in the 1780's by the historian David Ramsay. Although the colonists' books "were generally small in size and few in number: a great part of them consisted of those fashionable authors, who have defended the cause of liberty. Cato's Letters, the Independent Whig, and such productions were common in one extreme of the Colonies, while in the other, histories of the Puritans kept alive the remembrance of the sufferings of their forefathers, and inspired a warm attachment, both to the civil and the religious rights of human nature."[43]

For those Americans without books or access to libraries, newspapers and pamphlets provided a ready introduction to the ideas of "Cato" and the "Independent Whig." From Franklin's use in the 1720's, Alexander's in the 1730's, and Livingston's in the 1750's, the pattern of journalistic references and quotations from Trenchard and Gordon continued and grew in scope. Thus, the *Boston Gazette* paraphrased, quoted, and reprinted at length from *Cato's Letters* during the 1750's. It repeated its references to a particular favorite, Number 15 of the *Letters*, "Of Freedom of Speech," in 1767, 1771, and 1780.[44] The *Massachusetts Spy* followed the same pattern of repeated citations from Trenchard and Gordon during the early 1770's, and it admitted, in the course of one writer's attacks upon Governor Francis Bernard, this dependence upon

---

[42] While G. K. Smart, "Private Libraries in Colonial Virginia," *American Literature*, X (1938), 24–52, does not discuss the works of Trenchard and Gordon, E. G. Swem, *Virginia Historical Index* (2 vols., Roanoke: Stone, 1934–1936) reveals the presence of copies of *Cato's Letters* and *The Independent Whig* in private libraries and in books auction catalogues.

[43] David Ramsay, *History of the American Revolution* (Dublin: W. Jones, 1793), I, 26–27.

[44] *The Boston Gazette*, April 21, May 12 and 19, June 23, 1755, November 9, 1767, May 6, 1771, and August 14, 1780.

the popularity of the English "Cato": "*Cato's Letters* are now busily parceling out in almost every essay with which of late we are pretty plentifully served up . . . ."[45] Other journals, the *Pennsylvania Evening Post*, the *Maryland Gazette*, the *Providence Gazette*, tended to imitate the pattern of the New England papers.[46] Moreover, editors assumed their audiences would immediately identify the works of Trenchard and Gordon; writers often simply referred to the "Immortal Cato," the "British Cato," or the "Independent Whig."[47] Pamphleteers also cited or borrowed from the thoughts and phrasings of the earlier English Whig writers. Such an author as Tom Paine knew, at least indirectly, of the works of "Cato." Paine read and cited James Burgh's *Political Disquisitions*, a work favorable to the American protests against British policies, and Burgh, in turn, had used Trenchard and Gordon and quoted from them on such subjects as standing armies, freedom of the press, and hereditary titles.[48]

---

[45] *Massachusetts Spy* (Boston), March 7 and 28, and April 4, 1771. Quotation from issue of May 2, 1771.

[46] *Pennsylvania Evening Post* (Philadelphia), April 4, 1775; *Maryland Gazette*, January 21, 1768, April 19, 1770, June 24, 1773, March 7, 1776, August 16, 1787; *Providence Gazette*, February 2, 1782.

[47] *Boston News-Letter*, March 12, 1724, "the Celebrated BRITISH CATO"; *New York Weekly Journal*, December 10, 1733, "the following Sentiments of (I had almost said, the Divine) English CATO"; *ibid.*, February 4, 1733/34, "ADDISON STEEL and ENGLISH CATO have been Men ALMOST DIVINE"; *Maryland Gazette*, April 19, 1770, a paraphrase and excerpt of Number 32 of the *Letters*, signed "Cato"; *Massachusetts Spy*, August 5, 1773, "those excellent statesmen, Gordon and Trenchard."

[48] The ideas of Paine on hereditary monarchy were common property among eighteenth-century radicals and were very close to those of Trenchard and Gordon in *Cato's Letters*. Paine esteemed James Burgh and suggested that Burgh's works should be generally read. Burgh in his *Political Disquisitions: or, an Enquiry into Public Errors, Defects and Abuses* (3 vols., Philadelphia: Bell and Woodhouse, 1775), had borrowed arguments and facts from many sources and frequently used the pithier phrases of Trenchard and Gordon in his work.

After the Revolution

Having been so frequently exposed to the maxims of Trenchard and Gordon, members of the Revolutionary generation remained fond of the Englishmen's work even after the securing of American Independence. When, in 1789, Chief Justice Cushing of Massachusetts queried John Adams on the meaning of that state's guarantee of liberty of the press, he cited from *Cato's Letters* in support of his belief that the truthfulness of a statement should be a defense against a charge of libel on a public official.[49] And when Josiah Quincy, Junior, the ill-fated, tubercular friend and colleague of John Adams, made his will, he bequeathed to his son "Algernon Sidney's works, John Locke's works, Lord Bacon's works, Gordon's *Tacitus*, and Cato's *Letters*" and wished that "the spirit of liberty" might "rest" upon that boy.[50] While the impact of Trenchard and Gordon upon the son, cannot, of course be determined, that gentleman, also named Josiah, did in his own way live in the "spirit of liberty" and became a stubbornly independent political maverick. He survived until 1864, and was, successively, staunch Federalist and opponent of the War of 1812, Mayor of Boston, President of Harvard, and supporter of Lincoln and the Union cause.

Another instance of the liking for Trenchard and Gordon by the surviving leaders of the Revolution, and a clear-cut example of the continued use of the Whig authors, was certified by John Adams himself in 1817. In his last recorded reference to the work of Trenchard and Gordon, Adams wrote to Jefferson and reported the recent republication of *The Independent Whig* in Connecticut. The people of that state were debating the future of the Congregational Establishment

[49] See selections from the correspondence between Cushing and Adams, in Levy, *Legacy of Suppression*, pp. 193–196, and Levy's commentary on their views on pp. 196–201.

[50] Josiah Quincy, *Memoirs of Josiah Quincy, Jr.* (Boston, 1825), p. 350.

and the desirability of expanding religious liberty. Adams wrote that "Someone, no doubt instigated by the Devil," had reprinted the *Whig:* "These Volumes it is said, have produced a Burst of Indignation against Priestcraft Bigotry and Intollerance, and in conjunction with other causes have produced the late Election." In the election, the people of the state had indicated their support for a constitutional convention, and that convention subsequently adopted a new frame of government providing for religious freedom. To Adams, Jefferson replied, ". . . what need we despair of after the resurrection of Connecticut to light and liberality."[51]

In spite of the remnants of interest revealed in the wishes of Josiah Quincy for his son and in the words of John Adams, *Cato's Letters* and *The Independent Whig* did pass into obscurity in the nineteenth century and remained there for much of the twentieth. The reasons for the decline in popular admiration were several: the rejection of English authors by a nationalistic people; the triumph of a rougher and cruder democracy with a lack of patience for the learned arguments of an earlier generation; and, perhaps most important of all, the declining importance or the transformation of some of the old issues that had given meaning to Trenchard and Gordon, the changing nature, for example, of the relationships between church and state once established religions disappeared from the United States. Whatever the causes, the two English radical libertarians did pass from the popular consciousness and, as they did so, they, somewhat more surprisingly, passed from the realm of the historians' interest or even knowledge. Thus, early twentieth-century students of American political theory or constitutional development generally overlooked Trenchard and Gordon; in their principal books, such writers as Benjamin

---

[51] John Adams to Thomas Jefferson, April 19, 1817, in *The Adams-Jefferson Letters,* ed. Lester J. Cappon (Chapel Hill: University of North Carolina Press, 1959), II, 510; Jefferson to Adams, May 5, 1817, *ibid.,* II, 512.

Wright, Charles Merriam, Andrew C. McLaughlin, and Randolph G. Adams made no reference to Trenchard and Gordon or their works.[52] Trenchard and Gordon suffered the fate of popular authors whose writings did not involve ideas so complex as to excite the theoretician, whose great fame as "Cato" was obscured in the midst of the commonly used Revolutionary synonyms of "Brutus," "Caesar," and the rest, and whose books had been so often and so heavily used as literally to disintegrate and disappear from libraries. Not until the 1950's were *The Independent Whig* and *Cato's Letters* really discovered in America. Such writers as Clinton Rossiter, Caroline Robbins, Leonard W. Levy, Arthur M. Schlesinger, Sr., and Jackson T. Main have recently noted the significance of the work of Trenchard and Gordon for the New World.[53]

The present edition is the first modern selection from *Cato's Letters* and *The Independent Whig*. The works themselves were so widely known and admired in eighteenth-century America as to make modern knowledge of them necessary for an understanding of the "light and liberality" of that age of the American Revolution.

---

[52] See, for example, Randolph G. Adams, *Political Ideas of the American Revolution* (Durham: Trinity College Press, 1922); Andrew C. McLaughlin, *The Foundations of American Constitutionalism* (New York: New York University Press, 1932); Charles Merriam, *A History of American Political Theories* (New York: Macmillan, 1903); and Benjamin Wright, *American Interpretation of Natural Law* (Cambridge: Harvard University Press, 1931).

[53] Leonard W. Levy, *Legacy of Suppression* (Cambridge: Harvard University Press, 1960); Jackson T. Main, *The Anti-Federalists* (Chapel Hill: University of North Carolina Press, 1961); Caroline Robbins, *The Eighteenth Century Commonwealthman* (Cambridge: Harvard University Press, 1959); Clinton Rossiter, *Seedtime of the Republic* (New York: Harcourt, Brace, 1953); and Arthur M. Schlesinger, Sr., *Prelude to Independence* (New York: Knopf, 1958).

Table of Editions

The Publishing History of Selected Works of

John Trenchard and Thomas Gordon

The following list is based upon a careful check of the printed catalogues of major European and American libraries, of standard bibliographies, and of original copies or reproductions of many of the works. These sources probably do not include all editions of the works listed. In cases of differences among these sources, the editor has followed whichever source seemed the more authoritative. The actual texts have been preferred to library listings; the more detailed citations to the less circumstantial. The reader should also be cautioned that the French editions cited below were quite possibly not printed in the cities listed on their title pages. The work of d'Holbach, *L'Esprit du Clergé*, lists "Londres" as its place of publication; it was actually issued in Amsterdam. Something of the same possibly took place with the various French editions of Gordon's *Discours . . . sur Tacite* or *sur Salluste*. In the absence of definite evidence of such discrepancies, however, the citations for these works list the place of publication indicated in the texts or in library catalogues.

A. *The Independent Whig* by John Trenchard and Thomas Gordon:

The Character of an Independent Whig (London: J. Roberts, 1719–1720). At least four editions appeared.

Considerations Offered Upon the Approaching Peace and upon the Importance of Gibraltar to the British Empire, Being the Second Part of the Independent Whig (London: J. Roberts, 1719 and 1720). At least five editions were printed.

The Independent Whig (Appeared as fifty-three separate numbers issued from January 20, 1719/20 to January 5, 1720/21).

The Independent Whig (London: J. Peele, 1721).
(London: J. Peele, 1722). Second edition. The text from which the selections in this volume are taken.
(Philadelphia: S. Keimer, 1724). A partial serialization.
(London: J. Peele, 1726). Third edition.
(London: J. Peele, 1728). Fourth edition.
(2 vols., London: J. Osborn, 1732–1735). Fifth edition. The numbering for the various editions in the 1730's is highly erratic.
(3 vols., London: J. Peele, 1732–1735). An "enlarged" edition.
(London, 1736). Seventh edition.
(Philadelphia: Bradford, 1740).
(3 vols., London: J. Peele, 1743). Also called seventh edition.
(4 vols., London: J. Peele, 1747). Includes three volumes of 1743 plus a fourth and new volume.
(Dublin, 1748). A reprint of the greater part of the fourth volume of 1747).
(Manchester, 1750). Selections from Trenchard and Gordon and other writers.
(London: R. Ware, 1752).
L'Esprit du Clergé, ou le Christianisme primitif vengé des enterprises et des excès de nos prêtres modernes (2 vols., London [Amsterdam]: Weller, 1767). A translation of *The Independent Whig* done by Baron d'Holbach.

B. *Cato's Letters* by John Trenchard and Thomas Gordon:

A Collection of Cato's Letters (London: J. Roberts, 1721). A
partial collection of the letters to December 17, 1720. This
appeared in at least two editions, the second with a "new
Preface."

Political Letters in the London Journal (London: J. Roberts,
1721). A third partial collection including the letters published before the end of March, 1721. At least four further
collections were published in 1721 and 1722 by J. Roberts
and J. Peele.

Cato's Letters (4 vols., London: Wilkins, Walthoe, Woodward,
and Peele, 1724). The first full collection.

(4 vols., London: W. Wilkins, 1731).

(4 vols., London: W. Wilkins, 1733). Third edition.

(4 vols., London: W. Wilkins, 1737). Fourth edition.

(4 vols., London: Woodward and Walthoe, 1748). Fifth
edition.

(4 vols., London: Walthoe, 1754–1755). The final, "corrected" edition from which the selections in this volume
are taken.

*Brieven over de Vryheid en het Geluk des Volks onder pen
Goede Regeerung in't Englesch uitgegeeven op den Naam
van Cato* (3 vols., Amsterdam: Tongerlo, Houttayn, 1754).
One hundred and thirty-three of *Cato's Letters* translated
into Dutch.

*Dix-septième lettre de Caton, traduite de l'Anglais de Thomas
Gordon* (Paris: A. Baudoin, [1790]). Translated by J. L.
Chalmel.

C. *The Works of Tacitus* and *The Works of Sallust*
by Thomas Gordon:

The Works of Tacitus (London: Woodward and Peele, vol. I,
1728, and vol. II, 1731).

(Dublin: Gunne, Smith and Bruce, vol. I in two parts, 1728, and vol. II in two parts, 1732).

The Works of Tacitus (2 vols., London: Woodward and Peele, 1737).

Discours historiques, critiques, et politiques sur Tacite (2 vols., Amsterdam: F. Changuion, 1742). Translated by Pierre Daude.

The Works of Sallust (London: Woodward and Peele, 1744). (Dublin: John Smith, 1744).

Discours . . . sur Tacite (2 vols., Amsterdam: F. Changuion, 1749). (3 vols., Amsterdam, 1751).

The Works of Tacitus (5 vols., London: T. and T. Longman, 1753). (4 vols., London, 1757).

Discours . . . sur Salluste (2 vols., Geneva: Cramer, 1759). (2 vols., Geneva: Cramer, 1762). Translated by Pierre Daude.

Discours . . . sur Tacite (2 vols., Geneva: Cramer, 1759). Also translated by Pierre Daude.

Discours . . . sur Tacite (Geneva: Cramer, 1762).

The Works of Sallust (London, 1762). (Glasgow: R. Urie, 1762).

The Works of Tacitus (5 vols., London, 1770). (5 vols., Dublin, 1778).

Discours . . . sur Tacite et sur Salluste (3 vols., Paris: F. Buisson, 1794). A new edition by Pierre Daude.

The Works of Tacitus (2 vols., London, 1817).

Discurso sobre los partidos y facciones . . . traducido de Inglés al Francés, y de este al Español (Madrid, 1840). A translation of the first discourse on Sallust.

The Reign of Tiberius Out of the First Six Annals [of Tacitus] (London: W. Scott, 1886). A selection of part of the Gordon translation.

Selected Bibliography

Since the notes to the "Introduction" and to the text indicate the principal sources of information on Trenchard and Gordon, the editor has not included any formal bibliography. However, the following works, some of which are also cited in the notes, are particularly important as statements of the issues debated by Trenchard and Gordon or as discussions of eighteenth-century political thought.

CONTEMPORARY WORKS

BURGH, JAMES *Political Disquisitions: or, an Enquiry into Public Errors, Defects and Abuses.* 3 vols. Philadelphia: R. Bell, 1775.

GORDON, THOMAS *An Apology for the Danger of the Church.* London: J. Roberts, 1719. Printed anonymously. *A Sermon Preached before the Learned Society of Lincoln's-Inn.* London: J. Peele, 1733.

HARRINGTON, JAMES *The Common-wealth of Oceana.* London: D. Pakeman, 1656.

HOADLY, BENJAMIN *A Preservative Against the Principles and Practices of the Nonjurors both in Church and State.* London: Knapton and Childe, 1716. *A Sermon on the Nature of the Kingdom of Christ.* London: Knapton, 1717.

MOLESWORTH, ROBERT *An Account of Denmark.* London, 1694.

POWNALL, THOMAS *Principles of Polity.* London: E. Owen, 1752.

SIDNEY, ALGERNON   *Discourses Concerning Government*. London, 1698.

TRENCHARD, JOHN, and MOYLE, WALTER   *An Argument Showing . . . a Standing Army Inconsistent with a Free Government*. London, 1697.

TRENCHARD, JOHN   *A Short History of Standing Armies in England*. London: A. Baldwin, 1698.

COLLATERAL READING

BLITZER, CHARLES   *An Immortal Commonwealth; the Political Thought of James Harrington*. New Haven: Yale University Press, 1960.

BRIDENBAUGH, CARL   *Mitre and Sceptre*. New York: Oxford University Press, 1962.

BULLOCH, J. M.   "Thomas Gordon, The Independent Whig," University of Aberdeen Library *Bulletin*, III (1918), 598–612, 733–749.

HANSON, LAURENCE   *Government and the Press, 1695–1763*. Oxford: Oxford University Press, 1936.

JAMES, DAVID G.   *The Life of Reason; Hobbes, Locke, Bolingbroke*. London: Longmans, Green, 1949.

JOSHI, K. L.   "The London Journal, 1719–1738," *Journal* of the University of Bombay, IX (1940), 33–66.

KLEIN, MILTON, ed.   *The Independent Reflector* [by William Livingston]. Cambridge: Harvard University Press, 1963.

LAPRADE, WILLIAM T.   *Public Opinion and Politics in England in the Eighteenth Century*. New York: Macmillan, 1936.

LEVY, LEONARD W., *Legacy of Suppression*. Cambridge: Harvard University Press, 1960.

MACPHERSON, CRAWFORD B.   *The Political Theory of Possessive Individualism: Hobbes to Locke*. Oxford: Clarendon Press, 1962.

REALEY, CHARLES B. "The London Journal and Its Authors," University of Kansas *Humanistic Studies*. Lawrence: University of Kansas Press, 1935, 236–274.

ROBBINS, CAROLINE "Algernon Sidney's Discourses Concerning Government," *William and Mary Quarterly*, 3rd series, IV, (1947), 267–296. *The Eighteenth Century Commonwealthman*. Cambridge: Harvard University Press, 1959.

ROSSITER, CLINTON *Seedtime of the Republic*. New York: Harcourt, Brace, 1953.

WILLIAMS, BASIL *The Whig Supremacy, 1714–1760*. 2nd ed. Oxford: Clarendon Press, 1962.

Editor's Note

The text of the documents is taken from the 1722, or the second complete, edition of *The Independent Whig* and from the 1754–1755 edition of *Cato's Letters*, which was the final and "corrected" edition. (For the publishing history of these works, see the Table of Editions on pp. lxi–lxiv.) Punctuation and spelling follow the originals, including inconsistencies but with the exception of obvious printer's errors, such as "ir" for "it." These are indicated in the text by the use of square brackets (e.g., "i[t]").

Eighteenth-century printing conventions differed from those of today in that most nouns were capitalized, and italics were used not only for foreign words and for emphasis but also for many proper nouns and adjectives, for headings and the like, and for many direct and indirect quotations. These devices have also been retained.

Summaries and comments by the editor are to be found at the beginning of each of the two bodies of selections and at several points within the text of *Cato's Letters*, particularly where the content of omitted numbers requires mention. All numbered annotations are the work of the present volume's editor. Minor omissions are indicated by ellipses.

David L. Jacobson

Davis, California
April, 1965

The Independent Whig

[For each of the following selections, the title indicates the general topic. Reprinted here are seven numbers containing clear statements of the general views of Trenchard and Gordon on religious questions. The first selection, "The Design of this Paper," reveals Trenchard and Gordon's broad views and designs, particularly on the role of the clergy in society. Succeeding numbers discuss particular problems of church-state relations, the relationships among various faiths, and the problems of interpreting the Scriptures. Whatever the authors' qualifications of their argument, Number III of *The Whig*, the second piece in the following pages, very quickly contributed to the belief among their critics that Trenchard and Gordon were enemies of all religion. Number IX, "Of the Clearness of Scripture," suggests Trenchard and Gordon's doubts about most organized religious bodies and also states the authors' own general views. It, in common with the other letters and particularly Number XXIV, proclaims opposition to any enforced conformity or persecution for conscience' sake. Number XXXV emphasizes the compatibility of reason and Scripture and the author's own belief in a rational religion, one in which reason reveals "what is Scripture" and how it is to be interpreted. While the following selections represent the major points argued in *The Independent Whig*, they do not include some of the polemical numbers, in particular those addressed to contemporary detractors. Moreover, it should be noted that these selections are **not** entirely typical of the style of *The*

Whig; they are better than average, unburdened with an overly argumentative tone or numerous Scriptural obscurities. Even though they are less polemical than the average product of this period of Trenchard and Gordon's literary activities, the selections do reveal the vigor of argument, the bluntness of phrase, the occasional sarcasm, which came to maturity in the authors' later writings.]

Number II.

WEDNESDAY, JANUARY 27. 1720.

THE DESIGN OF THIS PAPER.

Religion was designed by Heaven, for the Benefit of Men alone: It teaches us to moderate our Desires, calm our Passions, and be useful and beneficent to one another; and whatever does not contribute to those Ends, ought not to be called by that Name. For, Almighty God has infinite Happiness in himself, which we can neither diminish nor add to; and therefore he can require nothing of us, but for our own Sakes; nor command any Thing but what tends to our own Good, both here and hereafter.

I say it with the utmost Sincerity, that no Man living desires to pay a more true and affectionate Esteem and Reverence than my self to those Clergymen, who answer this End of their Institution, and whose Lives and Manners grace and adorn their Profession and Doctrine.

I thank God, I know many such; and perceive, with Pleasure and Transport, a noble Spirit of Liberty and true Religion rising up among them; which will soon flame out far and wide, if it is not stifled by those, whose true Interest and Honour call aloud to them to give it Assistance and Protection.

That Profession must be always most honourable and deserving from Mankind, which is most useful and advantageous to them. As it is therefore impossible to shew too much Respect to virtuous Clergymen, so the corrupt Part of them cannot be too much expos'd. As the Possession which they have of the Fears and Panick of superstitious People, and in the tenderest Seasons too, enable them to do the greatest Mischief, so the strongest Antidotes ought to be applied to their Poison. It will be ridiculous to call for Protection from that Character, which they constantly disgrace, and to ask Assistance from the Religion, which they neither believe nor practise.

I here list my self under the Banners of the former sort; and design by this Work to illustrate the Beauty of Christianity, by exposing the Deformity of Priestcraft; and to distinguish the good Clergy from the bad, by giving to each his Share of Praise or Infamy, according to the different Deeds done by them. I will lose no Opportunity of doing Justice to the former, nor willingly to the latter.

In doing this, I shall go far backward; and taking Things from the Beginning, shew in the Course of these Papers, the Infinite Evils brought upon Mankind, from Age to Age, by the Pride and Imposture of corrupt Ecclesiasticks: I shall shew what a *Babel* they have built upon the Foundation of Christ and his Apostles, who were made to father Doctrines which they never taught, and to countenance Power which they always disclaimed. I shall shew by what Arts and Intrigues they came, from being Alms-Men of the People, to be Masters of Mankind; and how, by pretending to dispose of the *Other World,* they actually usurped and ruled *This.*

I shall shew, that notwithstanding Christianity was first propagated by Miracles and Mildness only, and the Teachers of it had no Power but to persuade; making it withal appear, in the whole Course of their Lives and Preaching, that they sought no Manner of personal Advantage, or any Manner of Jurisdiction over their Hearers and Converts; yet they who, without their Inspiration and Manners, called themselves their

Successors, did by Virtue of their Names, lay insolent Claim
to Dominion, and carried all Things before them, by the Dint
of Terror and Excommunication.

I shall shew, that though the Clergy, like other Militia, were
raised and paid for protecting Mankind from their Spiritual
Enemy, yet they soon made use of the Sword put into their
Hands against their Masters, and set up for themselves. I shall
shew, that notwithstanding the whole End of their Institution
was to make Men wiser and better, yet wherever *They* prevailed, Debauchery and Ignorance also prevailed; and the
constant Lesson they taught was blind Belief and blind Obedience, of both which they made themselves the Objects. So
that Superstition was an inseparable Creature of their Power,
and the perpetual Issue of it; and tainted Morals and darkened
Minds were the great Props of their Dominion. A good Understanding, and an inquisitive Spirit, led directly to Heresy; and
a pious Life was of ill Example, and a Reproach to the Clergy;
and if any one gave Offence this Way, it was but calling him
Heretick, and delivering him over to *Satan,* and the Man was
undone, and the Clergy safe.

I shall shew how they soon banished the meek Spirit of the
Christian Religion, and growing to as great Variance with
Mercy as they were with Reason, perverted Religion into
Rage, and Zeal into Cruelty. They made the peaceable Doctrine of Jesus a Doctrine of Blood; and excommunicated and
damned by that Name, by which alone Men could be saved.
It is true, they damned one another as much as they did other
People; for, agreeing in nothing but the great Principle of Interest, tho' they rode upon the Necks of their People, yet they
never could be at Peace, nor Ease, among themselves, so long
as each Individual was not in the highest Place: And therefore,
because every one of them could not be above the rest, they
were eternally quarrelling, and giving one another to the Devil.

If one of them held any Proposition, true or false, it was
Reason enough for another to deny it, and *curse* him into the

Bargain. At last, there was not one Principle in their System but what was contested; and they agreed in nothing but their own Power, tho' at the same Time they disputed what that was.

In this everlasting Scuffle and Civil War, they had so mangled Truth, and muffled it up, that few could distinguish it from the false Images they had made of it. And yet these Men, who, by their constant Discords and Debates, confessed themselves in endless Uncertainties, were the sure and infallible Guides to others, who were obliged to believe their Guesses and Contradictions, on Pain of Hell-Fire.

I shall shew what a shameful Hand they have always had in bringing and keeping Mankind under Tyranny and Bondage to such Princes, as would divide the Spoil with them. In such Case, it was a Point of Conscience, and a religious Duty, for Subjects to be miserable Slaves; and Damnation but to strive to be happy. But if the Prince happen'd to be a Lover of Mankind, and endeavoured to protect his People in their Civil and Sacred Rights; then were they the constant Incendiaries of every popular and wicked Faction: They preached nothing but Sedition and Blood, till they had worked up their blind and stupid Votaries to Rebellions and Assassinations; and to such Conduct is owing a great Part of their Power and Wealth.

I think no one, who is the least conversant with Ecclesiastical History, will deny but this was the Condition of Christianity before the *Reformation;* and the chief Intent of this Paper is to let all the World know it, that they may be upon their Guard against the like Mischiefs. It is certain, that the Demands of the High Clergy upon the Laity, are as great, if not greater, than they were at that Time: As *Father Paul* says of *England, The Horse is bridled and sadled, and the old Rider is just getting upon his Back.*

It is Time now to conclude this Paper, by saying, if my hearty Endeavours shall any ways contribute to detect the Impostures, and expose the wicked Practices of those, who, under the prostituted Name of Sanctity, are Foes to Truth, to

Liberty, and Virtue, I shall think my Time and Pains well spent. But if not, I shall have the Internal Satisfaction of having attempted at least to attack Vice and Corruption, however dignified or distinguished; and the worst which can be said of me is,

Magnis tamen excidit ausis[1]

WEDNESDAY, FEBRUARY 3. 1720.

OF THE CONTEMPT OF THE CLERGY.

Ring the Bells backward! The Temple, the Temple is on Fire! The High Priests look aghast, and the People stare, and all cry out, The Craft, the Craft is in Danger!

This I expected, and was prepared for, when I first engaged in the Undertaking: Touch a galled Horse and he will wince, tho' 'tis in order to cure him. I knew a Gentleman, who found out a Murtherer by looking stedfastly in his Face. When any one is conscious of his own Crimes or Infirmities, he is jealous of every Approach towards a Discovery, and often makes one by it.

It is remarkable, that no Order or Society of Men is so apprehensive of Disrespect, or can so little bear the Examination into their Pretensions, as the greatest Part of the Ecclesiasticks: If you ridicule or laugh at the Professions of Law and Physick, the Lawyers and Physicians will laugh with you: The same is true of Soldiers, Merchants, and the Professors of almost all

---

[1] This is part of a sentence which appears in Ovid, *Metamorphoses* II. 328: *"HIC SITUS EST PHAETHON CURRUS AURIGA PATERNI QUEM SI NON TENUIT MAGNIS TAMEN EXCIDIT AUSIS."* ("Here Phaethon Lies, In Phoebus' Car He Fared, And Though He Greatly Failed, More Greatly Dared.")

Arts and Sciences, who generally are the first to expose the Knaves and Fools amongst them.

If a Lawyer, Soldier, or Merchant, deserves the Pillory; neither *Westminster-Hall*, the *Army*, or the *East-India* Company, are in an Uproar; or complain that the Law, Trade, or the Soldiery, are wounded thro' his Sides; nor endeavour to raise a Mobb in his Behalf, or rebel in Token of their unlimited Submission to Government. The Fair Sex do not think themselves ill used, when a Bawd is ty'd to a Cart, or a naughty Nymph beats Hemp: The Eleven Apostles lost no Credit when *Judas* hang'd himself; nor would any honest Clergyman, tho' ever so many of the other Sort did the same, or if it was done for them.

But I do not know by what Judgment or Fatality it happens, that if you but touch the Pretences or Vices of the Meanest of the Ecclesiasticks, so many of their Body are in an Uproar: They roar loud, their Order is exposed, their Mysteries derided and profaned, and Religion it self in Danger of being subverted; and *Socinian*,[1] *Deist* or *Atheist*, is the best Word that is often given to their best Friend; and sometimes all of them are given.

All other Societies of Men are contented with the Esteem and Honour, which result from the Usefulness of their Employments and Professions, and the Worth and Capacity of their Members; and yet none stand in such a Situation, and have so many Advantages to acquire Respect and Homage, as the Clergy.

Their Office is evidently adapted to promote the Welfare of Human Nature, and to propagate its Peace and Prosperity in this World, as well as its eternal Felicity in the next: so that it is the Interest of all Men to honour it; and none but a Madman will condemn and ridicule what has a manifest Tendency to the Security and Happiness of all Mankind.

---

[1] A Socinian was a follower of two Italian religious leaders, uncle and nephew, whose Latinized name was Socinus. In essence, Socinianism amounted to a sixteenth-century brand of Unitarianism.

The Temporal Condition of the Clergy does likewise place them far above Contempt: They have great Revenues, Dignities, Titles, and Names of Reverence, to distinguish them from the rest of the World; and it is too well known that Wealth, Power, and Learning, carry to the Vulgar a kind of Mystery, and distant Grandeur, and command not only Admiration and Reverence, but often a superstitious Veneration.

Added to this, they have the Possession and Direction of our Fears, and are admitted in Health and Sickness: Every Sunday they have the sole Opportunity to gain our Esteem by worthy and useful Instructions, and all the Week by their good Lives: They educate us whilst young, influence us in our middle Age, and govern us in our Dotage, and we neither live nor die without them.

A numerous Body of Men, so constituted and endowed, so privileged and posted, are capable of being most useful and beneficent to Society, if their Actions are suitable to their Professions. All the World will acknowledge and pay a willing Homage to their Merit, and there will be no need of demanding, much less of extorting Respect, or of Complaints and Exclamations for want of it. The Danger lies on the other Side; for there are such Seeds of Superstition in human Nature, that all our Prudence and Caution will be little enough to prevent even Adoration to their Persons.

If, therefore, they want that Respect they are so fond of, they cannot be to seek for the true Reasons, *viz.* their own Corruptions and Worthlesness, which must be exceeding great to get the better of so many Advantages. When a certain late Dutchess was complaining to a Gentleman of more Wit than Complaisance, that (in Spite of her great Quality and Revenue) she was subject to continual Affronts; *Pray, Madam,* says he, *is not Mr.* Goodman *an excellent Actor?*

If Clergymen would avoid Contempt, let them avoid the Causes of it. Let them not be starting and maintaining eternal Claims to worldly Power: Let them not be hunting after Honours, courting Preferments, and bustling for Riches: Let them not be assuming to give Models of human Government, or to adjust and determine the Titles of Princes: Let them not pretend to punish any Man for his Way of Worship, and to give him to the Devil for his Money or Opinion: Let them not join in Factions, and foment Rebellions: Let them not defy Heaven by swearing falsly: Let them not promote Servitude in the People, and Barbarity in the Prince; and let them not flatter wicked Kings, and plague and disturb good Ones.

Let them win Respect, and wear it; but let them not earn Infamy, and demand Veneration. Let not those of them, who gratify Brutish Appetites, and live in all Vileness, add Want of Shame to their Want of Grace, and bewail that they are contemned, while they are deserving it. If a Man pretending to great Gravity and Regard, should dress himself up in a Fool's Coat, and a Pair of Horns, would not People laugh at him in Spite of themselves? And would not his Resentment and Rebukes add still to their Mirth? A Clergyman who is Drunk on *Saturday*, will but, with an ill Grace, talk of his Dignity and Ambassadorship on *Sunday*. Ought we to own and reverence that Man as our Guide to Heaven, who is himself going a contrary Road, and rioting in those Vices which his whole Duty is to restrain?

The Honour therefore of the good Clergy is consulted and promoted by exposing the bad. A profane Priest is the Disgrace and Bane of his own Order; and they who stand by him, adopt his Infamy, and defile themselves. If he neglects God, and disturbs human Society, how do the Clergy suffer tho' he is whip'd or hang'd? His Punishment is their Credit and Security, because by it is lopped off from their Body a gangrened Limb, that incumbred and deformed the rest.

Atheists, who are not restrained by the Fear of God, which is stronger than all the Laws in the World, ought, in the Opinion of Politicians, as well as Casuists, to be expelled from the Society of Men: And shall more Mercy be shewn to those who are so hardened in Impiety, that tho' they believe a God, yet dread not his Vengeance, but swear by his great and terrible

Name to an avowed Falshood? Or can the Clergy suffer by the Loss of such execrable Company?

An unfortunate *Levite,* some Years since, had his Head cleft by a Butcher, who caught him in Bed with his Wife; and neither the Number of Reverend Auditors, who attended the Tryal, a due Regard to the Cloth, or an Apprehension of the Carnage it might produce, could hinder the Judge from directing the Jury to call the Crime only *Man-Slaughter;* which so provoked the meek Spirit and Patience of a Holy Brother, then present, that he cried out in the Court, *Hey Day! Here's a fine World! if these Things are suffered, there will be no living for us.*

No chaste or sober Clergyman could be terrify'd with such an Example, or think the Church in any Danger by it. Does any vertuous Member of the Holy Order suffer either in his Person or Character, if *Biss* diverts his Spectators in a Pillory, or Parson *Paul* his Auditors upon a Gallows? None can share in their Disgrace, but those who sympathize in their Crimes, or censure their Punishment. How much more honest, as well as prudent, would it be to remove the Guilt from themselves, by throwing it all upon the devoted Head; to put the evil Thing out of the City; and to imitate the Sagacity of the horned Herd, who always drive the blown Deer from amongst them, where he seeks his Refuge, tho' at the Hazard of involving the whole Tribe in his Misfortune?

Number IV.

WEDNESDAY, FEBRUARY 10.   1720.

OF THE EXPLICATION OF THE SCRIPTURE.

To fear God, and keep his Commandments, is the Summary of the Old Testament; and to believe that Jesus Christ is come in the Flesh, is the Compendium of the New.

Whoever can prove his Obedience and Faith, by these two plain Duties, fulfils the Law and the Gospel.

It was most agreeable to the infinite Goodness and tender Mercies of God, to make every Thing, which he requires of us weak Men, obvious and clear. The Importance of the Duty implies its Certainty, which is not to be found in Phrases either doubtful or obscure. The Scriptures are justly stiled the *Revealed Will* of God, and are address'd to *all* Mankind, and given to remain as a Rule of Faith and Manners to the End of the World. It must therefore follow, that whatever is necessary to be known in them, is to be as easy and intelligible at one Time as another, and to all Men alike.

Where their Meaning cannot be positively determined, a new Inspiration will be necessary to reduce them to Certainty; and if that is wanting, every Thing else is but Conjecture. Whoever therefore goes about to put a Construction upon such Passages in Scripture, and enjoins us to believe his Interpretation, does not demand Submission to the Word of God, but to his own Authority and Imagination.

What Use is there of an unintelligible Proposition; or of a Revelation which wants to be reveal'd? Almighty God will never require of us to see in the Dark, till he has given us new Eyes; nor to believe any Article, or obey any Precept, till we understand him, and know what he means. A Rule which is not plain, is no Rule at all: Nor will he make a Law binding, or the Transgression of it a Sin, till we know what it is.

It is true, human Laws oblige all Men to submit to the Penalty annex'd to the Transgression, tho' many perhaps may never hear of them. But this is to prevent the constant Plea of Ignorance, which otherwise would be made by all Offenders. The Corruption and Imbecility of human Nature make this Procedure necessary. But it is far otherwise in the Dispensation of Providence: The Author of it sees our Hearts, penetrates the most secret Recesses of our Souls, makes indulgent Allowances for our Weaknesses, and expects nothing from us, but what he has given us the Means and Abilities of knowing and performing. He requires us not to make Brick without Straw. He judges by the Intention, not the Action. We cannot offend him, but voluntarily; much less offer him an Affront, when we design Respect and Obedience.

The Creator and Preserver of Mankind cannot take Delight in puzling his Creatures with Darkness and Ambiguities, and in Points too where their Souls are in Danger. He is not a rigid Master, who would reap where he did not sow. This would be a cruel Mockery, unworthy of the Divine Being, *Who has brought Life and Immortality to Light.*

Nothing is plainer than the Law and the Gospel. Whoever says the contrary, does no less than accuse the great and good God, and justify wicked and wilful Men, whom he has left without Excuse, by telling them clearly what he expects from them. *What does God require of thee, O Man, but to do Justice, to love Mercy, and to walk Humbly?* said One of his Prophets out of his Mouth. I am very sure there is no Difficulty in understanding this.

The obscure Passages in Scripture could not be intended for our Instruction. Infinite Wisdom has hid them from our Eyes, to be brought to Light in his own Time, and then to answer the Ends of his Providence; or perhaps to baffle our vain Pride and Curiosity. Who art thou, O Man, who wilt be wiser than the Omniscient; who wilt make those Things necessary, which he has not made so; wilt discover what he has thought fit to conceal, and know his Secrets whether he will or no? This would be to mend the Scripture; to make it more useful than God has made it; to help the Holy Ghost, and to teach the Almighty how to express himself.

How absurd would it be to send Cook-Maids and Day-Labourers to study *Aristotle* and *Suarez;* to rake into the Jargon of the Schools; to learn all Languages, examine all Systems, and to discover of themselves all Errors, Interpolations and Mistakes; or to do what is much more ridiculous, *that is,* wholly throw themselves and their Salvation, in most Countries, upon a Confederacy of Men, who have an Interest to deceive and oppress them, and ever did so when they had an Opportunity; who have been always at Variance with one another, and with themselves; and have agreed in nothing, but the misleading of those who trusted them! And yet One of these must be the unhappy Circumstance of the greatest Part of Mankind, if what I have said before is not true; which we may be sure the Divine Goodness cannot permit.

Nothing is more evident from History, than that most, if not all, the Improvements and Reformations of Religion have been made not only without, but in Opposition to these Men. There have been near a Million of them kept in constant Pay for the best Part of Seventeen Hundred Years, to teach the World by their Precepts, and reform it by their Example; and yet I am persuaded they will not pretend that Religion is plainer, the Scriptures better understood, or that Mankind are more wise or virtuous for all their Instructions. So little have we been benefited by their Labours, and for all the Money they have receiv'd! I wish I could not say that the World has gradually decreas'd in Piety and Virtue, as these its Teachers have advanced in Riches and Power. It is owned by the best of themselves.

It is the farthest from my Thoughts, by any Thing I have before said, to undervalue their true Office, much less to make it useless. I sincerely think it absolutely necessary to the Peace and Happiness of Society. The *Roman* Consuls had an Officer attending their Triumphial Chariots, whose Business it was to cry out *Memento mori.*[1]

I would have these too answer the same End of their Institution; to press the Reading of the Scriptures upon their Hearers;

---

[1] This line may be roughly translated, "Remember, thou must die." The full statement, supposedly made to those celebrating a triumph, was *"Respice post te, hominem te memento."* ("Look behind you, remember that you are but mortal.")

to shew their Excellency and Advantages; to inculcate the *plain Precepts* of Faith and Morality contained in them; and to demonstrate the Goodness of God to Men, by proving that he has laid down to us, in plain Words, every Duty which he requires of us, either to himself, our Neighbour, or our selves. But let them not distract, instead of instructing; and confound ignorant People with Metaphysical Subtilties, which the Wisest cannot comprehend. Let them not strain ridiculous and selfish Consequences from obscure Parts of Scripture, and make the Almighty mean what he never said.

Let them give us God's Will in God's Words.

Another End of their Office is to execute those Duties of our most Holy Religion, which the Word of God has left at large for every one to do, but which indeed are necessary to be perform'd by single Persons in the several Churches or Societies of Christians; such as reading the Scriptures and publick Prayers aloud to the Congregation, and administring the Sacraments: What by the Gospel Liberty is the Right of every one (as shall be unanswerably made out hereafter) is by the Consent of Voluntary and National Churches become the Duty and Business of particular Persons, who are set aside and paid for that Purpose.

In what I have before said, I have the Concurrence of the best and wisest of our own Clergy, who acknowledge and contend that we are not to take the Almighty's Meaning at second-hand, nor receive that for his Will which we our selves do not find to be so; but that we are to enquire before we believe, and to be convinc'd before we assent; every Assertion or Proposition, before it is examin'd, being alike to the Understanding, as every Colour is to the Blind: They own that our Judgment ought to be at no Man's Service, nor our Minds controuled in religious Matters, but by God alone; for as no Man's Soul can be saved by Proxy, so no Man ought to exercise his Faith by Proxy.

WEDNESDAY, FEBRUARY 24. 1720.

OF CREEDS AND CONFESSIONS OF FAITH.

I Have shewn in my Fourth Paper, the Boldness and Absurdity of the Exposition of Holy Scripture, when that Exposition is maintained and imposed for Canonical Truth. I shall here prosecute the same Subject, merely as it relates to *Creeds* and *Confessions of Faith.*

In our dispu[t]es with the Church of *Rome,* we contend that the Scripture alone is a sufficient Rule of Faith and Practice; and our Divines have proved it unanswerably. But when our High-Church Priests argue with Dissenters, and those whom they are pleased to christen Hereticks, Holy Writ is not so highly complemented: It is then very subject to lead us into Mistakes, and hard to be understood. It is true 'tis infallible, and was given us from Heaven to *be a Light unto our Feet, and a Lamp unto our Paths;* but still it is dark and insufficient without *Human Aid and Explication.* For, though it be exceeding plain to us of the Established Church of *England,* and proves us to be in the Right in every Article, Ceremony and Habit whatsoever; yet it is utterly hid from those who will not accept of *our* Guidance, and submit to *our* Authority. And therefore, if they refuse to believe and obey our *Supplements* and *Improvements* of the Bible, and to accept of the Salvation which is to be had in our Church, and the Church of *Rome,* they shall have no Salvation at all. It is fit and Orthodox that Men should perish for following their Consciences, and for understanding the Scripture without the Leave of the Ordinary.

Thus when they debate with the Papists, they praise the Scriptures, inveigh against the imposing of Opinions, and speak in the Stile of Dissenters: But when they are pleased to rebuke Non-conformists, they borrow the Language of Papists, and urge the Authority of our Apostolick Church, and her divine Right to judge for others; and deal hard Language, and worse Usage, to all that take the same Privilege which they do. There is, however, this small Difference between us Conformists and the Schismaticks; We have good Pay for being Orthodox, and the Separatist pays dear for being in the Wrong. If these are not two good Reasons for delivering him over to Satan, I despair of finding better.

In Consequence of this Power in High-Churchmen to be the Mouthsmen of the Bible, which if we take their Word cannot speak for it self, they claim a Right to make *Creeds* for others: And this is what I am now to examine.

I think it but Justice to the Goodness of God to affirm, that Belief or Disbelief can neither be a Virtue or a Crime in any One, who uses the best Means in his Power of being informed. If a Proposition is evident, we cannot avoid believing it; and where is the Merit or Piety of a necessary Assent? If it is not evident, we cannot help rejecting it, or doubting of it; and where is the Crime of not performing Impossibilities, or not believing what does not appear to us to be true? Are Men who have good Eyes, the more righteous for seeing? Or do they offend in seeing too well? Or do blind Men sin, in not distinguishing Colours?

When we clearly see the Connexion of a Proposition, or know that we have God's Word for it, our Assent is inevitable. But if we neither comprehend it our selves, nor see God's Authority for it, and yet swallow it, this is *Credulity*, and not *divine Faith*, which can have nothing less than *divine Truth* for its Object. When we are sure that God Almighty speaks to us, we readily believe him, who cannot lie, nor be mistaken, nor deceive us: But when Men speak, though from God himself, our Belief in them is but human Confidence, if we have only their own Authority that they had it from God. Their being Bishops, their being learned, their meeting together in Synods; all this alters not the Case: We can judge of their Opinions no otherwise than as of the Opinions of Men, and of their Decisions, but as of human Decisions.

When the Articles of any *Creed* appear to be contained in Scripture, whoever believes *that,* does in Consequence believe *them;* and then such Creed is unnecessary: But when we cannot, or think we cannot, find them in Scripture, and yet give equal Credit to them, we depreciate and profane the divine Authority it self, by accepting the Words of Man's Invention as wiser and more significant than the Words of God's own chusing.

We are sure that the Scripture Phrases were inspired by the Holy Ghost, and as sure that our own Forms and Injunctions are Human, and framed by Priests. It is therefore strange, that the former should be insufficient and unintelligible, and the latter infallible, and to be embraced and obey'd on the pain of Damnation; and that the Priests must do what God Almighty has, without Success, endeavoured to do.

Besides, as the Imposition of human Creeds is contrary to Reason, so is it also to Charity. They were generally made in a Passion, not to edify, but to plague those for whom, or rather against whom, they were intended. They were the Engines of Wrath and Vengeance, nor could they serve any other Purpose. Those who believed them already, did not want them; and those who disbelieved them, were not the better for them. But this was not the worst of it; for they who did not receive them against their Conscience, were curs'd; and they who did, deserved it. So that either the Wrath of God on one Hand, or the Wrath and Cruelty of the Clergy on the other, was unavoidable. If People said they believed, and did not, they mocked God, and shipwrecked their Souls; and if they did not believe and owned it, though they saved their Souls, they provoked their Reverend Fathers, and were destroyed.

Whenever these Dictators in Faith had a Mind to be mischievous, and to undo one who gave them signal Offence, either by his good Reputation, or good Bishoprick, they began his Ruin by their great Care for his Soul; and so invented a Creed for him, which ruined him effectually, by giving him, as they said, to Satan, but, in Truth, to Beggary, Stripes, or Flames. He therefore who had any Virtue or Religion, was a certain Sufferer by those Systems of Faith, which were contrived for that Purpose. The Man that had no Conscience nor Honesty, was not worthy of their Anger; or, which is most likely, was on the Orthodox Side, or at least quickly became a Convert to it, being, like themselves, able to swallow any Thing.

So that Creeds, as they were the Result of Revenge, Pride, or Avarice, so were they the constant Preludes and Introductions to Ignorance, Cruelty and Blood; and the wretched Laity were craftily, as well as inhumanly, made the deluded and unnatural Instruments of Butchering one another, to prove the Infallibility of the Faith-Makers; who, while they were wantonly shedding Christian Blood, and dooming to Damnation those who called upon the Name of the true God, had the shameless Assurance to miscal themselves the Ambassadors of the meek Jesus.

And indeed, what better could be expected from Men so chosen, so unqualify'd, and so interested, as the Members of these general Creed-making Councils for the most Part were? They were chosen from several Parts by a Majority of Votes; and they who were most aspiring, factious or crafty, carried it. They sprung from the meanest of the People: They were bred in Cells: They popped into the World without Experience or Breeding: They knew little of Mankind, and less of Government, and had not the common Qualifications of Gentlemen: They were governed by Passion, and led by Expectation: And, either eager for Preferment, or impatient of missing it, they were the perpetual Flatterers or Disturbers of Princes.

These were the Men, this their Character. When these Reverend Fathers were got together in a Body, by the Order of a Prince or a Pope; who, having his Necessities, or the Ends of his Ambition to serve, chose proper Tools for those Purposes; they were directed to form such Creeds and Systems of Faith, as his present Views or Interests made requisite for Mankind to believe.

In this new Employment every Member, we may be sure, was forward to shew his Talents in starting new Tenets, or in contradicting those already started, and so to make himself considerable enough for the Preferment which he was resolved to earn one way or another. And this being the great Aim of them all, Jealousies and hard Words were carried to the most violent Pitch. There was no End of their Wrangling and Reviling: Not content to abuse each other by Word of Mouth, they sometimes scolded in Writing; and every Reverend Father drew up a bitter *Billinsgate* Petition against another Reverend Father. Sometimes, not satisfied with Vollies of Scurrility, unheard of in Assemblies of Gentlemen, they had Recourse to Club-Law, and made good their Inventions and Distinctions with Blows and Blood. And if the Truth could not be found out by Scolding, Contradiction, and Battle, it was not found out at all.

Thus any Emperor or Pope might have what Creed he pleased, provided he would be at the Pains and Price of it. And for the rest of Mankind, they had this short Choice, *To comply*, or be undone.

Number IX.

WEDNESDAY, MARCH 16.   1720

OF THE CLEARNESS OF SCRIPTURE.

I Shall in this Paper endeavour to confirm what I have said in my last; by shewing, that God Almighty, in revealing his Will to Mankind, has always taken effectual Care that it could not be mistaken, and therefore made it so plain, as to need no farther Explanation, in all Things which are necessary for us to know.

When God would have his Pleasure known to Men, it is agreeable to his Goodness to make it evident; when he would not, it is agreeable to his Wisdom to make it impenetrable. Scripture was not given to make work for Interpreters; nor to teach Men how to doubt, but how to live. The Holy Spirit has made undeniably clear and manifest all those Precepts which enjoin Faith and Obedience, which are the great Points of Religion; and weak Men cannot correct him, and do it better themselves.

I think it is generally granted, that Revelations are no more, and that Prophecy hath ceased. The Reason given for this, I take to be a very good one; namely, that God has already sufficiently discovered his Mind to Men, and made his Meaning manifest. If it were otherwise, we should doubtless have his extraordinary Presence still; but as we have not, it is to be presumed there is no Occasion. He appeared himself whilst Men were in Darkness; but now that he hath shewn them his *marvellous Light*, he appears no more. His Presence is supplied by his Word; which being addressed to all Men equally, and not to *one Tribe of Men* to interpret it for the rest, it follows, that all Men have in their Power the Means to understand it. *Old Revelation* therefore does not want the Assistance of *New*, nor has the Omnipotent any need of *Prolocutors*.

While God is delivering his Law to the World, he is plain even to Exactness; and his Orders are full and circumstantial, even about the minutest Points. This is eminently proved by his Manner of giving Laws to the *Jews*. Every Ceremony, and every Instrument and Garment, used in their Worship, is precisely described and directed. The Trumpets, the Candlesticks, the Lamps, the Spoons, the Snuffers, are all of his own Appointment, both as to the Materials and the Use of them. He makes it impossible to mistake him. He calls the Priests by their Names, points out their Persons, and shews them every Branch of their Office. He limits and governs their Behaviour while they are about it; and does not leave it to *their* Wisdom to invent such Postures and Ceremonies, as *they* think fit to call *decent* and *significant*. They had not the Privilege to chuse their own Garments. *Moses,* who was the *Civil Magistrate,* had it in his Charge to *Sanctify* and *Consecrate* their Persons: Their Business in the Sacrifices, is pointed out to them: They are to put their Hands upon the Head of the Beast, and to receive its Blood, and to make Fires. They are not, as I remember, once made use of to speak God's Mind to his People; *that* is the Duty and Commission of the *Civil Magistrate,* and *Moses* performs it. They had not the least Hand in the Celebrating of the *Passover,* the *Jewish Sacrament,* to which ours of the *Lord's Supper* hath, it is said, succeeded: And as little were they employed in that other of *Circumcision,* the reputed Ancestor of *Baptism.* In short, their whole Function was to be *Servants* and Journeymen in the *House of* S[a]*crifice.*

If Almighty God was thus punctual and particular in the Rituals and Outside of his Worship, can we imagine that he was defective or obscure, in declaring the more weighty Points of the Law? No—When our first Parents broke the Covenant, they did it wilfully, and could not pretend that they understood it not; *Of the Tree of the Knowledge of Good and Evil, thou shalt not eat of it,* was all the Injunction that was laid upon them: And there was no need of a Commentator here. The Text might have been rendered more perplext, but not more plain.

The Covenant which he made with *Abraham* was not less clear: He was to *be the God of* Abraham *and of his Seed;* and *every Male of his Race, and those that were bought with Money, were to be circumcised.* There were no more Words to this Contract; and the Patriarch and his Issue had but one short System of Divinity, most intelligible of it self, and in no wise darkened with Glosses.

The Decalogue, or the Law of the Ten Commandments, delivered by God himself from *Mount Sinai*, with great Glory and astonishing Circumstances, was little else but the Law of Nature reduced into Tables, and expressed in Words of God's own chusing: And they were worthy of the Omnipotent and Infallible Author; for they were so plain and indisputable, that not a single Person of all the Twelve Tribes, so addicted on other Occasions to Contradiction and Wrangling, so much as pretended not to understand them: Nor was there one Man, much less a *Body of Men*, set apart to explain them.

When God spoke to the *Jews* by his Prophets, the same Method of Clearness was observed. The Admonitions given, and the Judgments denounced, were adapted to the Capacity of every one concerned. The *Jews*, it is true, did not often believe them, at least not mind them; but it was never pleaded that they did not comprehend them. God inspired, and the Prophets spake, and all understood; but neither *Creeds* nor *Paraphrases* were made, for they were not necessary. At last, indeed, the *Priests* and *Pharisees made void the Word of God by their Traditions, and* very rigidly *tithing Mint and Cummin, neglected the greater Things of the Law, and taught for Doctrines the Commandments of Men*. But we know what Thanks and Character they had for their Pains from the Saviour of the World, and what a terrible Doom he pronounced against them. Read the 23d Chapter of St. *Matthew*'s Gospel, and see the Description of these vile Hypocrites, and then consider whether they be at this Day without Heirs or Successors. Indeed it seems to me to be the only Succession which has not been interrupted.

The Gospel, when it came, as it was to excel all other Laws in its Ends and Usefulness, so was it the shortest and plainest Institution in the World. It only added the Duty of Faith to that of Good Works, which was the great, if not the only, Business of the Moral Law. To believe that *Jesus Christ was the only Son of God*, was the great Principle of the Christian Religion. Nor was the Practice of this Belief attended with the least Difficulty, since our Saviour proved his Mission and Omnipotence, by Miracles that were undeniable and convincing. For the Truth of them he appealed to Men's Senses, and there was neither Mystery nor Jugling in his Actions, nor did they want any Body to explain them.

All this is further confirmed by the Conduct of the Apostles. The constant Drift and Tenour of their Lives and Preaching, was to perswade Mankind to believe in *Jesus Christ*. In order to which they worked Miracles, and gave the Holy Ghost. The Precept was thus short, and the Motives to comply with it were thus irresistible. Hence it was, that sometimes Thousands were convinced in a Moment, without either *Commentaries*, or *Creeds*, or *Catechisms*. And indeed who could avoid believing a Proposition that proved it self?

The Apostles, when they had converted one City, did not stay to establish a Hierarchy there only, and to tell the *same Thing* over and over again to those that knew it already: No,— when they had planted the Faith in one Place, they travelled to another, and preached the Gospel to the unconverted World; leaving those already converted, to perform Christian Worship *their own Way*. If they believed in Christ, and lived soberly, the Apostles desired no more. Those were the *Two Things needful;* nor were they more needful than clear.

In this plain manner did God Almighty always discover himself and his Will, whenever he dispensed his Laws to the World. On the other Hand, while he hid himself from the Heathen World, did their Priests ever discover him? No,— they had Deities without Number; They worshipped Stocks and Stones, Trees, Rivers, Bulls, Serpents, Monkeys and Garlick. Both their Religion and their Gods were of the Priests making, and therefore we may be sure they were hopeful Ones. They created their Deities *after their own Likeness;* angry, cruel, covetous and lustful. Their Mysteries were full of Horror, Obsceneness, Craft and Delusion. The Will of their God was searched in the Guts and Ordure of dead Beasts, and a Coop of Chickens were his Privy Councillors. His Favour or

Displeasure depended upon their Craws; if they had puny Stomacks, the God was in a Fit of the Spleen; if ravenous, he was in a giving Humour, and would grant you any Thing, even to the Cutting of the Throats of a whole Army, or Burning of a City, or Plundering a Province: And when he was tired of his Kindness to you, he would perhaps in a Day or Two, do all this for your Enemy.

Upon the whole, when Almighty God reveals his Will, he does it effectually; but when he disguises it in dark and doubtful Expressions, it is plain the Time of making himself *further* known to Men, is not yet come, and it is in vain for them to pry into his Secrets.

The all-merciful Being does never require of us, that which we cannot find he requires. It is not consistent with his Wisdom and Goodness, to make that necessary which he hath not made plain. He has with the greatest Perspicuity, described the Candlesticks, Tongs, and other *Tools* of Worship under the *Jewish* Law; and yet in the Gospel has not said one Word of some Doctrines, which we are told are necessary to Salvation. Altars and Priests are divinely appointed in the *Old Dispensation,* but are neither directed nor described in the *New;* and yet we know of what Importance they are at present in the *Popish Church* and *elsewhere.* The Priest's Office is particularized and circumscribed, even to the Killing of a Goat, or a Pair of Pigeons; and yet under the Gospel it is not so much as hinted, that a Priest shall administer either of the Sacraments; though, if we will take their own Words for it, there can be no Sacrament without them. In the *Levitical* Law, the *Sons of Levi* are expresly appointed to be Priests continually; but it is not once said in the Christian Law, that there must be an uninterrupted Race of Bishops, or Popes, or Priests, to the End of the World; and that there can be no Church where it is not; tho', if this had been needful, it must have been particularized: So essential a Part of the Christian Religion, and so absolutely necessary to every Man's Salvation, could never have been wholly omitted, or so much as left in Doubt.

As by the Law of *Moses,* the Priest's Office and Duty were minutely described, so their Maintenance was ascertained: But by the Law of Christ, there is not any Priesthood at all appointed, (as I shall fully make out hereafter) and consequently no certain Provision made for them. It is indeed said, that *The Labourer is worthy of his Hire;* and I acknowledge it is fit that those who hire them should pay them: But sure this Text leaves every one at Liberty to chuse his own *Labourer,* and to make as good a Bargain as he can, or to do his own Business himself. What Pretence is there of a Divine Right to just a Tenth Part; and not only of our Estates, but of our Stock and Industry too, which in some Corn Lands comes to Double the Rent that the Landlord receives?

The *Tribe of Levi* amongst the *Jews* were the twelfth Tribe of *Israel,* and, in the Division of the Lands, had a Right to the Twelfth Share, without any Regard had to their Priestly Office; and consequently were allowed but a very small Proportion towards their *Hire,* and much less than, I doubt, their pretended Successors would be satisfy'd with. I would therefore, as a sincere Friend to their Order, recommend to their Consideration, whether it would not be most adviseable, to quit their Divine Right, and be even content with the Laws of the Land.

Number XXIV.

WEDNESDAY, JUNE 29. 1720.

OF PERSECUTION.

There are but two Ways of propagating Religion, namely, Miracles and Exhortation. The one depends upon divine Power, and the other upon the Strength of Reason.

Where the Finger of God appears, all further Testimony is needless; and where the Truth is obvious to Reason, Miracles are needless. God never wills us to believe that which is above our Reason, but he at the same Time commands our Faith by Miracles. He does not leave necessary Things doubtful; and for this Reason alone it is, that Men are said to be *left without Excuse*.

Every Point of Belief therefore must be supported either by Reason or Miracle, or else it is no Point of Belief at all. Both the *Jewish* and the Christian Law were delivered and enforced with manifest Signs and Demonstrations of God's extraordinary Presence and Power. And it has been very justly boasted of the Christian Religion in particular, that it spread and prospered by Miracles, Persuasion, and Clemency, in Opposition to Violence and Cruelty.

But when Christianity became tainted and defaced by Priestcraft, it grew necessary to have many Points believed, which contradicted both Revelation and common Sense: Therefore its *Foster Fathers,* who to the Worship of God added the Worship of themselves, had no other Way to prove their System but by Wrath and Vengeance. Reason was against them, and Miracles not for them: So their whole Dominion stood upon Falshood, guarded by Force. This Force, when it is exercised upon a religious Account, is called *Persecution;* which is what I am now to consider and expose.

To punish Men for Opinions that were even plainly False and Absurd, is barbarous and unreasonable. We possess different Minds as we do different Bodies; and the same Proposition carries not the same Evidence to every Man alike, no more than the same Object appears equally clear to every Eye. A cholerick Temper, when it is not corrected with Reason, and seasoned with Humanity, is naturally zealous. A phlegmatick Temper, on the other side, as it is naturally slow, so is it lukewarm and indifferent. Is there any Merit in having a warm Complexion, or any Sin in being dull?

But further; to punish a Man for not seeing the Truth, or for not embracing it, is in the first Place, to make him miserable, because he is already so; and in the second Place, to pluck Vengeance out of God's Hands, to whom alone it belongs, if we will take his own Word for it. If this Severity is pretended to be for his Good; I would ask, Is manifest Cruelty any Token of Kindness, or was it ever taken for such? Does it not always encrease the Evil which it is employed to cure? Is Destruction the Means to Happiness? Absurd and terrible!

But what, if, after all, the Person persecuted should be found an Adherent to Truth and Honesty, and *his* Enemies should prove *their* Enemies? Would not this be adding Cruelty to Falshood, and heaping up Guilt with both Hands? This indeed is often the Case. And where it is not altogether so, the Persecutors are still inexcusable. He who, in the Search of Truth, does all he can, does as much as he ought. God requires no more; and what Man dares do it, who fears him? When *he* acquits, who is it that condemns?

Besides, he that suffers, or at least dies, for Religion, gives a Testimony by so doing, that his Conscience is dearer to him than Ease or Interest: Whereas the Patrons of Persecution have manifestly personal Motives and self Ends in it. It gratifies their Pride, awes Mankind, and brings them Obedience and Gain.

Our blessed Saviour, who had no View but the Redemption of the World, never used his Omnipotence, or the least Force, to subdue his Enemies, though he knew their Hearts to be malicious and implacable. He neither delivered them to Death nor the Devil, even for the hellish Designs to kill him; much less for Points of Error or Speculation. He reasoned with all Men, but punished none. He used Arguments, he worked Wonders; but Severities he neither practised, nor recommended. His was a different Spirit. He rebuked his Apostles with Sharpness, when being yet full of the Spirit of this World, and void of the Spirit of God, they were for bringing down Fire from Heaven upon the *Heretical Samaritans*. The merciful

Jesus would not hurt these half Heathens, though they rejected him in Person; for he *came not to destroy Mens Lives, but to save them:* And they who take another Method, give the Lye to the Lord of Life, and disown him for their Head.

His Apostles, as soon as they had received the Holy Ghost, grew wiser and more merciful. They shewed by Miracles, that they were endowed with the Divine Power; but they never used either to compel or to burn, though they were beset with false Teachers, and opposed by Gain-sayers. They were so far from giving ill Usage, that they never returned i[t]. The Exercise of *Wholsome Severities* was no part of their Doctrine. Prayers and Perswasions were their only Arms, and such as became the *Gospel of Peace.*

This was the mild and heavenly Behaviour of Christ and his Apostles, towards those who did not believe, or believed wrong; and it was followed by all their Successors who aimed at the Good of Souls. But those who used the Sacred Function as a Stirrup to Power and Gain, made a new Gospel of their own Decisions, and forced it upon the World, partly by *Fighting,* and partly by *Cursing.* The Apostles taught Christ, and their Successors taught Themselves. It was not enough to believe the Doctrine of Christianity, but you must believe it in Words of their *inventing.* To dispute their Decrees, though they contradicted common Sense and the Spirit of God, was Heresy; and Heresy was Damnation. And when, in Consequence of this, they had allotted a pious Christian to eternal Flames, for his Infidelity in *them,* they dispatched him thither with all speed; because he was to be damned in the *other* World, therefore he was to be hanged or burned in *this.* A terrible Gradation of Cruelty! to be cursed, burned, and damned! But it was something natural; it began from persecuting Priests, and ended in Hell, and the Devil was the *last* and *highest* Executioner.

Thus they became *Prelates* of both Worlds, and Proprietors of the Punishments of both. Even where the Civil Sword was not at their Command, their Vengeance was as successfully, and in my Opinion more terribly executed without it, by the temporal Effect of their Excommunication. For the Person under it was looked upon as a Daemon, and one in the Power of the Devil; and so driven out, like a wild Beast, from all the Comforts of Life, and human Society, to perish in a Desart, by Hunger, or the Elements, or Beasts of Prey. And all this, perhaps, for denying a Word or a Phrase, which was never known in Scripture, though impudently pretended to be fetch'd from thence.

Such dreadful Dominion had they usurped over the Bodies and Souls of Men, and so implacably did they exercise it! And, to fill up the Measure of their Falshood and Cruelty, they blasphemously pretended to be serving God, when they were acting as if there was none.

Those who set up for Infallibility have found a good Excuse, if it were true, for the insupportable Tyranny, infinite Murthers, and wide Devastations, which their Religion has every where introduced. But those, who exact a blind Obedience to Decrees, which they own to be human; and annex Penalties to Positions, which we know to be false, and they know to be disputable; and, in fine, act and dictate as if they were infallible, without pretending to be so; are so utterly without all Excuse, that I know no Language which affords a Name proper for their Behaviour.

The *Mahometan* Imposture was professedly to be spread by the Sword. It had nothing else but that and Libertinism to recommend it. But to propagate the Christian Religion by Terror or Arms, is to deny it. It owns no such Spirit. It rendered it self amiable, and gained Ground, by a Principle of Peace and Love. These were the Means of Christ's instituting, for the Recommendation and Defence of his Gospel; and they, who would chuse contrary ones, charge him with Folly, and have Ends to serve very different from his. Ambition, Pride, and Revenge, may make good Use of Violence and Persecution; but they are the Bane of Christianity, which always sinks when Persecution rises. The vilest and most profligate Men are ever the greatest Promoters of it; and the most virtuous are the greatest Sufferers by it. Libertines stick at nothing; but they who have the Fear of God, cannot comply with all Things.

Persecution is therefore *the War of Craft against Conscience,* and of Impiety against Truth. Reason, Religion, and Liberty, are its great Foes; but Ignorance, Tyranny, and Atheism, its great Seconds and Support. We ought then constantly to oppose all Claims of Dominion in the Clergy; for they naturally end in Cruelty. I believe it will be hard to shew, that ever the Priesthood, at any Time, or in any Place, enjoyed the Power of Persecution, without making use of it.

Number XXXV.

WEDNESDAY, SEPTEMBER 14.   1720.

OF REASON.

REASON is the only Guide given to Men in the State of Nature, to find out the Will of God, and the Means of Self-preservation. 'The Senses are its subordinate Instruments and Spies: They bring it Intelligence; and it forms a Judgment, and takes Measures, according to the Discoveries which they make. It compares Things one with another, and chooses them, if they are good; or neglects them, if they are indifferent; or shuns them, if they are bad. It discovers a first Cause, the Maker, Contriver, and Preserver of all Things; and therefore it teaches Submission to his Will, Admiration of his Wisdom and Power, and Thankfulness for his Goodness and Mercy. It distinguishes Subjects from Slaves; and shews the Loveliness of Liberty, and the Vileness of Vassalage: It shews that, as to political Privileges, all Men are born equal; and consequently, that he who is no better than others, can have no Right to command others, who are as good as himself; unless for the Ends of their own Interest and Safety, they confer that Right upon him, during *their* good Pleasure, or *his* good Behaviour.

REASON has invented all *Science*, pointed out all Commerce, and framed all Schemes for social Happiness. It has polished Mankind, set the *Greeks* above the *Barbarians*, and the *Romans* above the *Greeks*. It has been observed, in Praise of its great Power and Excellency, by a celebrated Moralist, that *we have not sufficient Strength to follow our Reason as far as it would carry us.*

To REASON we are beholden for all the Comforts and Conveniencies of Life, next after the first Author of them; and for our Defence against the Assaults of Beasts of Prey, and of one another; and for our Shelter from the Inclemencies of uncertain Weather, freezing us, or scorching us, according to the different Seasons of the Year. The Earth, with all its Abundance, affords but rude and unpleasing Entertainment, without the Dexterity and Refinements of Reason. Thus, even the Gifts of *Nature*, before they arrive at us, and are made fit for our Use, become also the Gifts of REASON. Without REASON, we had lived like the *Brute Creation*, upon raw Fruit, tasteless Herbs, and the cold Spring; or exposed to the merciless Jaws of Famine, when a severe Winter had frozen up the Stores of the Earth, and locked the Waters under Ice.

REASON checks tumultuous Passion, the greatest Enemy to the Peace of the Mind, and to the Peace of Society. Hence it has been observed, by the same Moralist, that all our *rational* Pursuits are *temperate* Pursuits; and that what we pursue with REASON, we never pursue *with Violence*. REASON, subdues Anger, and prevents Cruelty; it makes a Man less fierce than a Lyon, and less ravenous than a Bear. It is not *human Shape*, but human Reason, that places a *Man* above the *Beasts* of the Field, and lifts him into a Resemblance with God himself. Hence it is justly stiled *Divinae particula Aurae; A Ray, or*

Impulse of the Divinity. And, in what Sense can a Man be said to be *made after the Image of God,* unless by his possessing that REASON, which is a *divine Particle of the GODHEAD;* We *resemble* not our MAKER in *Person* or *Complexion;* and therefore can only *resemble* him in REASON, and in *Mercy,* which is the Child of this *Divine Reason.*

Were we not *rational Creatures,* we could not be *religious Creatures,* but upon a Level with *Brutes,* to whom God has made no Revelation of himself, because they want Reason to discern it, and to thank him for it. *Revelation* therefore presupposes *Reason,* and addresses it self to *Reason;* and God himself, by perswading us, as he does in his Word, by the Voice of *Reason,* appeals to our *Reason.* We cannot glorify God but with our Understandings; and we are convinced of his Goodness before we adore it. To praise him, without *Reason,* is a Contradiction, and an Impossibility. The Devotion which he requires, must be *free, rational* and *willing;* and where it is not so, it is *Folly* or *Hypocrisy.*

Nor is there any Opposition between *Reason* and *Grace,* whatever some may weakly, or dishonestly, maintain. In Truth, *Grace* is never given, but where *Reason* was already given; and the former *cannot* subsist, where the latter *does not.* We may have worldly Wisdom without Piety; but cannot possess Piety without Understanding; nor does Grace, tho' given in the greatest Abundance, at all supply the ordinary Offices of Reason. We do not find that St. *Luke* was a better Physician, for having written a *Gospel;* or St. *Paul* a better *Sailor,* or better *Tent-Maker,* for being an *Apostle.* But neither could St. *Luke* have been an *Evangelist,* nor St. *Paul* an *Apostle,* unless God had given them *Reason* as well as *Grace.* Indeed they are both the Gifts of God; only the One is *ordinary,* and the Other is *extraordinary.*

REASON, even without the Light of *Revelation,* teaches us to investigate Nature, and praise God for the Wonderfulness of his Works. It must judge of Revelation it self, what is so, and what not; and of the Words and Language, in which the Holy Oracles were at first convey'd; and of the Words and Language into which they were afterwards translated. Now Words, many of them, being obscure or equivocal, and signifying different Things to different Men, it is left to our Reason to determine, in what Sense these Words are to be understood. The Spirit of God has invented for us no *New Ones,* or such as carry in their Sound certain and determinate Ideas, which cannot be mistaken, but must *infallibly* be the same to every Man.

By the *Light* of REASON we see about us. It warns us against Craft, and arms us against Force; and the same *Reason,* which commands us to believe in God *implicitly,* and obey him *passively,* does also command us to trust to no Man without Inquiry, and to submit to no Man without Cause. Thus, what is our Duty in Relation to God, would be Madness in Relation to one another: The good *GOD* cannot deceive us; but MEN have Pride, Folly, Interest and Complexion, all conspiring to deceive themselves and others.

Our first Attempt to make Converts, is an Appeal to their REASON, by which they are to judge *for themselves* of the *Reasonableness* of our Religion, and of the Arguments which we bring for the Defence and Recommendation of our Religion: Which Method would be exceeding absurd and dishonest, if we did not suffer them to judge of our Religion with the same Freedom, after they are come into it, as they did before they embraced it. This would be Trepanning one's Reason into Captivity, with its own Assistance; first to make *use* of it, and then to vote it useless: A strange inconsistent Piece of Treachery, and a flat Contradiction to that *Liberty with which CHRIST has made us free!* As if we were to receive any *System* upon the Grounds of our *Reason,* without which it never can be sincerely receiv'd, and then to reject *our Reason* upon the Grounds of our *System!*

Pray, how do we distinguish the Beauty and Truth of the

Gospel, from the Imposture and Absurdity of the *Alcoran,*[1] but by our *Reason?* How do we detect the impudent and senseless Doctrine of *Transubstantiation,*[2] but by our *Sense* and *Reason?* Why did we, or how could we, leave *Popery,* and embrace the *Reformation,* but because our own *private Reason* told us; and *Scripture,* of which we made *our selves* the *Judges,* told us; that we left Slavery, Falshood, and Cruelty, for Truth, Freedom and Innocence? How did our *Saviour* prove himself *the Son of God,* but by Miracles, which every Eye saw, and every Ear heard? He appealed to the *Sense* and *Reason* of Mankind; and all were convinced, that would be convinced. How do we know the Scripture to be the Word of God, but by the Deductions and Information of *Reason?* How can we prove our own Church, *as by Law established,* to be the *purest* and *best constituted Church in the World,* but by the Testimony of impartial, *disinterested* REASON? For, it is plain, from the great Number of *Gainsayers,* and *Arians,*[3] that her *genuine Sons* have not the miraculous Gift of inspiring, *from above,* all Men with their own *Orthodox* Sentiments. How can we distinguish Religion from Enthusiasm; Grace from Superstition; Faith from Credulity; the Love of the Church from the Love of Power; and the Authority of God from the Impositions of Men; but by *Reason,* or by the *Scripture,* interpreted by *Reason?*

---

[1] This is Trenchard and Gordon's usual terminology for the Moslem Koran.

[2] In the theology of the Eucharist, this is the Roman Catholic doctrine affirmed by the Council of Trent. It had been rejected by Martin Luther and was rejected by the Church of England. By the Test Act of 1673, Englishmen about to assume political office had to take Oaths of Supremacy and Allegiance and to make the "Declaration against Transubstantiation," that is, to swear that they did not accept the Catholic doctrine. For Trenchard and Gordon, the doctrine simply served as an example of clerical mumbo jumbo.

[3] The Arians were upholders of the heresy identified as Arianism (after Arius, *ca.* 250 to *ca.* 336). In essence, Arius denied the divinity of Christ.

In short, all who are Friends to TRUTH, are Friends to REASON, the Discoverer and Champion of TRUTH; and none are Foes to *Reason*, but those who have *Truth* and *Reason* for their Foes. He, who has dark Purposes to serve, must use dark Means: Light would discover him, and Reason expose him: He must endeavour to shut out both; and make them look frightful, by giving them ill Names; for farther than Names the Vulgar inquire not.

From this Cause, Religion and Liberty flourish, where *Reason* and Knowledge are encouraged; and where-ever the latter are stifled, the former are extinguished. In *Turkey*, Printing is forbid, *Enquiry* is dangerous, and *Free-speaking* is CAPITAL; because they are all inconsistent with the *MAHO-METANISM by Law established*. Hence it comes to pass, that the wretched *Turks* are all stupidly ignorant, are all Slaves, all Infidels. Nor have the *Papists* much Advantage to boast above the *Mahometans*. Their Guides and Governors lock up from them the Scripture, which is the Book of Knowledge: They teach them, that *Ignorance is the Mother of Devotion:* They banish Liberty, they brow-beat *Reason*, they persecute Truth. In Consequence of all which, the deluded Votaries of the *Romish Church* are as ignorant as the *Mahometans*, as great Slaves, greater Idolaters, and greater Persecutors; that is, they exceed the *Turks* in their Barbarity, who exceed most others.

Here, in *England*, why are we *free*, why *Protestants;* but because we are guided by *Reason*, and judge for our selves? And none amongst us complain of the *Liberty of the Press*, or the *Growth of Free-Thinking*, but those who would found a Dominion upon *Stupidity* and Persecution. Vile and woeful is that Cause, which must be supported by Ignorance and Misery! And yet there are those in *Great-Britain*, who, tho' they wear a holy and venerable Livery, yet have the Boldness and Blasphemy to christen that *impious Cause*, the *Cause of God* and *of his Church*.

To conclude; *Scripture* and *Reason*, without which Scripture can have no Effect, are the only Tests of every Falshood and Imposture, and every Superstition. Suppose, for Example, a Reverend Doctor is touched with an odd Zeal for *Bowing* to the *East;* he ought to convince my *Reason* that *Bowing* to the *East* is enjoined in Scripture, before he enjoins me to bow also. If he says, it is enjoined by the Authority of the Church; he then must satisfy my Reason, that the Scripture teaches the Church to teach her Members to make Bows. If he answers, that neither does the Scripture teach to bow to the *East,* but that the *Church* thinks *Bowing* decent and edifying; he must then prove, by rational Evidence, that what every Church thinks decent is a Duty. If he replies, that this is only true of the one Orthodox Church; then he must prove that his Church is the sole Orthodox Church, according to the Rules of the Gospel. And if the Doctor cannot do this to my Satisfaction, then there will be an End of his Argument for his Ecclesiastical *Bowings.*

As we must judge from Scripture what is Orthodoxy; so we must judge from Reason, what is Scripture.

Cato's Letters

[The following pages include thirty-five of the one hundred and thirty-eight numbers of *Cato's Letters*. In the selection and editing of these writings, the following rules have been applied:

1. Included are the letters most often cited or quoted by later English and, especially, by later American writers.

2. The numbers dealing primarily with the details of contemporary controversies (e.g., the several letters dealing with the "South Sea Bubble") are not reprinted, except where they contain some statements of general importance in clarifying the views of Trenchard and Gordon.

3. While Trenchard and Gordon were fond of examples and stories from the past and often used them to add persuasiveness to their writings, they had a tendency to repeat their examples and sometimes to lose arguments in the midst of historical erudition. Moreover, the authors themselves made clear their view that examples were only illustrations of rationally derived political principles. For these reasons, the editor has excluded a considerable portion of the historical material, where it is repetitive or not connected to the main line of argument.

4. Trenchard and Gordon's writings have considerable value in that they outline the English view of Europe and its politics in the early eighteenth century. The two writers contrasted England's liberties with the oppression they believed character-ized life on the Continent. Since their viewpoint was a common

one in England and America, examples of its expression are reprinted in the following pages.

5. Notes are included for quotations and for some of the obscurer historical examples. Trenchard and Gordon's writings were filled with material drawn from the history of ancient Rome. Many of their arguments can be understood only with some knowledge of that Republic and Empire. Therefore, the editor has included longer explanatory notes for such references.

6. The capital letter at the end of each number indicated the identity of the principal author (i.e., "G" for Gordon and "T" for Trenchard). These identifying marks were added after the original printing of the *Letters* in the *London Journal.*]

Number 15.

SATURDAY, FEBRUARY 4, 1720.

Of Freedom of Speech: That the same is inseparable from Publick Liberty.

SIR,

Without Freedom of Thought, there can be no such Thing as Wisdom; and no such Thing as publick Liberty, without Freedom of Speech: Which is the Right of every Man, as far as by it he does not hurt and controul the Right of another; and this is the only Check which it ought to suffer, the only Bounds which it ought to know.

This sacred Privilege is so essential to free Government, that the Security of Property; and the Freedom of Speech, always go together; and in those wretched Countries where a Man cannot call his Tongue his own, he can scarce call any Thing else his own. Whoever would overthrow the Liberty of the Nation, must begin by subduing the Freedom of Speech; a Thing terrible to publick Traytors.

This Secret was so well known to the Court of King *Charles* I. that his wicked Ministry procured a Proclamation to forbid the People to talk of Parliaments, which those Traytors had laid aside.[1] To assert the undoubted Right of the Subject, and defend his Majesty's Legal Prerogative, was called Disaffection, and punished as Sedition. Nay, People were forbid to talk of Religion in their Families: For the Priests had combined with the Ministers to cook up Tyranny, and suppress Truth and the Law. While the late King *James*, when Duke of *York*, went avowedly to Mass; Men were fined, imprisoned, and undone, for saying that he was a Papist: And, that King *Charles* II. might live more securely a Papist, there was an Act of Parliament made, declaring it Treason to say that he was one.

That Men ought to speak well of their Governors, is true, while their Governors deserve to be well spoken of; but to do publick Mischief, without hearing of it, is only the Prerogative and Felicity of Tyranny: A free People will be shewing that they are so, by their Freedom of Speech.

The Administration of Government is nothing else, but the Attendance of the Trustees of the People upon the Interest and Affairs of the People. And as it is the Part and Business of the People, for whose Sake alone all publick Matters are, or ought to be, transacted, to see whether they be well or ill transacted; so it is the Interest, and ought to be the Ambition, of all honest Magistrates, to have their Deeds openly examined, and publickly scanned: Only the wicked Governors of Men dread what is said of them; *Audivit* Tiberius *probra queis*

---

[1] For eleven years (1629–1640), Charles I ruled without summoning Parliament. Troubles in Scotland led to his calling Parliament into session, and subsequent strife led to the Civil Wars, to Charles's eventual defeat, and to his execution in 1649.

lacerabitur, atque perculsus est. The publick Censure was true, else he had not felt it bitter.[2]

Freedom of Speech is ever the Symptom, as well as the Effect, of good Government. In old *Rome,* all was left to the Judgment and Pleasure of the People; who examined the publick Proceedings with such Discretion, and censured those who administered them with such Equity and Mildness, that in the Space of Three Hundred Years, not Five publick Ministers suffered unjustly. Indeed, whenever the Commons proceeded to Violence, the Great Ones had been the Aggressors. . . .

The best Princes have ever encouraged and promoted Freedom of Speech; they knew that upright Measures would defend themselves, and that all upright Men would defend them. *Tacitus,* speaking of the Reign of some of the Princes above-mention'd, says with Extasy, *Rara temporum felicitate, ubi sentire quae velis, & quae sentias dicere liceat:* A blessed Time, when you might think what you would, and speak what you thought! . . .[3]

I doubt not but old *Spencer* and his Son, who were the chief Ministers and Betrayers of *Edward.* II. would have been very

---

[2] The line is a misquotation from Tacitus, the great Roman historian (A.D. 55 to *ca.* 119). Extant portions of Tacitus' *Histories* and *Annals* cover most of the period from the death of Augustus to the year 96. The correct quotation would be: ". . . *audivit Tiberius probra, quis per occultum lacerabatur, adeoque perculsus est.* . . (*Annals* IV. 42). ("Tiberius thus heard the scurrilities with which he was attacked in private and such was the shock. . . .") The altering of the text to suit the situation was characteristic of Gordon's use of Latin sources. He was familiar enough with them to repeat them from memory. The consequence was that many of his quotations differed slightly from the original text.

[3] The quotation comes from Tacitus, *Histories* I. 1. There Tacitus refers to the reigns of Nerva and Trajan as the subject for a history which he would like to write at a later time: "Yet if my life but last, I have reserved for my old age the history of the deified Nerva's reign and of Trajan's rule, a richer and less perilous subject [than that of the earlier period he was studying], because of the rare good fortune of an age in which we may feel what we wish and may say what we feel." Tacitus did not live to complete this project.

glad to have stopped the Mouths of all the honest Men in *England*. They dreaded to be called Traytors, because they were Traytors. And I dare say, Queen *Elizabeth's Walsingham*, who deserved no Reproaches, feared none.[4] Misrepresentation of publick Measures is easily overthrown, by representing publick Measures truly: When they are honest, they ought to be publickly known, that they may be publickly commended; but if they be knavish or pernicious, they ought to be publickly exposed, in order to be publickly detested.

To assert, that King *James* was a Papist and a Tyrant, was only so far hurtful to him, as it was true of him; and if the Earl of *Stafford* had not deserved to be impeached, he need not have feared a Bill of Attainder.[5] If our Directors and their Confederates[6] be not such Knaves as the World thinks then, let them prove to all the World, that the World thinks wrong, and that

---

[4] Edward II (1284–1327) was King of England from 1307. He lost the battle of Bannockburn to the famed Robert the Bruce of Scotland. Generally incompetent, he was deposed by the Barons in Parliament and murdered in 1327. His favorites were the Despencers, Hugh le Despencer and his son, who were once banished from England, returned, were defeated by the Barons, and finally executed for treason. Sir Francis Walsingham (1530?–1590) was the great minister of Elizabeth. A determinedly anti-Spanish diplomat, he warned of the dangers of the Armada.

[5] Thomas Wentworth, First Earl of Strafford (1593–1641), was an energetic and highly capable minister of Charles I. He attempted to aid Charles by creating an army in Ireland which would be independent of the control of the English Parliament. When Charles was compelled to call Parliament into session, Strafford was sentenced by an Act of Attainder and executed. For Trenchard and Gordon, Strafford was the very symbol of Stuart tyranny and, particularly, of the dangers of unregulated military forces.

[6] The Directors of the South Sea Company are repeatedly mentioned throughout *Cato's Letters*. The Directors were blamed by Trenchard and Gordon for the scandals surrounding the collapse of that Company and particularly for the skulduggery involved in its spectacular proposal for funding the national debt of England. In succeeding letters, even when the Directors are not explicitly cited, Trenchard and Gordon often had the Company in mind as an example of the dangers of public corruption.

they are guilty of none of those Villainies which all the World lays to their Charge. Others too, who would be thought to have no Part of their Guilt, must, before they are thought innocent, shew that they did all that was in their Power to prevent that Guilt, and to check their Proceedings.

Freedom of Speech is the great Bulwark of Liberty; they prosper and die together: And it is the Terror of Traytors and Oppressors, and a Barrier against them. It produces excellent Writers, and encourages Men of fine Genius. *Tacitus* tells us, that the *Roman* Commonwealth bred great and numerous Authors, who writ with equal Boldness and Eloquence: But when it was enslaved, those great Wits were no more.—*Postquam bellatum apud Actium; atque omnem potestatem ad unum conferri pacis interfuit, magna illa ingenia cessere.*[7] Tyranny had usurped the Place of Equality, which is the Soul of Liberty, and destroyed publick Courage. The Minds of Men, terrified by unjust Power, degenerated into all the Vilenes[s] and Methods of Servitude: Abject Sycophancy and blind Submission grew the only means of Preferment, and indeed of Safety; Men durst not open their Mouths, but to flatter. . . .

All Ministers, therefore, who were Oppressors, or intended to be Oppressors, have been loud in their Complaints against Freedom of Speech, and the Licence of the Press; and always restrained, or endeavoured to restrain, both. In consequence of this, they have brow-beaten Writers, punished them violently, and against Law, and burnt their Works. By all which they shewed how much Truth alarmed them, and how much they were at Enmity with Truth.

There is a famous Instance of this in *Tacitus:* He tells us, that *Cremutius Cordus,* having in his Annals praised *Brutus*

---

[7] Tacitus, *Histories* I. 1: "But after the battle of Actium, when the interests of peace required that all power should be concentrated in the hands of one man, writers of like ability disappeared. . . ." Tacitus referred to the decline of objective historical studies.

and *Cassius,* gave Offence to *Sejanus,*[8] First Minister, and to
some inferior Sycophants in the Court of *Tiberius;* who, conscious of their own Characters, took the Praise bestowed on
every worthy *Roman,* to be so many Reproaches pointed at
themselves: They therefore complain of the Book to the Senate;
which, being now only the Machine of Tyranny, condemned it
to be burnt. But this did not prevent its spreading.—*Libros
cremandos censuere Patres; sed manserunt occultati & editi:*
Being censured, it was the more sought after.[9] *From hence,* says
*Tacitus, we may wonder at the Stupidity of those Statesmen,
who hope to extinguish, by the Terror of their Power, the
Memory of their Actions;* for quite otherwise, *the Punishment
of good Writers gains Credit to their Writings: Nam contra,
punitis ingeniis, gliscit auctoritas.*[10] Nor did ever any Government, who practised impolitick Severity, get any thing by it,
but Infamy to themselves, and Renown to those who suffered
under it. This also is an Observation of *Tacitus: Neque aliud
reges, qui ea saevitiae usi sunt, nisi dedecus sibi, atque gloriam
illis peperere.*

Freedom of Speech, therefore, being of such infinite Impor-

---

[8] Lucius Aelius Sejanus (d. A.D. 31) served as commander of the
Praetorian Guard and consul and was executed on suspicion of a plot
against the Emperor Tiberius. For Trenchard and Gordon, he was the
tyrannical minister who had led his master into many misdeeds and had
eventually even plotted against Tiberius. The Trenchard and Gordon
version of Sejanus was largely drawn from Tacitus, and, to a lesser extent,
from Suetonius, *Lives of the Twelve Caesars.*

[9] The line appears in Tacitus, *Annals* IV. 35. 14–16: *"Libros per
aediles cremandos censuere patres: set manserunt, occultati et editi. . . ."*
("The Fathers ordered his books to be burned by the aediles; but copies
remained, hidden and afterwards published. . . .")

[10] This and the following quotation come from Tacitus, *Annals* IV. 35.
18–21: *"Nam contra punitis ingeniis gliscit auctoritas, neque aliud externi
reges aut qui eadem saevitia usi sunt, nisi dedecus sibi atque illis gloriam
peperere."* ("On the contrary, genius chastised grows in authority; nor
have alien kings or the imitators of their cruelty effected more than to
crown themselves with ignominy and their victims with renown.")

tance to the Preservation of Liberty, every one who loves Liberty ought to encourage Freedom of Speech. Hence it is that I, living in a Country of Liberty, and under the best Prince upon Earth, shall take this very favourable Opportunity of serving Mankind, by warning them of the hideous Mischiefs that they will suffer, if ever corrupt and wicked Men shall hereafter get Possession of any State, and the Power of betraying their Master. . . .

Valerius Maximus tells us, that *Lentulus Marcellinus*, the *Roman* Consul, having complained, in a popular Assembly, of the overgrown Power of *Pompey;* the whole People answered him with a Shout of Approbation: Upon which the Consul told them, *Shout on, Gentlemen, shout on, and use those bold Signs of Liberty while you may; for I do not know* [how] *long they will be allowed you.*[11]

God be thanked, we *Englishmen* have neither lost our Liberties, nor are in Danger of losing them. Let us always cherish this matchless Blessing, almost peculiar to ourselves; that our Posterity may, many Ages hence, ascribe their Freedom to our Zeal. The Defence of Liberty is a noble, a heavenly Office; which can only be performed where Liberty is: For, as the same *Valerius Maximus* observes, *Quid ergo Libertas sine* Catone? *Non magnis quam* Cato *sine Libertate.*[12]

G   *I am, &c.*[13]

---

[11] Lentullus Marcellinus was governor of Syria in 60 B.C., consul in 56, and an opponent of the triumvirs. Valerius Maximus was a Roman historian who lived during the reign of Tiberius. He published a handbook of illustrative examples for moral precepts. The last English translation of his work appeared in 1678.

[12] The quotation may be roughly translated: "What liberty would there be without Cato? Just as much, what would Cato be without liberty."

[13] For further discussions of free speech see this volume, particularly *Letters* number 32, 100, and 101.

Number 16.

SATURDAY, FEBRUARY 11, 1720.

The Leaders of Parties, their usual Views.—Advice to all Parties to be no longer misled.

SIR,

The wise *Sancho Pancha* desired that his Subjects, in the promised Island, might be all Blacks, because he would sell them.[1] And this seems to be the first modest, and, as I think, the only reasonable Desire of the Leaders of all Parties; for no Man will be at the Expence and Fatigue of Body and Conscience, which is necessary to lead a Faction, only to be disturbed and annoyed by them.

A very great Authority* has told us, that *'Tis worth no Man's Time to serve a Party, unless he can now and then get good Jobbs by it.* This, I can safely say, has been the constant Principle and Practice of every leading Patriot, ever since I have been capable of observing publick Transactions; the *primum Mobile*, the *Alpha* and *Omega* of all their Actions: They all professed to have in View only the Publick Good; yet every one shewed he only meant his own; and all the while the great as well as little Mob, the *procerum turba Mobilium*, contended as fiercely for their Leaders, as if their Happiness or Misery depended upon the Face, the Cloaths, or Title of the Persons who robbed and betrayed them. Thus the Highwayman

---

* This was said to have been spoken by a certain Lord Chancellor in former times.[2]

[1] Sancho Panza was the "round, selfish, and self-important" squire of Don Quixote in Cervantes' novel *Don Quixote*.

[2] The reference is probably to William Cowper, who twice served as Lord Chancellor in the early eighteenth century and wrote several short tracts on political parties.

said to the Traveller, *Pray, Sir, leave your Watch and Money in my Hands; or else, by G—, you will be robbed.*

Pound a Fool in a Mortar, and he comes out never the wiser; no Experience will make the Bulk of Mankind so, or put them upon their Guard; they will be caught over and over again by the same Baits and Stale Stratagems: No sooner is a Party betrayed by one Head, but they rail at him, and set up another; and when this has served them in the same Manner, they choose a Third; and put full Confidence in every one of them successively, though they all make the same Use of their Credulity; that is, put a Price upon their Calves Heads, and sell them; which, however, they have the less Reason to complain of, because they would have all done the same.

I assure you, Sir, that I have not the least Hopes in this Letter to make Men honester, but I would gladly teach them a little more Wit; that is, I would advise any one who is contented to be sold, that he receive the Money himself, and take good Care of One, whatever becomes of his Neighbours; as some discreet Persons have lately done. Whatever Bargains are struck up amongst the Betrayers of their Country, we must find the Money, and pay both Sides. How wise and advantageous would it then be for us, not to interest ourselves in the Agreements or Squabbles of ambitious Men, who are building their Fortunes upon our Ruin? Once upon a Time, a *French* Embassador desired an Audience of the Grand Vizier, and in pompous *French* Fustian notified to him, that his Master had won a great Victory over the *Germans;* to which that wise Minister answered laconically, *What is it to me, if the whole Herd of Unbelievers, like Dogs, mutually worry one another, so that my Master's Head be safe?*

This Letter of Advice is not intended for those who share already in the publick Spoils, or who, like Jackalls, hunt down the Lion's Prey, that they may have the picking of the Bones, when their Masters are glutted. But I would persuade the poor, the injured, the distressed People, to be no longer the Dupes and Property of Hypocrites and Traytors. But very few can share in the Wages of Iniquity, and all the rest must suffer; the People's Interest is the publick Interest; it signifies the same Thing: Whatever these Betrayers of their Country get, the People must lose; and, what is worse, must lose a great deal more than the others can get; for such Conspiracies and Extortions cannot be successfully carried on, without destroying or injuring Trade, perverting Justice, corrupting the Guardians of the publick Liberty, and the almost total Dissolution of the Principles of Government.

Few can receive the Advantages arising from publick Misfortunes; and therefore methinks few should desire them. Indeed, I can easily see how Men of desperate Circumstances, or Men guilty of desperate Crimes, can find their Account in a general Confusion of all Things. I can see how those Priests, who aim at Tyranny, can find their Interest in the Loss of publick Liberty, in the Restraint of the Press, and in introducing a Religion which destroys Christianity: There are Reasons too at hand, why ambitious Men should, *per fas & nefas*,[3] grasp at the Possession of immense Wealth, high Honours, and exorbitant Power: But that the Gentry, the Body of the People in a free Nation, should become the Tools and Instruments of Knaves and Pick-pockets; should list themselves in their Quarrels, and fight their Battles; and this too, often at the Expence, and by the Violation of good Neighbourhood, near Relation, private Friendship: That Men of great Estates and Quality, for small and trifling Considerations, and sometimes none at all, should promote wild, villainous Projects, to the Ruin of themselves and Country, by making precarious their own Titles to their Lives, Estates, and Liberties, is something so stupendous, that it must be thought impossible, if daily Experience did not convince us that it is more than possible.

---

[3] "Per fas et nefas" roughly equals the expression "by fair means or foul."

I have often seen honest *Tories* foolishly defending knavish *Tories;* and untainted *Whigs* protecting corrupt *Whigs*, even in Instances where they acted against the Principles of all *Whigs;* and by that Means depreciated *Whiggism* itself, and gave the stupid Herd Occasion to believe that they had no Principles at all, but were only a factious Combination for Preferment and Power.

It is high Time, at last, for the Bubbles of all Parties, for *Whigs* and *Tories,* for High Church and Low Church, to come to an *Eclaircissement,* and no longer suffer themselves to be bought and sold by their Drivers: Let them cease to be Calves and Sheep, and they will not be used like Calves and Sheep. If they can be persuaded now and then to confer Notes, they will find, that for the most part the Differences between them are not material; that they take only different Measures to attain the same Ends; that they have but one common Interest, which is the Interest of their Country; and that is, to be freed from Oppression, and to punish their Oppressors: Whose Practice, on the contrary, will always be to form Parties, and blow up Factions to mutual Animosities, that they may find Protection in those Animosities.

Let us not therefore, for the Time to come, suffer ourselves to be engaged in empty and pernicious Contentions; which can only tend to make us the Property and Harvest of Pickpockets: Let us learn to value an honest Man of another Party, more than a Knave of our own: Let the only Contention be, who shall be most ready to spew out their own Rogues; and I will be answerable that all other Differences will soon be at an End. Indeed, there had been no such Thing as Party now in *England,* if we had not been betrayed by those whom we trusted.

Through the Villainy and knavish Designs of Leaders, this Nation has lost several glorious Opportunities of rescuing the Constitution, and settling it upon a firm and solid Basis: Let us not therefore, by the like Practices, lose the present favourable Offer: Let us make Earnings of our Misfortunes, and accept our

Calamities as an Opportunity thrown into our Laps by indulgent Providence, to save ourselves; and not again foolishly and ungratefully reject and spurn at the Intimations and Invitations of Heaven, to preserve our Prince and Country.

Machiavel[4] tells us, that no Government can long subsist, but by recurring often to its first Principles; but this can never be done while Men live at Ease and in Luxury; for then they cannot be persuaded to see distant Dangers, of which they feel no Part. The Conjunctures proper for such Reformations, and when Men are awakened by Misfortunes, and frighted with the Approach and near View of present Evils; then they will wish for Remedies, and their Minds are prepared to receive them, to hear Reasons, and to fall into Measures proposed by wise Men for their Security.

The great Authority just quoted informs us what Measures and Expedients are necessary to save a State under such Exigencies: He tells us, that as a Tyranny cannot be established but by destroying *Brutus;* so a free Government is not to be preserved but by destroying *Brutus's* Sons.[5] Let us therefore put on a Resolution equal to the mighty Occasion: Let us exert a Spirit worthy of *Britons,* worthy of Freemen who deserve Liberty. Let us take advantage of the Opportunity, while Mens Resentments boil high, whilst lesser Animosities seem to be laid aside, and most Men are sick of Party and Party-Leaders; and let us, by all proper Methods, exemplarily punish the Parricides, and avowed Enemies of all Mankind.

Let neither private Acquaintance, personal Alliance, or Party Combination, stand between us and our Duty to our

---

[4] Niccolo Machiavelli (1649–1527) wrote the famous *The Prince,* but was of more interest to Trenchard and Gordon as the author of the *Discourses on the First Ten Books of Titus Livius.* The quotations from Machiavelli in *Cato's Letters* were generally drawn from the *Discourses.*

[5] The reference here is to Lucius Junius Brutus, the founder of the Roman Republic. According to early legend, this Brutus passed a capital sentence upon his sons for their crimes.

Country: Let all those who have a common Interest in the publick Safety, join in common Measures to defend the publick Safety: Let us pursue to Disgrace, Destruction, and even Death, those who have brought this Ruin upon us, let them be ever so great, or ever so many: Let us stamp and deep engrave, in Characters legible to all *Europe* at present, and to all Posterity hereafter, what Vengeance is due to Crimes, which have no less Objects in View than the Ruin of Nations, and the Destruction of Millions: They have made many bold, desperate, and wicked Attempts to destroy us; let us strike one honest and bold Stroke to destroy them.

Though the Designs of the Conspirators should be laid as deep as the Center, though they should raise Hell itself in their Quarrel, and should fetch Legions of Votaries from thence to avow their Proceedings; yet let us not leave the Pursuit, till we have their Skins and Estates: We know, by past Experience, that there are those amongst us, who will be glad to quit the Chase, when our Villains, like Beavers, drop what they are usually hunted for; but the Nation is now too much provoked, and too much injured, to suffer themselves to be again so betrayed.

We have Heaven to direct us, a glorious King to lead us, and a wise and faithful Parliament to assist and protect us: Whilst we have such a King, and such a Parliament, every worthy *Briton* cries out aloud,

Manus haec inimica Tyrannis
Ense petit placidam, sub libertate quietem.[6]

T   *I am, &c.*

---

[6] This was the famed Latin motto of the Whig martyr Algernon Sidney (1622–1683). In 1842, the motto was paraphrased by John Quincy Adams in the following lines:

This hand to tyrants ever sworn the foe,
For freedom only deals the deadly blow,

SATURDAY, FEBRUARY 18, 1720.

What Measures are actually taken by wicked and desperate Ministers to ruin and enslave their Country.

SIR,

As under the best Princes, and the best Servants to Princes alone, it is safe to speak what is true of the worst; so, according to my former Promise to the Publick, I shall take the Advantage of our excellent King's most gentle Government, and the virtuous Administration of an uncorrupt Ministry, to warn Mankind against the Mischiefs which may hereafter be dreaded from corrupt ones. It is too true, that every Country in the World has sometimes groaned under that heavy Misfortune, and our own as much as any; though I cannot allow it to be true, what Monsieur *de Witt*[1] has long since observed, that the

---

That sheathes in calm repose the vengeful blade,
For gentle peace in freedom's hallowed shade.

(Robert C. Winthrop, *Algernon Sidney: A Lecture Delivered Before the Boston Mercantile Library* [Boston: S. K. Whipple, 1854]). Sidney was arrested, tried, and executed for treason in the reign of Charles II. The chief evidence against him at his trial was an unpublished manuscript that later appeared in print under the title *Discourses Concerning Government.* Both the *Discourses* and Sidney's *Dying Speech,* a short statement delivered to the sheriff at the time of his execution, were favorite Whig texts after the Glorious Revolution. They were well known in America throughout the eighteenth century. Trenchard and Gordon borrowed the greater part of several numbers of *Cato's Letters* directly from Sidney and expounded upon several of his ideas on limiting the power of the monarchy, on the right of revolution, the contractual nature of government, and so on.

---

[1] Jan De Witt (1625–1672) was a foremost Dutch statesman and opponent of the House of Orange. He was overthrown and murdered by a mob after Louis XIV's invasion of the United Netherlands in 1672.

English Court has always been the most thievish Court in *Europe.*

Few Men have been desperate enough to attack openly, and barefaced, the Liberties of a free People. Such avowed Conspirators can rarely succeed: The Attempt would destroy itself. Even when the Enterprize is begun and visible, the End must be hid, or denied. It is the Business and Policy of Traytors, so to disguise their Treason with plausible Names, and so to recommend it with popular and bewitching Colours, that they themselves shall be adored, while their Work is detested, and yet carried on by those that detest it.

Thus one Nation has been surrendered to another under the fair Name of mutual Alliance: The Fortresses of a Nation have been given up, or attempted to be given up, under the frugal Notion of saving Charges to a Nation; and Commonwealths have been trepanned into Slavery, by Troops raised or increased to defend them from Slavery.

It may therefore be of Service to the World, to shew what Measures have been taken to corrupt Ministers, in some of our neighbouring Countries, to ruin and enslave the People over whom they presided; to shew by what Steps and Gradations of Mischief Nations have been undone, and consequently what Methods may be hereafter taken to undo others: And this Subject I rather choose, because my Countrymen may be the more sensible of, and know how to value the inestimable Blessing of living under the best Prince, and the best established Government in the Universe, where we have none of these Things to fear.

Such Traytors will probably endeavour first to get their Prince into their Possession, and, like *Sejanus,*[2] shut him up in a little Island, or perhaps make him a Prisoner in his Court; whilst, with full Range, they devour his Dominions, and plunder his Subjects. When he is thus secluded from the Access

---

[2] See note 8 to *Letter* 15. p. 43.

of his Friends, and the Knowledge of his Affairs, he must be content with such Misrepresentations as they shall find expedient to give him. False Cases will be stated, to justify wicked Counsel; wicked Counsel will be given, to procure unjust Orders. He will be made to mistake his Foes for his Friends, his Friends for his Foes; and to believe that his Affairs are in the highest Prosperity, when they are in the greatest Distress; and that publick Matters go on in the greatest Harmony, when they are in the utmost Confusion.

They will be ever contriving and forming wicked and dangerous Projects, to make the People poor, and themselves rich; well knowing that Dominion follows Property; that where there are Wealth and Power, there will be always Crowds of servile Dependents; and that, on the contrary, Poverty dejects the Mind, fashions it to Slavery, and renders it unequal to any generous Undertaking, and incapable of opposing any bold Usurpation. They will squander away the publick Money in wanton Presents to Minions, and their Creatures of Pleasure or of Burthen, or in Pensions to mercenary and worthless Men and Women, for vile Ends and traiterous Purposes.

They will engage their Country in ridiculous, expensive, fantastical Wars, to keep the Minds of Men in continual Hurry and Agitation, and under constant Fears and Alarms; and, by such Means, deprive them both of Leisure and Inclination to look into publick Miscarriages. Men, on the contrary, will, instead of such Inspection, be disposed to fall into all Measures offered, seemingly, for their Defence, and will agree to every wild Demand made by those who are betraying them.

When they have served their Ends by such Wars, or have other Motives to make Peace, they will have no View to the publick Interest; but will often, to procure such Peace, deliver up the Strong-Holds of their Country, or its Colonies for Trade, to open Enemies, suspected Friends, or dangerous Neighbours, that they may not be interrupted in their domestick Designs.

They will create Parties in the Commonwealth, or keep them

up where they already are; and, by playing them by Turns upon each other, will rule both. By making the *Guelfs* afraid of the *Ghibelines,* and these afraid of the *Guelfs,* they will make themselves the Mediums and Balance between the two Factions; and both Factions, in their Turns, the Props of their Authority, and the Instruments of their Designs.[3]

They will not suffer any Men, who have once tasted of Authority, though personally their Enemies, and whose Posts they enjoy, to be called to an Account for past Crimes, though ever so enormous. They will make no such Precedents for their own Punishment; nor censure Treason, which they intend to commit. On the contrary, they will form new Conspiracies, and invent new Fences for their own Impunity and Protection; and endeavour to engage such Numbers in their Guilt, as to set themselves above all Fear of Punishment.

They will prefer worthless and wicked Men, and not suffer a Man of Knowledge or Honesty to come near them, or enjoy a Post under them. They will disgrace Men of Virtue, and ridicule Virtue itself, and laugh at Publick Spirit. They will put Men into Employments, without any Regard to the Qualifications for those Employments, or indeed to any Qualifications at all, but as they contribute to their Designs, and shew a stupid Alacrity to do what they are bid. They must be either Fools or Beggars; either void of Capacity to discover their Intrigues, or of Credit and Inclination to disappoint them.

They will promote Luxury, Idleness, and Expence, and a general Depravation of Manners, by their own Example, as well

---

[3] A Guelph belonged to one of the two great parties in medieval Italian politics and opposed the pretensions of the Hohenstaufens as Holy Roman Emperors, while a Ghibelline supported the imperial forces. When the House of Brunswick gained the English throne in the person of George I, the Elector of Hanover, the term "Guelph" was transmitted into English politics through his family's claim of Guelph ancestry. In this context, "Guelf" and "Ghibeline" simply denote the extremes of political partisanship.

as by Connivance and publick Encouragement. This will not only divert Mens Thoughts from examining their Behaviour and Politicks, but likewise let them loose from all the Restraints of private and publick Virtue. From Immorality and Excesses they will fall into Necessity; and from thence into a servile Dependence upon Power.

In order to this, they will bring into Fashion Gaming, Drunkenness, Gluttony, and profuse and costly Dress. They will debauch their Country with foreign Vices, and foreign Instruments of vicious Pleasures; and will contrive and encourage publick Revels, nightly Disguises, and debauched Mummeries.

They will, by all practicable Means of Oppression, provoke the People to Disaffection; and then make that Disaffection an Argument for new Oppression, for not trusting them any further, and for keeping up Troops; and, in fine, for depriving them of Liberties and Privileges, to which they are entitled by their Birth, and the Laws of their Country.

If such Measures should ever be taken in any free Country, where the People choose Deputies to represent them, then they will endeavour to bribe the Electors in the Choice of their Representatives, and so to get a Council of their own Creatures; and where they cannot succeed with the Electors, they will endeavour to corrupt the Deputies after they are chosen, with the Money given for the publick Defence; and to draw into the Perpetration of their Crimes those very Men, from whom the betrayed People expect the Redress of their Grievances, and the Punishment of those Crimes. And when they have thus made the Representatives of the People afraid of the People, and the People afraid of their Representatives; then they will endeavour to persuade those Deputies to seize the Government to themselves, and not to trust their Principals any longer with the Power of resenting their Treachery and Ill-Usage, and of sending honester and wiser Men in their room.

But if the Constitution should be so stubbornly framed, that it will still preserve itself and the People's Liberties, in spite of all villainous Contrivances to destroy both; then must the Constitution itself be attacked and broken, because it will not bend. There must be an Endeavour, under some Pretence of publick Good, to alter a Balance of the Government, and to get it into the sole Power of their Creatures, and of such who will have constantly an Interest distinct from that of the Body of the People.

But if all these Schemes for the Ruin of the Publick, and their own Impunity, should fail them; and the worthy Patriots of a free Country should prove obstinate in Defense of their Country, and resolve to call its Betrayers to a strict Account; there is then but one thing left for such Traytors to do; namely, to veer about, and, by joining with the Enemy of their Prince and Country, complete their Treason.

I have somewhere read of a Favourite and First Minister to a neighbouring Prince, long since dead, who played his Part so well, that, though he had, by his evil Counsels, raised a Rebellion, and a Contest for the Crown; yet he preserved himself a Resource, whoever got the better: If his old Master succeeded, then this *Achitophel*, by the Help of a baffled Rebellion, ever favourable to Princes, had the Glory of fixing his Master in absolute Power: But, as his brave Rival got the Day, *Achitophel* had the Merit of betraying his old Master to plead; and was accordingly taken into Favour.

Happy therefore, thrice happy, are we, who can be unconcerned Spectators of the Miseries which the greatest Part of *Europe* is reduced to suffer, having lost their Liberties by the Intrigues and Wickedness of those whom they trusted; whilst we continue in full Enjoyment of ours, and can be in no Danger of losing them, while we have so excellent a King, assisted and obeyed by so wise a Parliament.

T   *I am, &c.*

Number 18.

SATURDAY, FEBRUARY 25, 1720.

The terrible Tendency of publick Corruption to ruin a State, exemplified in that of ROME, and applied to our own.

SIR,

Venalis civitas mox peritura si emptorum invenias!
"Mercenary City, ripe for Destruction, and just ready to deliver up thyself, and all thy Liberties, to the first Bidder, who is able to buy thee!" said the great King *Jugurtha*, when he was leaving *Rome*.[1] *Rome* the Nurse of Heroes, the Mistress of Nations, the Glory of Empires, the Source, the Standard, and Pattern of Virtue and Knowledge, and, indeed, of every Thing which ever was praise-worthy and valuable amongst Men, was soon after fallen, fallen Ten Thousand Thousand Fathoms deep in the Abyss of Corruption and Impiety: No more of that publick Spirit appeared, that rendered it amiable, as well as terrible, to the World: It had conquered by its Virtue more than its Arms: It had commanded a willing Subjection from the numerous Nations, who readily acknowledged its superior Genius and natural Right to Empire, and afterwards their own Condition to be graced by the Dignity of such a Mistress.

"But (says the Abbot *Vertot*[2]) about this Time another Nation seemed to appear upon the Stage: A general Corruption soon spread itself through all Degrees of the State: Justice was publickly sold in the Tribunals: The Voices of the People went

---

[1] Jugurtha was a Numidian King (rule 111–106 B.C.) whose power was eventually destroyed by the Romans. He was the principal subject of Sallust's *Bellum Iugurthinum,* a work later translated by Gordon.

[2] René Aubert, Abbé de Vertot (1655–1735), was a French historical writer.

to the highest Bidder; and the Consuls, having obtained that great Post by Intrigues, or by Bribery, never now made War but to enrich themselves with the Spoils of Nations, and often to plunder those very Provinces, which their Duty bound them to protect and defend. —The Provinces were obliged to supply these prodigious Expences: The Generals possessed themselves of the Revenues of the Commonwealth; and the State was weakened in proportion as its Members became powerful. —It was sufficient Colour for rifling the People, and laying new Imposts, if they did but give those Exactions a new Name.

"There arose on a sudden, and as it were by Enchantment, magnificent Palaces, whose Walls, Roofs, and Cielings were all gilded: It was not enough that their Beds and Tables were all of Silver; that rich Metal must also be carved and adorned with *Basso Relievo's*, performed by the most excellent Artists. —All the Money of the State was in the Hands of the Great Men, the Publicans, and certain Freed-men richer than their Masters.

He says, "It would make a Volume to represent the Magnificence of their Buildings, the Richness of their Habits, the Jewels they wore, the prodigious Number of Slaves, Freed-men, and Clients, by which they were constantly attended, and especially the Expence and Profusion of their Tables: They were not contented, if, in the midst of Winter, the *Falernian* Wine that was presented them was not strewed with Roses; and cooled in Vessels of Gold in Summer: Their Side-Boards groaned under the Weight and Load of Plate, both Silver and Gold: They valued the Feast only by the Costliness of the Dishes that were served up; Pheasants must be fetched for them through all the Dangers of the Sea; and, to complete their Corruption, after the Conquest of *Asia,* they began to introduce Women-Singers and Dancers into their Entertainments.

"What Defenders of Liberty, *says he,* are here? What an Omen of approaching Slavery? None could be greater, than to see Valour less regarded in a State than Luxury? to see the poor Officer languishing in the obscure Honours of a Legion, whilst the Grandees concealed their Cowardice, and dazzled the Eyes of the Publick, by the Magnificence of their Equipage, and the Profusion of their Expence."

But what did all this Profusion and Magnificence produce? Pleasure succeeded in the room of Temperance, Idleness took place of the Love of Business, and private Regards extinguished that Love of Liberty, that Zeal and Warmth, which their Ancestors had shewn for the Interest of the Publick; Luxury and Pride became fashionable; all Ranks and Orders of Men tried to outvie one another in Expence and Pomp; and when, by so doing, they had spent their private Patrimonies, they endeavoured to make Reprisals upon the Publick; and, having before sold every thing else, at last sold their Country.

The publick Treasure was squandered away, and divided amongst private Men; and new Demands made, and new Taxes and Burdens laid upon the People, to continue and support this Extravagance. Such Conduct in the Great Ones occasioned Murmurings, universal Discontent, and at last Civil Wars. The People threw themselves under different Heads or Leaders of Parties, who all aspired to make themselves Masters of the Commonwealth, and of the publick Liberty; and, during the Struggle, *Rome* and all *Italy* was but one Slaughter-House. Thousands, Hundreds of Thousands, fell Sacrifices to the Ambition of a few: Rivers of Blood ran in the publick Streets, and Proscriptions and Massacres were esteemed Sport and Pastime; till at length Two Thirds of the People were destroyed, and the rest made Slaves to the most wicked and contemptible Wretches of Mankind.

Thus ended the greatest, the noblest State that ever adorned the worldly Theatre, that ever the Sun saw: It fell a Victim to Ambition and Faction, to base and unworthy Men, to Parricides and Traytors; and every other Nation must run the same Fortune, expect the same fatal Catastrophe, who suffer themselves to be debauched with the same Vices, and are actuated by the same Principles and Passions.

I wish I could say, that the Abbot *Vertot's* Description of the *Roman* State, in its last Declension, suited no other State in our own Time. I hope that we ourselves have none of these Corruptions and Abuses to complain of: I am sure, if we have, that it is high Time to reform them, and to prevent the dismal Evils which they threaten. It is wild to think that there is any other Way to prevent the Consequence, without preventing the Corruption, and the Causes which produce it: Mankind will be always the same, will always act within one Circle; and when we know what they did a Thousand Years ago in any Circumstance, we shall know what they will do a Thousand Years hence in the same. This is what is called Experience, the surest Mistress and Lesson of Wisdom.

Let us therefore grow wise by the Misfortunes of others: Let us make Use of the *Roman* Language, as a Vehicle of good Sense, and useful Instruction; and not use it like Pedants, Priests, and Pedagogues. Let their Virtues and their Vices, and the Punishment of them too, be an Example to us; and so prevent our Miseries from being an Example to other Nations: Let us avoid the Rocks upon which they have suffered Shipwreck, and set up Buoys and Sea-marks to warn and guide Posterity. In fine, let us examine and look narrowly into every Part of our Constitution, and see if any Corruptions or Abuses have crept or galloped into it. Let us search our Wounds to the Core, without which it is beyond the Power of Surgery to apply suitable Remedies.

Our present Misfortunes will rouse up our Spirits, and, as it were, awaken us out of a deep Lethargy. It is true, indeed, that they came upon us like a Storm of Thunder and Lightning in a clear Sky, and when the Heavens seemed more serene; but the combustible Matter was prepared before: Steams and Exhalations had been long gathering from Bogs and Jakes; and though they some Time seemed dispersed and far removed by the Heat of a warm Sun, yet the Firmament was all the while impregnating with Fire and Brimstone; and now, on a Sudden, the Clouds thicken, and look black and big on every Side, and threaten us with a Hurricane.

Let us therefore act the Part of skilful Pilots, and call all Hands to labour at the Oars and at the Ropes: Let us begin with throwing all our Luggage and useless Trumpery overboard; then let us lower or take down all superfluous Sails, to prevent the Boat from being overset; and when we have done all in our Power to save the Ship, let us implore the Assistance of Heaven; and I doubt not but we shall out-ride the Storm. . . .

T   *I am, &c.*

Number 24.

SATURDAY, APRIL 8, 1721.

Of the natural Honesty of the People, and their reasonable Demands. How important it is to every Government to consult their Affections and Interest.

SIR,

I Have observed, in a former Letter, that the People, when they are not misled or corrupted, generally make a sound Judgment of Things. They have natural Qualifications equal to those of their Superiors; and there is oftener found a great Genius carrying a Pitch-fork, than carrying a White Staff. The poor Cook preferred by the Grand Seignior to be his First Vizier, in order to cure the publick Disorder and Confusion occasioned by the Ignorance, Corruption, and Neglect of the former Ministry, made good effectually his own Promise, and did Credit to his Master's Choice: He remedied the publick

Disorders, *and proved*, says Sir *Paul Ricaut, an able and excel-lent Minister of State.*[1]

Besides, there are not such mighty Talents requisite for Gov-ernment, as some, who pretend to them without possessing them, would make us believe: Honest Affections, and common Qualifications, are sufficient; and the Administration has been always best executed, and the publick Liberty best preserved, near the Origin and Rise of States, when plain Honesty and common Sense alone governed the publick Affairs, and the Morals of Men were not corrupted with Riches and Luxury, nor their Understandings perverted by Subtleties and Distinctions. Great Abilities have, for the most part, if not always, been employed to mislead the honest, but unwary, Multitude, and to draw them out of the open and plain Paths of publick Virtue and publick Good.

The People have no Biass to be Knaves; the Security of their Persons and Property is their highest Aim. No Ambition prompts them; they cannot come to be great Lords, and to possess great Titles, and therefore desire none. No aspiring or unsociable Passions incite them; they have no Rivals for Place, no Com-petitor to pull down; they have no darling Child, Pimp, or Relation, to raise: they have no Occasion for Dissimulation or Intrigue; they can serve no End by Faction; they have no Inter-est, but the general Interest.

The same can rarely be said of Great Men, who, to gratify private Passion, often bring down publick Ruin; who, to fill their private Purses with many Thousands, frequently load the People with many Millions; who oppress for a Mistress, and, to save a Favourite, destroy a Nation; who too often make the Publick sink and give way to their private Fortune; and, for a private Pleasure, create a general Calamity. Besides, being edu-

---

[1] Paul Rycaut (d. 1700) was an English diplomat, traveler, and historian. His works included a *Present State of the Ottoman Empire* (1670) and a *History of the Turks 1623–1699* (1680–1700). His views of the Turks corresponded nicely with Trenchard and Gordon's view of the Ottoman Empire as the most awful of tyrannies. "The Grand Seignior," mentioned in this same context, was the Ottoman Sultan.

cated in Debauchery, and pampered in Riot and Luxury, they have no Sense of the Misfortunes of other Men, nor Tenderness for those who suffer them: They have no Notion of Miseries which they do not feel. There is a Nation in *Europe*, which, within the Space of an Hundred Years last past, has been blessed with Patriots, who, void of every Talent and Inclination to do Good, and even stinted in their Ability for Roguery, were forced to be beholden, for most of the Mischief which they did, to the superior Arts and Abilities of humble Rogues and Brokers.

The first Principles of Power are in the People; and all the Projects of Men in Power ought to refer to the People, to aim solely at their Good, and end in it: And whoever will pretend to govern them without regarding them, will soon repent it. Such Feats of Errantry may do perhaps in *Asia:* but in Countries where the People are free, it is Madness to hope to rule them against their Wills. They will know, that Government is appointed for their Sakes, and will be saucy enough to expect some Regard and some Good from their own Delegates. Those Nations who are governed in spite of themselves, and in a Manner that bids Defiance to their Opinions, their Interests, and their Understandings, are either Slaves, or will soon cease to be Subjects.

Dominion that is not maintained by the Sword, must be maintained by Consent; and in this latter Case, what Security can any Man at the Head of Affairs expect, but from pursuing the People's Welfare, and seeking their Good-Will? The Government of One for the Sake of One, is Tyranny; and so is the Government of a Few for the Sake of Themselves: But Government executed for the Good of All, and with the Consent of All, is Liberty; and the Word *Government* is profaned, and its Meaning abused, when it signifies any Thing else.

In free Countries the People know all this. They have their Five Senses in as great Perfection, as have those who would treat them as if they had none. They are not wont to hate their Governors, till their Governors deserve to be hated; and when this happens to be the Case, not absolute Power itself, nor the Affections of a Prince invested with it, can protect or employ Ministers detested by the People. Even the Grand Seignior, with all his boundless Authority, is frequently forced to give up his First Minister (who is sometimes his Son-in-Law, or Brother-in-Law) a Sacrifice to appease the People's Rage.

The People, rightly managed, are the best Friends to Princes; and, when injured and oppressed, the most formidable Enemies. Princes, who have trusted to their Armies or their Nobility, have been often deceived and ruined; but Princes, who have trusted wholly to the People, have seldom been deceived or deserted: The Reason is, that in all Governments, which are not Violent and Military, the People have more Power than either the Grandees or the Soldiery; and their Friendship is more sincere, as having nothing to desire but Freedom from Oppression. And whilst a Prince is thus beloved by his People, it will rarely happen that any can be so rash and precipitate as to conspire against him; and such Conspiracies have never the intended Success: but, as *Machiavel* well observes, *When the People are dissatisfied, and have taken a Prejudice against their Governors, there is no Thing nor Person that they ought not to fear.*

It is therefore of vast Importance to preserve the Affections of the People even in those Governments where they have no Share in the Administration. The wise States of *Holland* are so apprized of the Truth of this Maxim, that they have preserved themselves and their State by religiously observing it. Their Government consists of many little Aristocracies, where the Magistrates choose each other, and the People have nothing to do; but in Spirit and Effect it is a Democracy, and the Dispositions and Inclinations of the People have above all Things the greatest Weight in their Counsels. The Jealousy of the People makes a vigilant Magistracy, who are honest out of Fear of provoking them, and, by never doing it, are in great Safety.

But, Thanks be to Heaven and our worthy Ancestors, our

Liberties are better secured. We have a Constitution, in which the People have a large Share: They are one Part of the Legislature, and have the sole Power of giving Money; which includes in it every Thing that they can ask for the publick Good; and the Representatives, being neither awed nor bribed, will always act for their Country's Interest; their own being so interwoven with the People's Happiness, that they must stand and fall together.

But what if our Delegates should not be suffered to meet; or, when met, should be so awed by Force (as formerly in *Denmark*[2]) or so corrupted by Places and Pensions (as in the Reign of *Charles* II.[3]) as to be ready to give up publick Liberty, and betray the Interest of their Principals to secure their own? This we may be sure can never happen under his Majesty's most just and gentle Reign: However, it has happened formerly; and what has been, may be again in future Reigns.

What, in such a Case, is to be done? What Remedies have our Laws provided against so fatal a Mischief? Must the People patiently crouch under the heaviest of all Evils? Or has our Constitution pointed out the Means of Redress? It would be absurd to suppose that it has not; and, in effect, the People have a legal Remedy at hand: It is their undoubted Right, and acknowledged to be so in the *Bill of Rights*[4] passed in the Reign

---

[2] The fall of Denmark to absolutist rule was an example frequently used by Whig writers of the early eighteenth century. Trenchard and Gordon drew particularly from the work of Robert Molesworth, the great Whig leader, *An Account of Denmark*. Molesworth had seen in Denmark the case of an ancient constitution giving way to hereditary tyranny and had feared a like fate for England. Thus, Denmark was cited by Trenchard and Gordon as a parallel for what might happen in their own country.

[3] Charles II was the son of Charles I. He dated his rule from the time of his father's execution in 1649 and ruled in England from 1660 to 1689.

[4] The meaning here is unclear. The famous Bill of Rights was enacted in 1689. The authors may have meant the Petition of Right of 1628, a famous example of the Parliamentary use of the petition form to gain a redress of grievances.

of King *Charles* I. and since, by the Act of Settlement[5] of the Crown at the *Revolution;* humbly to represent their publick Grievances, and to petition for Redress to those whose Duty it is to right them, or to see them righted: And it is certain, that in all Countries, the People's Misfortunes are greater or less, in Proportion as this Right is encouraged or checked.

It is indeed the best and the only just Way that they can take to breathe their Grievances; and whenever this Way has been taken, especially when it has been universally taken, our Kings have always accepted so powerful an Application. Our Parliaments too, who are the Keepers and Barriers of our Liberty, have shewn themselves ready and willing to receive the modest Complaints and Representations of their Principals, and to apply quick Remedies to the Grievances contained in them. It has, indeed, been always thought highly imprudent, not to say dangerous, to resist the general Groans and Entreaties of the People, uttered in this Manner.

This has been a Method, which has always had great Weight with good Men, and has been always a great Terror to bad. It has therefore always been encouraged or discouraged, according to the Innocence or Guilt of Men in Power. A Prince, who minds the Welfare and desires the Affections of his Subjects, cannot wish for a better Expedient to know how his Servants are approved, and how his Government is liked, than by this Way of countenancing his People in laying their Hearts, their Wishes, and their Requests before him; and Ministers never can be averse to such Representations of the Complaints of the People, unless they have given the People Occasion to complain.

Titus and *Trajan*, conscious of their own virtuous Administration, and worthy Purposes, cour[t]ed Addresses and Infor-

---

[5] The authors refer not to the Act of Settlement of 1701, which established the Hanoverian succession, but to the Bill of Rights of 1689, which gave constitutional recognition to certain rights, among them the right to petition, and settled the crown on William and Mary.

mations of this kind, from their Subjects: They wisely knew, that if the *Roman* People had free Leave to speak, they would not take Leave to act; and that, whilst they could have Redress, they would not seek Revenge.[6]

None but desperate Parricides will make the People desperate.

G   *I am, &c.*

Number 25.

SATURDAY, APRIL 15, 1721.

Considerations on the destructive Spirit of arbitrary Power. With the Blessings of Liberty, and our own Constitution.

SIR,

The Good of the Governed being the sole End of Government, they must be the greatest and best Governors, who make their People great and happy; and they the worst,

---

[6] Titus Flavius Vespasianus (A.D. 39–81) was the son of the Emperor Vespasian and himself Emperor from A.D. 79 to 81. In spite of his brief reign and a later reputation gained from his war against the Jews and capture of Jerusalem in 70, he was popularly regarded as a good emperor who generously aided the sufferers after the eruption of Vesuvius. He was labeled, for example, by Suetonius "the delight and darling of the human race" (*Lives,* "Titus" I).

Marcus Ulpius Trajanus was another of the good emperors of Rome. He was a successful soldier adopted by the Emperor Nerva as his heir. He ruled from A.D. 98 to 117, at the period of Tacitus' greatest literary activity. Although he did not live to write Trajan's history, Tacitus thought highly of him, and the general public seems to have regarded this Emperor as humane and progressive.

Thus, Titus and Trajan stood for Trenchard and Gordon as examples of good rulers, occasionally betrayed because of the wideness of their powers, but earnestly striving to rule well.

who make their People little, wicked, and miserable. Power in a free State, is a Trust committed by All to One or a Few, to watch for the Security, and pursue the Interest, of All: And, when that Security is not sought, nor that Interest obtained, we know what Opinion the People will have of their Governors.

It is the hard Fate of the World, that there should be any Difference in the Views and Interests of the Governors and Governed; and yet it is so in most Countries. Men who have a Trust frankly bestowed upon them by the People, too frequently betray that Trust, become Conspirators against their Benefactors, and turn the Sword upon those who gave it; insomuch that in the greatest Part of the Earth, People are happy if they can defend themselves against their Defenders.

Let us look round this great World, and behold what an immense Majority of the whole Race of Men crouch under the Yoke of a few Tyrants, naturally as low as the meanest of themselves, and, by being Tyrants, worse than the worst; who, as Mr. *Sidney*[1] observes, *use their Subjects like Asses and Mastiff Dogs, to work and to fight, to be oppressed and killed for them.* Even the good Qualities and Courage of such Subjects are their Misfortune, by strengthening the wicked Hands of their brutal Masters, and strengthening their own Chains. Tyrants consider their People as their Cattle, and use them worse, as they fear them more. Thus the most of Mankind are become the wretched Slaves of those, who are or should be their own Creatures; they maintain their haughty Masters like Gods, and their haughty Masters often use them like Dogs: A fine Specimen of Gratitude and Duty!

Yet this cruel Spirit in Tyrants is not always owing naturally to the Men, since they are naturally like other Men; but it is owing to the Nature of the Dominion which they exercise. Good Laws make a good Prince, if he has a good Understanding; but the best Men grow mischievous when they are set above Laws.

---

[1] On Algernon Sidney, see note 6, *Letter* 16, pp. 50–51.

Claudius was a very harmless Man, while he was a private Man; but when he came to be a Tyrant, he proved a bloody one, almost as bloody as his Nephew and Predecessor *Caligula;* who had also been a very good Subject, but when he came to be the *Roman* Emperor, grew the professed Executioner of Mankind.[2]

There is something so wanton and monstrous in lawless Power, that there scarce ever was a human Spirit that could bear it; and the Mind of Man, which is weak and limited, ought never to be trusted with a Power that is boundless. The State of Tyranny is a State of Wàr; and where it prevails, instead of an Intercourse of Confidence and Affection, as between a lawful Prince and his Subjects, nothing is to be seen but Jealousy, Mistrust, Fear, and Hatred: An arbitrary Prince and his Slaves often destroy one another, to be safe: They are continually plotting aginst his Life; he is continually shedding their Blood, and plundering them of their Property. . . .

As arbitrary Power in a single Person had made greater Havock in human Nature, and thinned Mankind more, than all the Beasts of Prey and all the Plagues and Earthquakes that ever were; let those Men consider what they have to answer for, who would countenance such a monstrous Evil in the World, or would oppose those that would oppose it. A Bear, a

---

2 Tiberius Claudius Nero Germanicus (10 B.C.-A.D. 54) was Emperor of Rome from A.D. 41. He was famous partially for the circumstances of his coming to power; he was discovered cowering behind a curtain in the palace and then proclaimed Emperor by the Praetorian Guard. His rule was not so evil as suggested by Trenchard and Gordon. They base their account largely on Tacitus, whose coverage of the good years of Claudius is no longer extant. He was also famed for the method of his death; he succumbed from poisoned mushrooms probably fed him by his niece.

Gaius Julius Caesar Germanicus (A.D. 12–41) was known as "Caligula," a nickname derived from the "Baby-boots" he once wore as a child. He was the infamous, certainly unstable, and perhaps mentally unbalanced successor of Tiberius and predecessor of Claudius. In Trenchard and Gordon's thinking, he was the very symbol of the misuse of autocratic power.

Lion, or a Tyger, may now and then pick up single Men in a Wood, or a Desert; an Earthquake sometimes may bury a Thousand or Two Inhabitants in the Ruins of a Town; and the Pestilence may once in many Years carry off a much greater Number: But a Tyrant shall, out of a wanton personal Passion, carry Fire and Sword through a whole Continent, and deliver up a Hundred Thousand of his Fellow Creatures to the Slaughter in one Day, without any Remorse or further Notice, than that they died for his Glory. I say nothing of the moral Effect of Tyranny; though 'tis certain that Ignorance, Vice, Poverty, and Vileness, always attend it.

He who compares the World now with what it was formerly, how populous once, how thin now; and considers the Cause of this doleful Alteration, will find just Reason to fear, that Spiritual and Temporal Tyranny, if they go on much longer, will utterly extinguish the human Race. Of *Turkey* I have spoken already: The great Continent of *America* is almost unpeopled, the *Spaniards* having destroyed, 'tis thought, about Forty Millions of its Natives; and for some Kingdoms in *Europe,* especially towards the North, I do not believe that they have now half the Inhabitants that they had so lately as a Hundred Years ago.

Blessed be God, there are still some free Countries in *Europe,* that abound with People and with Plenty, and *England* is the foremost. This demonstrates the inestimable Blessing of Liberty. Can we ever over-rate it, or be too jealous of a Treasure which includes in it almost all Human Felicities? Or can we encourage too much those that contend for it, and those that promote it. It is the Parent of Virtue, Pleasure, Plenty, and Security; and 'tis innocent, as well as lovely. In all Contentions between Liberty and Power, the latter has almost constantly been the Aggressor. Liberty, if ever it produce any Evils, does also cure them: Its worst Effect, Licentiousness, never does, and never can, continue long. Anarchy cannot be of much Duration: and where 'tis so, it is the Child and Companion of Tyranny;

which is not Government, but a Dissolution of it, as Tyrants are the Enemies of Mankind.

Power is like Fire; it warms, scorches, or destroys, according as it is watched, provoked, or increased. It is as dangerous as useful. Its only Rule is the Good of the People; but because it is apt to break its Bounds, in all good Governments nothing, or as little as may be, ought to be left to Chance, or the Humours of Men in Authority: All should proceed by fixed and stated Rules, and upon any Emergency, new Rules should be made. This is the Constitution, and this the Happiness of *Englishmen;* as hath been formerly shewn at large in these Letters.

We have a Constitution that abhors absolute Power; we have a King that does not desire it; and we are a People that will never suffer it: No free People will ever submit to it, unless it steal upon them by Treachery, or they be driven into it by Violence. But a State can never be too secure against this terrible, this last of all human Evils; which may be brought upon them by many Causes, even by some that at first Sight do not seem to threaten any such Thing: And of all those Causes, none seems more boding than a general Distress, which certainly produces general Discontent, the Parent of Revolutions; and in what such a Circumstance of Affairs may end, no Man can ever foresee: Few are brought about without Armies; a Remedy almost always worse than the Disease. What is got by Soldiers, must be maintained by Soldiers; and we have, in this Paper, already seen the frightful Image of a Military Government; a Government, which, at best, is violent and bloody, and eternally inconsistent with Law and Property.

It is therefore a dreadful Wickedness to have any Share in giving Occasion for those Discontents, which are so apt to burst into Rage and Confusion. A State sometimes recovers out of a Convulsion, and gains new Vigour by it; but it much oftener expires in it. Heaven preserve me from ever beholding contending Armies in *England!* They are different Things from what they once were. Our Armies formerly were only a Number of the People armed occasionally; and Armies of the People are the only Armies which are not formidable to the People. Hence it is, that, in the many Revolutions occasioned by the Strife between the two Royal Houses of *York* and *Lancaster,* there never was any Danger of Slavery from an armed Force: A single Battle decided the Contention; and next Day these popular Soldiers went Home, and resumed their ordinary Arms, the Tools of Husbandry. But since that Time Armies have not been so easily parted with; but after the Danger was over for which they were raised, have often been obstinately kept up, and by that Means created Dangers still as great.

Some Quacks in Politicks may perhaps venture publick Disturbances, out of an Opinion that they shall be able to prevent them by Art, or suppress them by Force. But this shews their Capacity, as well as their Wickedness: For, not to mention the Malignity of their Hearts, in risquing publick Ruin, to gratify a private Appetite; how can any Event be certainly foreseen, when the Measure of the Cause cannot be certainly known? They can never ascertain the Degree of Opposition; they cannot foreknow what Circumstances may happen, nor into whose Hands Things may fall. *Cicero* did not dream, when he employed *Octavius* for the Commonwealth, that his young Champion for Liberty would ever be the Tyrant of his Country. Who could foresee that *Cromwel* would enslave those whom he was employed to defend? But there is no trusting of Liberty in the Hands of Men, who are obeyed by great Armies.

From hence may be seen what a fatal and crying Crime it would be, in any free Country, to break the Confidence between the Prince and his People. When Loyalty is once turned into Indifference, Indifference will soon be turned into Hatred; Hatred will be returned with Hatred; Resentment may produce Tyranny, and Rage may produce Rebellion. There is no Mischief which this mutual Mistrust and Aversion may not bring forth. They must therefore be the blackest Traytors, who are the first Authors of so terrible an Evil, as are they who would endeavour to protect them.

Henry III. of Castile said, *That he feared the Curse of his People more than he did the Arms of his Enemies:* In which Saying he shewed as much Wisdom as Humanity; since, while he was beloved at Home, he had nothing to fear from Abroad, and the Curses of his Subjects were the likeliest Means to bring upon him the Arms of his Enemies.[3]

G   *I am, &c.*

Number 32.

SATURDAY, JUNE 10, 1721.

Reflections upon Libelling.

SIR,
I Design in this Letter to lay before the Town some Thoughts upon Libelling; a Sort of Writing that hurts particular Persons, without doing Good to the Publick; and a Sort of Writing much complained of amongst us at this Time, with great Ground, but not more than is pretended.

A Libel is not the less a Libel for being true. This may seem a Contradiction; but it is neither one in Law, or in common Sense: There are some Truths not fit to be told; where, for Example, the Discovery of a small Fault may do great Mischief; or where the Discovery of a great Fault can do no Good, there ought to be no Discovery at all: And to make Faults where there are none, is still worse.

But this Doctrine only holds true as to private and personal Failings; and it is quite otherwise when the Crimes of Men come to affect the Publick. Nothing ought to be so dear to us as our Country, and nothing ought to come in Competition with its Interests. Every Crime against the Publick is a great Crime,

---

[3] Henry III of Castile (1379–1406) reigned from 1390 and was better known by the name "Henry the Sickly."

though there be some greater than others. Ignorance and Folly may be pleaded in Alleviation of private Offences; but when they come to be publick Offences, they lose all Benefit of such a Plea: We are then no longer to consider only to what Causes they are owing, but what Evils they may produce; and here we shall readily find, that Folly has overturned States, and private Ignorance been the Parent of publick Confusion.

The exposing therefore of publick Wickedness, as it is a Duty which every Man owes to Truth and his Country, can never be a Libel in the Nature of Things; and they who call it so, make themselves no Compliment. He who is affronted at the reading of the Ten Commandments, would make the Decalogue a Libel, if he durst; but he tempts us at the same Time to form a Judgment of his Life and Morals not at all to his Advantage: Whoever calls publick and necessary Truths, Libels, does but apprize us of his own Character, and arm us with Caution against his Designs. I doubt not but if the late Directors had been above the Parliament, as they once thought themselves, they would have called the *Votes of the House of Commons* against them, *false and scandalous Libels.*[1]

Machiavel[2] says, *Calumny is pernicious, but Accusation beneficial, to a State;* and he shews Instances where States have suffered or perished for not haveing, or for neglecting, the Power to accuse Great Men who were Criminals, or thought to be so; and hence grew the Temptation and Custom of slandering and reviling, which was the only Remedy that the People had left them: So that the Evil of Calumny was owing to the Want of Justice, and the People were more blameless than those whom they reviled; who, having forced them upon a Licentiousness of Speech, did very unkindly chide and punish

---

[1] Trenchard and Gordon here again refer to the Directors of the South Sea Company, who obviously would have preferred to keep from public knowledge the details of the collapse of that Company and its corrupt dealings with prominent politicians. See note 6, *Letter* 15, p. 41.

[2] On "Machiavel," see note 4, *Letter* 16, p. 49.

them for using it. Slander is certainly a very base and mean Thing: But surely it cannot be more pernicious to calumniate even good Men, than not to be able to accuse ill ones.

I have long thought, that the World are very much mistaken in their Idea and Distinction of Libels. It has been hitherto generally understood that there were no other Libels but those against Magistrates, and those against private Men: Now, to me there seems to be a third Sort of Libels, full as destructive as any of the former can possibly be; I mean, Libels against the People. It was otherwise at *Athens* and *Rome;* where, though particular Men, and even great Men, were often treated with much Freedom and Severity, when they deserved it; yet the People, the Body of the People, were spoken of with the utmost Regard and Reverence: *The sacred Privileges of the People, The inviolable Majesty of the People, The awful Authority of the People,* and *The unappealable Judgment of the People,* were Phrases common in these wise, great, and free Cities. Other Modes of Speech are since grown fashionable, and popular Madness is now almost proverbial: But this Madness of theirs, whenever it happens, is derived from external Causes. *Oppression,* they say, *will make a wise Man mad;* and Delusion has not less Force: But where there are neither Oppressors nor Imposters, the Judgment of the People in the Business of Property, the Preservation of which is the principal Business of Government, does rarely err. Perhaps they are destitute of Grimace, Mystery, Refinements, Shrugs, Dissimulation, and Reserve and the other Accomplishments of Courtiers: But as these are only Masks to conceal the Absence of Honesty and Sense, the People, who possess as they do the Substance, have Reason to despise such insipid and contemptible Shadows.

Machiavel, in the Chapter where he proves that a Multitude is wiser and more constant than a Prince, complains, that the Credit which the People should be in declines daily; *For,* says he, *every Man has Liberty to speak what he pleases against them; but against a Prince no Man can talk without a thousand*

Apprehensions and Dangers. I have indeed often wondered, that the inveighing against the Interest of the People, and calling their Liberties in Question, as has been and is commonly done among us by old Knaves and young Fools, has never been made an express Crime.

I must own, I know not what Treason is, if sapping and betraying the Liberties of a People be not Treason, in the eternal and original Nature of Things. Let it be remembered for whose Sake Government is, or could be, appointed; then let it be considered, who are more to be regarded, the Governors or the Governed. They indeed owe one another mutual Duties; but if there be any Transgressions committed, the Side that is most obliged ought doubtless to bear the most: And yet it is so far otherwise, that almost all over the Earth, the People, for One Injury that they do their Governors, receive Ten Thousand from them: Nay, in some Countries, it is made Death and Damnation, not to bear all the Oppressions and Cruelties, which Men made wanton by Power inflict upon those that gave it them.

The Truth is; If the People are suffered to keep their own, it is the most that they desire: But even this is a Happiness which in few Places falls to their Lot; they are frequently robbed by those whom they pay to protect them. I know that it is a general Charge against the People, that they are turbulent, restless, fickle, and unruly: Than which there can be nothing more untrue; for they are only so where they are made so. As to their being fickle, it is so false, that, on the contrary, they have almost ever a strong Bent to received Customs, and as strong a Partiality to Names and Families that they have been used to: And as to their being turbulent, it is as false; since there is scarce an Example in an Hundred Years of any People's giving Governors any Uneasiness, till their Governors had made them uneasy: Nay, for the most part, they bear many Evils without returning One, and seldom throw off their Burdens so long as they can stand under them.

But intending to handle this Subject more at large in another Letter, I return more directly to the Business of Libels.

As to Libels against Government, like all others, they are always base and unlawful, and often mischievous; especially when Governments are impudently charged with Actions and Designs of which they are not guilty. It is certain, that we ought not to enter into the private Vices or Weaknesses of Governors, any further than their private Vices enter into their publick Administration; and when they do, it will be impossible to stop People's Mouths: They will be provoked, and shew that they are so, in spite of Art and Threats, if they suffer Hardships and Woe from the private Gratifications of their Superiors, from whom they have a Right to expect Ease and Happiness; and if they be disappointed, they will be apt to deal very freely with their Characters.

In Truth, most Libels are purely personal; they fly at Men rather than Things; which Proceeding is as injudicious as it is unmanly. It is mean to be quarrelling with Faces, Names, and private Pleasures; Things perfectly indifferent to the World, or Things out of a Man's own Power; and 'tis silly, as it shews those whom we attack, that we attack them not for what they do, but for what they are: And this is to provoke them without mending them. All this therefore is Libelling; an Offence against which the Laws of almost every Country, and particularly of our own, have furnished a Remedy in proportion to the Consequence and Quality of the Person offended. And it is as just that Reputation should be defended by Law, as that Property should.

The Praise of Well-doing is the highest Reward that worthy and disinterested Men aim at, and it is villainous and ungrateful to rob them of it; and those that do it, are Libellers and Slanderers. On the other hand, while Censure and Infamy attend Evil-doers, it will be some Restraint, if not upon them, yet upon others, from following their Example: But if Men be ever suffered to do what they please without hearing of it, or being accountable for it; Liberty and Law will be lost, though their Names may remain. And whether acting wickedly with Impunity, or speaking falsly with Impunity, be likely to do most Hurt to human Society and the Peace of the World, I leave all the World to judge: Common Equity says, that they both ought to be punished, though not both alike.

All Libels, the higher they aim, the more Malignity they acquire; and therefore when they strike at the Person of the Prince, the Measure of their Guilt is complete. The Office of a Prince is to defend his People and their Properties; an excellent and a painful Office; which, where it is executed with Honesty and Diligence, deserves the highest Applause and Reward; and whoever vilifies and traduces him, is an Enemy to Society and to Mankind, and will be punished with the Consent of all who love either. And yet it is scarce possible, in a free Country, to punish by a general Law any Libel so much as it deserves; since such a Law, consisting of so many Branches, and being of such vast Latitude, would make all Writing whatsoever, how innocent soever, and even all Speaking, unsafe. Hence it is, that in *Turkey*, though Printing were permitted, it would be of no Use, because no body would dare to make any Use of it.

As long as there are such Things as Printing and Writing, there will be Libels: It is an Evil arising out of a much greater Good. And as to those who are for locking up the Press, because it produces Monsters, they ought to consider that so do the Sun and the *Nile;* and that it is something better for the World to bear some particular Inconveniencies arising from general Blessings, than to be wholly deprived of Fire and Water.

Of all Sorts of Libels, scurrilous ones are certainly the most harmless and contemptible: Even Truth suffers by Ill-Manners; and Ill-Manners prevent the Effect of Lyes. The Letter in the *Saturday's Post* of the 27th past does, I think, exceed all the Scurrilities which I have either heard, or seen, from the Press or the Pulpit. The Author of it must surely be mad: He talks as if Distraction were in his Head, and a Firebrand in his Hand;

and nothing can be more false, than the Insinuations which he makes, and the ugly Resemblances which he would draw. The Paper is a Heap of Falshood and Treason, delivered in the Style and Spirit of *Billingsgate;* and indeed most of the Enemies to his Majesty's Person, Title, and Government, have got the Faculty of Writing and Talking, as if they had their Education in that Quarter.

However, as bad as that Letter is, (and, I think, there cannot be a worse) Occasion will never be taken from scurrilous and traiterous Writing, to destroy the End of Writing. We know that in all Times there have been Men lying upon the Watch to stifle Liberty, under a Pretence of suppressing Libels; like the late King *James,* who, having Occasion for an Army to suppress *Monmouth's* Rebellion, would needs keep it up afterwards; because, forsooth, other Rebellions might happen, for which he was resolved to give Cause.

I must own, that I would rather many Libels should escape, than the Liberty of the Press should be infringed; yet no Man in *England* thinks worse of Libels than I do; especially of such as bid open Defiance to the present Protestant Establishment.

Corrupt Men, who have given Occasion for Reproach, by their base and dark Practices with the late Directors, being afraid of Truths that affect them from the Press, may be desirous of shutting it up: But honest Men, with clear Reputations, which they know foul Mouths cannot hurt, will always be for preserving it open, as a sure Sign of Liberty, and a Cause of it.

The best Way to escape the Virulence of Libels, is not to deserve them; but as Innocence itself is not secure against the Malignity of evil Tongues, it is also necessary to punish them. However, it does not follow that the Press is to be sunk, for the Errors of the Press. No body was ever yet so ridiculous to propose a Law for restraining People from travelling upon the Highway, because some who used the Highway committed Robberies.

It is commonly said, that no Nation in the World would allow such Papers to come Abroad as *England* suffers; which is only saying, that no Nation in the World enjoys the *Liberty* which *England* enjoys. In Countries where there is no Liberty, there can be no ill Effects of it. No body is punished at *Constantinople* for Libelling: Nor is there any Distinction there between the Liberty of the Press, and the Licentiousness of the Press; a Distinction ever to be observed by honest Men and Freemen.

G   *I am, &c.*

Number 33.

SATURDAY, JUNE 17, 1721.

Cautions against the natural Encroachments of Power.

SIR,

Considering what sort of a Creature Man is, it is scarce possible to put him under too many Restraints, when he is possessed of great Power: He may possibly use it well; but they act most prudently, who, supposing that he would use it ill, inclose him within certain Bounds, and make it terrible to him to exceed them.

Men that are above all Fear, soon grow above all Shame. *Rupto pudore & metu, suo tantum ingenio utebatur,* says *Tacitus* of *Tiberius.*[1] Even *Nero* had lived a great while inoffensively, and reigned virtuously: But finding at last that he might

---

[1] This is another variant from Tacitus, *Annals* VI. 51: ". . . *Postremo in scelera simul ac dedecora prorupit, postquam remoto pudore et metu suo tantum ingenio utebatur.*" ". . . Finally, when the restraints of shame and fear were gone, and nothing remained but to follow his own bent, he plunged impartially into crime and into ignominy."

do what he would, he let loose his Appetite for Blood, and committed such mighty, such monstrous, such unnatural Slaughters and Outrages, as none but a Heart bent on the Study of Cruelty could have devised. The good Counsels of *Seneca* and *Burrhus* were, for some Time, Checks upon his wolfish Nature; and doubtless he apprehended, that if he made direct and downright War upon his People, they would use Resistance and make Reprisals: But discovering, by degrees, that they would bear any thing, and his Soldiers would execute every thing, he grew into an open Defiance with Mankind, and daily and wantonly wallowed in their Blood. Having no other Rival, he seemed to rival himself, and every Day's Wick[ed]-ness was blacker than another.

Yet *Nero* was not the worst of all Men: There have been Thousands as bad as he, and only wanted the same Opportunity to shew it. And there actually have been many Princes in the World who have shed more Blood, and done more Mischief to Mankind, than *Nero* did. I could instance in a late One, who destroyed more Lives than ever *Nero* destroyed, perhaps an Hundred to One. It makes no Difference, that *Nero* committed Butcheries out of Cruelty, and the other only for his Glory: However the World may be deceived by the Change of Names into an Abhorrence of the One, and an Admiration of the Other; it is all one to a Nation, when they are to be slaughtered, whether they be slaughtered by the Hangman or by Dragoons, in Prison or in the Field; nor is Ambition better than Cruelty, when it begets Mischief as great.

It is nothing strange, that Men, who think themselves unaccountable, should act unac[c]ountably, and that all Men would be unaccountable if they could: Even those who have done nothing to displease, do not know but some time or other they may; and no Man cares to be at the entire Mercy of another. Hence it is, that if every Man had his Will, all Men would exercise Dominion, and no Man would suffer it. It is therefore owing more to the Necessities of Men, than to their Inclinations, that they have put themselves under the Restraint of Laws, and appointed certain Persons, called Magistrates, to execute them; otherwise they would never be executed, scarce any Man having such a Degree of Virtue as willingly to execute the Laws upon himself; but, on the contrary, most Men thinking them a Grievance, when they come to meddle with themselves and their Property. *Suarum legum auctor & eversor,* was the Character of *Pompey:* He made Laws when they suited his Occasions, and broke them when they thwarted his Will.[2] And it is the Character of almost every Man possessed of *Pompey's* Power: They intend them for a Security to themselves, and for a Terror to others. This shews the Distrust that Men have of Men; and this made a great Philosopher[3] call the *State of Nature, a State of War;* which Definition is true in a restrained Sense, since human Societies and human Laws are the Effect of Necessity and Experience: Whereas were all Men left to the boundless Liberty which they claim from Nature, every Man would be interfering and quarrelling with another; every Man would be plundering the Acquisitions of another; the Labour of one Man would be the Property of another; Weakness would be the Prey of Force; and one Man's Industry would be the Cause of another Man's Idleness.

Hence grew the Necessity of Government; which was the mutual Contract of a Number of Men, agreeing upon certain Terms of Union and Society, and putting themselves under Penalties, if they violated these Terms, which were called Laws,

---

[2] Gnaeus Pompeius (106–48 B.C.) was, of course, the successful general and violent politician who joined Caesar and Crassus in the First Triumvirate. For Trenchard and Gordon, he stands again as a symbol of the dangers of unlimited military power, of standing armies, of personal and whimsical violations of constitutional provisions. "*Suarem legem auctor & eversor,*" may be translated, "Author and violator of his own laws."

[3] Thomas Hobbes (1588–1679) argued, most notably in the thirteenth chapter of his *Leviathan,* that "Out of Civil States, there is always Warre of every one against every one."

and put into the Hands of one or more Men to execute. And thus Men quitted Part of their Natural Liberty to acquire Civil Security. But frequently the Remedy proved worse than the Disease; and human Society had often no Enemies so great as their own Magistrates; who, where-ever they were trusted with too much Power, always abused it, and grew mischievous to those who made them what they were. Rome, while she was free (that is, while she kept her Magistrates within due Bounds) could defend herself against all the World, and conquer it: But being enslaved (that is, her Magistrates having broke their Bounds) she could not defend herself against her own single Tyrants, nor could they defend her against her foreign Foes and Invaders; for by their Madness and Cruelties they had destroyed her Virtue and Spirit, and exhausted her Strength. This shews that those Magistrates that are at absolute Defiance with a Nation, either cannot subsist long, or will not suffer the Nation to subsist long; and that mighty Traytors, rather than fall themselves, will pull down their Country.

What a dreadful Spirit must that Man possess, who can put a private Appetite in balance against the universal Good of his Country, and of Mankind! *Alexander* and *Caesar* were that Sort of Men; they would set the World on fire, and spill its Blood, rather than not govern it. *Caligula* knew that he was hated, and deserved to be hated; but it did not mend him. *Oderint dum metuant*, was his By-word:[4] All that the Monster aimed at, was to be great and terrible. Most of these Tyrants died as became them; and, as they had reigned, by Violence: But that did not mend their Successors, who generally earned the Fate of those that went before them, before they were warm in their Place. *Invenit etiam aemulos infelix nequitia: Quid si floreat vigeatque?*

---

[4] On Caligula, see note 2, *Letter* 25, p. 69. The motto, *"Oderint dum metuant,"* may be translated, "Let them hate, so long as they fear." It was attributed to Caligula by Suetonius (*Lives of the Twelve Caesars*, "Caligula," XXX) and was quoted from the tragic poet Accius (or Attius, b. 170 B.C.) and his play *Atreus* (Accius, *Plays*, 168).

"If unfortunate Villainy thus finds Rivals, what shall we say, when it exalts its Head and prospers?" [5]

There is no Evil under the Sun but what is to be dreaded from Men, who may do what they please with Impunity: They seldom or never stop at certain Degrees of Mischief when they have Power to go farther; but hurry on from Wickedness to Wickedness, as far and as fast as human Malice can prompt human Power. *Ubi semel recto deerratum est, in praeceps per-venitur——a rectis in vitia, a vitiis in prava, a pravis in prae-cipitia,* says a *Roman* Historian; who in this speaks the Truth, though in other Instances he tells many Lies; I mean that base Flatterer of Power, *Velleius Paterculus.*[6] So that when we see any great Mischief committed with Safety, we may justly apprehend Mischiefs still greater.

The World is governed by Men, and Men by their Passions; which, being boundless and insatiable, are always terrible when they are not controuled. Who was ever satiated with Riches, or surfeited with Power, or tired with Honours? There is a Tradition concerning *Alexander,* that having penetrated to the Eastern Ocean, and ravaged as much of this World as he knew, he wept that there was never another World for him to conquer. This, whether true or no, shews the Spirit of the Man, and indeed of human Nature, whose Appetites are infinite.

---

[5] The word order is changed slightly from Tacitus, *Histories* IV. 42, but the sense remains the same: "Wickedness, even if unlucky, finds rivals. What would be the case if it should flourish and be strong?"

[6] Gaius Velleius Paterculus was a Roman soldier and minor political figure (*ca.* 19 B.C. to after A.D. 31). Only fragments survive of his admiring account of the Emperor Tiberius. The quotation combines two parts of two different lines from Paterculus' *Res Gestae Divi Augusti.* The first may be found in II. 3. 4: ". . . *ubi semel* . . .," ("When once the path of right is abandoned, men are hurried into wrong in headlong haste . . ."); the second in II. 10. 1, in slightly different words: ". . . *adeo nature a rectis in prava, a pravis in vitia, a vitiis in praecipitia pervenitur."* ("Thus does nature pass from the normal to the perverted, from that to the vicious, and from the vicious to the abyss of extravagance.")

People are ruined by their Ignorance of human Nature; which Ignorance leads them to Credulity, and too great a Confidence in particular Men. They fondly imagine that he, who, possessing a great deal of their Favour, owes them great Gratitude, and all good Offices, will therefore return their Kindness: But, alas! how often are they mistaken in their Favourites and Trustees; who, the more they have given them, are often the more incited to take All, and to return Destruction for generous Usage. The common People generally think that great Men have great Minds, and scorn base Actions; which Judgment is so false, that the basest and worst of all Actions have been done by great Men: Perhaps they have not picked private Pockets, but they have done worse; they have often disturbed, deceived, and pillaged the World: And he who is capable of the highest Mischief, is capable of the meanest: He who plunders a Country of a Million of Money, would in suitable Circumstances steal a Silver Spoon; and a Conqueror, who steals and pillages a Kingdom, would, in an humbler Fortune, rifle a Portmanteau, or rob an Orchard.

Political Jealousy, therefore, in the People, is a necessary and laudable Passion. But in a Chief Magistrate, a Jealousy of his People is not so justifiable, their Ambition being only to preserve themselves; whereas it is natural for Power to be striveing to enlarge itself, and to be encroaching upon those that have none. The most laudable Jealousy of a Magistrate is to be jealous *for* his People; which will shew that he loves them, and has used them well: But to be jealous *of* them, would denote that he has evil Designs against them, and has used them ill. The People's Jealousy tends to preserve Liberty; and the Prince's to destroy it. *Venice* is a glorious Instance of the former, and so is *England;* and all Nations who have lost their Liberty, are melancholy Proofs of the latter.

Power is naturally active, vigilant, and distrustful; which Qualities in it push it upon all Means and Expedients to fortify itself, and upon destroying all Opposition, and even all Seeds of Opposition, and make it restless as long as any Thing stands in its Way. It would do what it pleases, and have no Check. Now, because Liberty chastises and shortens Power, therefore Power would extinguish Liberty; and consequently Liberty has too much Cause to be exceeding jealous, and always upon her Defence. Power has many Advantages over her; it has generally numerous Guards, many Creatures, and much Treasure; besides, it has more Craft and Experience, less Honesty and Innocence: And whereas Power can, and for the most part does, subsist where Liberty is not, Liberty cannot subsist without Power; so that she has, as it were, the Enemy always at her Gates.

Some have said, that Magistrates being accountable to none but God, ought to know no other Restraint. But this Reasoning is as frivolous as it is wicked; for no good Man cares how many Punishments and Penalties lie in his Way to an Offence which he does not intend to commit: A Man who does not mean to commit Murder, is not sorry that Murder is punished with Death. And as to wicked Men, their being accountable to God, whom they do not fear, is no Security to us against their Folly and Malice; and to say that we ought to have no Security against them, is to insult common Sense, and give the Lie to the first Law of Nature, that of Self-Preservation. Human Reason says, that there is no Obedience, no Regard due to those Rulers, who govern by no Rule but their Lust. Such Men are no Rulers; they are Outlaws; who, being at Defiance with God and Man, are protected by no Law of God, or of Reason. By what Precept, moral or divine, are we forbid to kill a Wolf, or burn an infected Ship? Is it unlawful to prevent Wickedness and Misery, and to resist the Authors of them? Are Crimes sanctified by their Greatness? And is he who robs a Country, and murders Ten Thousand, less a Criminal, then he who steals single Guineas, and takes away single Lives? Is there any Sin in preventing, and restraining, or resisting the greatest Sin that can be committed, that of oppressing and destroying Mankind by wholesale? Sure there never were such open, such shameless, such selfish Impostors, as the Advocates for lawless Power! It is a damnable Sin to oppress Them; yet it is a damnable Sin to oppose Them when They oppress, or gain by Oppression of others! When they are hurt themselves ever so little, or but think themselves hurt, they are the loudest of all Men in their Complaints, and the most outrageous in their Behaviour: But when others are plundered, oppressed, and butchered, Complaints are Sedition; and to seek Redress, is Damnation. Is not this to be the Authors of all Wickedness and Falshood?

To conclude: Power, without Controul, appertains to God alone; and no Man ought to be trusted with what no Man is equal to. In Truth there are so many Passions, and Inconsistencies, and so much Selfishness, belonging to human Nature, that we can scarce be too much upon our Guard against each other. The only Security which we can have that Men will be honest, is to make it their Interest to be honest; and the best Defence which we can have against their being Knaves, is to make it terrible to them to be Knaves. As there are many Men wicked in some Stations, who would be innocent in others; the best Way is to make Wickedness unsafe in any Station.

I am, &c.

P. S. This Letter is the Sequel of that upon Human Nature; and both are intended for an Introduction to a Paper which I intend to write upon the Restraints which all wise Nations put upon their Magistrates.

G

Number 35.

SATURDAY, JULY 1, 1721.

Of publick Spirit.

SIR,

The Love of one's Country, or *Publick Spirit,* is a Phrase in every Body's Mouth, but it seldom goes deeper; it is talked of without being felt: Some mention it without having any Ideas at all of it, but only as a fine Thing which every Body likes, and a good Quality which one would not seem to be without.

Others, when they name it, intend only some poor and selfish Gratification of their own: Thus with Great Men, it is Wealth and Empire, to do what they list, and to get what they can; which is direct Faction, or promoting, under Colour of the Publick, those Views which are inconsistent with it. Thus with the Trader and Artificer, it is the encouraging only that Sort of Art or Ware in which he himself deals; and this is Monopoly and Engrossing, ever mischievous to the Public.

In Popish Countries, it is Publick Spirit to build and beautify many Churches, at the Expence of the poor People; who must also maintain, at a further Expence, a long Band of luxurious Ecclesiasticks, to play Tricks in them; or, in other Words, to keep the Heads and Pockets of their deluded Hearers as empty as they can. It is moreover great Publick Spirit, to adorn an old Skull with Pearl and Diamonds, and to enrich a venerable rotten Tooth with Gold and Emeralds, of a Value sufficient to maintain a City and all its Inhabitants, who yet perhaps are starved by doing it. It is likewise very publick-spirited there, for a Man to starve his Family and his Posterity, to endow a Monastery, and to feed, or rather gorge, a Fraternity of Reverend Gluttons, professed Foes to Truth and Peace, and to the

Prosperity of the World; Idlers, maintained to gormandize and deceive. This, forsooth, is Publick Spirit; to rob the Country of its Hands, to rear up a pernicious and turbulent Mob of Drones, in Principles destructive of Liberty, and to bring up Enemies to a Country at its own Charges.

In arbitrary Countries, it is Publick Spirit to be blind Slaves to the blind Will of the Prince, and to slaughter or be slaughtered for him at his Pleasure: But in Protestant free Countries, Publick Spirit is another Thing; it is to combat Force and Delusion; it is to reconcile the true Interests of the Governed and Governors; it is to expose Impostors, and to resist Oppressors; it is to maintain the People in Liberty, Plenty, Ease, and Security.

This is Publick Spirit; which contains in it every laudable Passion, and takes in Parents, Kindred, Friends, Neighbours, and every Thing dear to Mankind; it is the highest Virtue, and contains in it almost all others; Stedfastness to good Purposes, Fidelity to one's Trust, Resolution in Difficulties, Defiance of Danger, Contempt of Death, and impartial Benevolence to all Mankind. It is a Passion to promote universal Good, with personal Pain, Loss, and Peril: It is one Man's Care for Many, and the Concern of every Man for All.

Consider this Picture, O ye great Patriots and Guardians of the Earth, and try if you resemble it! Whom have ye exalted for his own Merits, whom cast down for the Sake of your Country? What Advantages have you acquired to your Nation, with Loss to yourselves? And have your People's Losses never been your Gains?

Out of *England* these Questions cannot well be answered; nor could they in *England* formerly.

If my Character of Publick Spirit be thought too heroick, at least for the living Generation, who are indeed but Babes in that Virtue; I will readily own, that every Man has a Right and a Call to provide for himself, to attend upon his own Affairs, and to study his own Happiness. All that I contend for is, that this Duty of a Man to himself be performed subsequently to the general Welfare, and consistently with it. The Affairs of All should be minded preferably to the Affairs of One, as every Man is ready to own when his own Particular is embarked with the Whole; as indeed every Man's will prove to be sooner or later, though for a while some may thrive upon the publick Ruins, but their Fate seldom fails to meet them at last, them or their Posterity.

It is a favourable Sign of Publick Spirit, though not a certain Sign, when the Interest and Reputation of Men rise and increase together; and there is Policy and Wisdom in it. He who acquires Money in spite of Fame, pays dear for his Avarice, while it returns him Hatred and Curses, as well as Gold; and to be rich and detested, is to me no pleasing Character. The same holds true in regard to Ambition, and every other Passion, which breaks its Bounds, and makes a Captive of its Owner. It is scarce possible to be a Rogue and be beloved; and when Men are arrived to an Insensibility of popular Censure and Opinion concerning their Honesty and Dishonesty, it is a Sign that they are at Defiance with the Community where they live, and that the rest ought to be upon their Guard against them; they do as it were cut themselves off from the Society, and teach the People what to call them.

It is true, that great ill Men never fail to have great Court paid to their Fortunes; which Court their own Self-Love always construes to be paid to their Persons: But there is a Way to undeceive them, and it often happens; let them but sink into Meanness, and they will soon find themselves sunk into Contempt, which is the End of Hatred when the Object of Hatred diminishes.

There is a Sort of Men found almost every where, who having got a Set of gainful and favourite Speculations, are always ready to spread and enforce them, and call their doing so *Publick Spirit,* though it often turns the World topsy-turvy: Like the mad Monk at *Heidelberg*, who was for knocking every

Man on the Head who did not like *Rhenish* Wine, which it seems was his beloved Liquor; perhaps he thought it was as reasonable to make all the World swallow *Rhenish*, as to make them swallow Transubstantiation.

Opinions, bare Opinions, signify no more to the World, than do the several Tastes of Men; and all Mankind must be made of one Complexion, of one Size, and of one Age, before they can be all made of the same Mind. Those Patrons therefore of dry Dreams, who do Mischief to the World to make it better, are the Pests and Distressers of Mankind, and shut themselves out from all Pretence to the Love of their Country: S[t]range Men! They would force all Men into an absolute Certainty about absolute Uncertainties and Contradictions; they would ascertain Ambiguities, without removing them; and plague and punish Men for having but five Senses.

I would assert another Proposition, as true as the Last, though it may seem stranger; namely, That the taking a Thousand or Ten Thousand Pounds a Year for the Merit of helping to draw a Hundred Times as much from the People, is not Publick Spirit, whatever Use may call it; and to grasp at All, and put a whole Country in two or three Pockets, is a Sort of Publick Spirit, which I hope in God never to see, though there have been Nations who have sorrowfully felt it.

As Liberty can never subsist without Equality, nor Equality be long preserved without an *Agrarian* Law,[1] or something like it; so when Mens Riches are become immeasurably or surprizingly great, a People, who regard their own Security, ought to make a strict Enquiry how they came by them, and oblige them to take down their own Size, for fear of terrifying the Community, or mastering it. In every Country, and under every Government, particular Men may be too rich.

If the *Romans* had well observed the *Agrarian* Law, by

[1] The term derived from the Roman *Lex agraria*, a law providing for the division of conquered lands. In general usage, it connoted a law intended for the more nearly equal division of the soil.

which the Extent of every Citizen's Estate was ascertained, some Citizens could never have risen so high as they did above others; and consequently, one Man would never have been set above the rest, and have established, as *Caesar* did at last, a Tyranny in that great and glorious State. I have always thought, that an Enquiry into Mens Fortunes, especially monstrous Fortunes raised out of the Publick, like *Milton's* infernal Palace,[2] as it were in an Instant, was of more Importance to a Nation, than some other Enquiries which I have heard of.

But, will some say, Is it a Crime to be rich? Yes, certainly, at the Publick Expence, or to the Danger of the Publick. A Man may be too rich for a Subject; even the Revenues of Kings may be too large. It is one of the Effects of arbitrary Power, that the Prince has too much, and the People too little; and such Inequality may be the Cause too of arbitrary Power. It is as astonishing as it is melancholy, to travel through a whole Country, as one may through many in *Europe,* g[as]ping under endless Imposts, groaning under Dragoons and Poverty, and all to make a wanton and luxurious Court, filled for the most with the worst and vilest of all Men. Good G[o]d! What Hardheartedness and Barbarity, to starve perhaps half a Province, to make a gay Garden! And yet sometimes even this gross Wickedness is called Publick Spirit, because forsooth a few Workmen and Labourers are maintained out of the Bread and the Blood of half a Million.

In those Countries, were the Judgment of the People consulted, Things would go better: But they are despised, and esteemed by their Governors happy enough, if they do not eat Grass; and having no Representatives, or Share in the Government, they have no Remedy. Such indeed is their Misery, that their Case would be greatly mended, if they could change Conditions with the Beasts of the Field; for then, being des-

---

[2] The reference is to John Milton's *Paradise Lost,* Book I, lines 670–730, where "Pandemonium, the Palace of Satan rises, suddenly built out of the Deep."

tined to be eaten, they would be better fed: Such a Misfortune is it to them that their Governors are not *Cannibals!* Oh happy *Britain,* mayest thou continue ever so!

For a Conclusion: As the Preservation of Property is the Source of National Happiness; whoever violates Property, or lessens or endangers it, common Sense says, that he is an Enemy to his Country; and Publick Spirit says, that he should feel its Vengeance. As yet in *England,* we can speak such bold Truths; and we never dread to see the Day, when it will be safer for one Man to be a Traytor, than for another Man, or for a whole People, to call him so. Where-ever Publick Spirit is found dangerous, she will soon be seen dead.

G   *I am, &c.*

SATURDAY, JULY 22, 1721.

The Right and Capacity of the People to judge of Government.

SIR,

The World has, from Time to Time, been led into such a long Maze of Mistakes, by those who gained by deceiving, that whoever would instruct Mankind, must begin with removeing their Errors; and if they were every where honestly apprized of Truth, and restored to their Senses, there would not remain one Nation of Bigots or Slaves under the Sun: A Happiness always to be wished, but never expected!

In most Parts of the Earth there is neither Light nor Liberty; and even in the best Parts of it they are but little encouraged, and coldly maintained; there being, in all Places, many engaged, through Interest, in a perpetual Conspiracy against them. They are the two greatest Civil Blessings, inseparable in their Interests, and the mutual Support of each other; and whoever would destroy one of them, must destroy both. Hence it is, that we every where find Tyranny and Imposture, Ignorance and Slavery, joined together; and Oppressors and Deceivers mutually aiding and paying constant Court to each other. Where-ever Truth is dangerous, Liberty is precarious.

Of all the Sciences that I know in the World, that of Government concerns us most, and is the easiest to be known, and yet is the least understood. Most of those who manage it would make the lower World believe that there is I know not what Difficulty and Mystery in it, far above vulgar Understandings; which Proceeding of theirs is direct Craft and Imposture: Every Ploughman knows a good Government from a bad one, from the Effects of it: he knows whether the Fruits of his Labour be his own, and whether he enjoy them in Peace and Security: And if he do not know the Principles of Government, it is for want of Thinking and Enquiry, for they lie open to common Sense; but People are generally taught not to think of them at all, or to think wrong of them.

What is Government, but a Trust committed by All, or the Most, to One, or a Few, who are to attend upon the Affairs of All, that every one may, with the more Security, attend upon his own? A great and honourable Trust; but too seldom honourably executed; those who possess it having it often more at Heart to encrease their Power, than to make it useful; and to be terrible, rather than beneficent. It is therefore a Trust, which ought to be bounded with many and strong Restraints, because Power renders Men wanton, insolent to others, and fond of themselves. Every Violation therefore of this Trust, where such Violation is considerable, ought to meet with proportionable Punishment; and the smallest Violation of it ought to meet with some, because Indulgence to the least Faults of Magistrates may be Cruelty to a whole People.

Honesty, Diligence, and plain Sense, are the only Talents

necessary for the executing of this Trust; and the public Good is its only End: As to Refinements and Finesses, they are often only the false Appearances of Wisdom and Parts, and oftener Tricks to hide Guilt and Emptiness; and they are generally mean and dishonest: they are the Arts of Jobbers in Politicks, who, playing their own Game under the publick Cover, subsist upon poor Shifts and Expedients; starved Politicians, who live from Hand to Mouth, from Day to Day, and following the little Views of Ambition, Avarice, Revenge, and the like personal Passions, are ashamed to avow them, yet want Souls great enough to forsake them; small wicked Statesmen, who make a private Market of the Publick, and deceive it, in order to sell it.

These are the poor Parts which great and good Governors scorn to play, and cannot play; their Designs, like their Stations, being purely publick, are open and undisguised. They do not consider their People as their Prey, nor lie in Ambush for their Subjects; nor dread, and treat and surprize them like Enemies, as all ill Magistrates do; who are not Governors, but Jaylors and Spunges, who chain them and squeeze them, and yet take it very ill if they do but murmur; which is yet much less than a People so abused ought to do. There have been Times and Countries, when publick Ministers and publick Enemies have been the same individual Men. What a melancholy Reflection is this, that the most terrible and mischievous Foes to a Nation should be its own Magistrates! And yet in every enslaved Country, which is almost every Country, this is their woful Case.

Honesty and Plainness go always together, and the Makers and Multipliers of Mysteries, in the political Way, are shrewdly to be suspected of dark Designs. *Cincinnatus*[1] was taken from

---

[1] Lucius Quinctius Cincinnatus, Roman dictator, lived in the fifth century B.C. His real career was subsequently embellished richly with legendary events. He apparently was called from the farm, and did serve briefly as dictator, save a Roman army from extinction, and then return promptly to his agricultural pursuits, leaving behind all his tremendous political power.

the Plough to save and defend the *Roman* State; an Office which he executed honestly and successfully, without the Grimace and Gains of a Statesman. Nor did he afterwards continue obstinately at the Head of Affairs, to form a Party, raise a Fortune, and settle himself in Power: As he came into it with universal Consent, he resigned it with universal Applause.

It seems that Government was not in those Days become a Trade, at least a gainful Trade. —Honest *Cincinnatus* was but a Farmer: And happy had it been for the *Romans,* if, when they were enslaved, they could have taken the Administration out of the Hands of the Emperors, and their refined Politicians, and committed it to such Farmers, or any Farmers. It is certain, that many of their Imperial Governors acted more ridiculously than a Board of Ploughmen would have done, and more barbarously than a Club of Butchers could have done.

But some have said, *It is not the Business of private Men to meddle with Government.* A bold, false, and dishonest Saying; and whoever says it, either knows not what he says, or cares not, or slavishly speaks the Sense of others. It is a Cant now almost forgot in *England,* and which never prevailed but when Liberty and the Constitution were attacked, and never can prevail but upon the like Occasion.

It is a Vexation to be obliged to answer Nonsense, and confute Absurdities: But since it is and has been the great Design of this Paper to maintain and explain the glorious Principles of Liberty, and to expose the Arts of those who would darken or destroy them; I shall here particularly shew the Wickedness and Stupidity of the above Saying; which is fit to come from no Mouth but that of a Tyrant or a Slave, and can never be heard by any Man of an honest and free Soul, without Horror and Indignation: It is, in short, a Saying, which ought to render the Man who utters it for ever incapable of Place or Credit in a free Country, as it shews the Malignity of his Heart, and the Baseness of his Nature, and as it is the pronouncing of a Doom upon our Constitution.—A Crime, or rather a Complication of

Crimes, for which a lasting Infamy ought to be but part of the Punishment.

But to the Falshood of the Thing: Publick Truths ought never to be kept Secrets; and they who do it, are guilty of a Solaecism, and a Contradiction: Every Man ought to know what it concerns All to know. Now, nothing upon Earth is of a more universal Nature than Government; and every private Man upon Earth has a Concern in it, because in it is concerned, and nearly and immediately concerned, his Virtue, his Property, and the Security of his Person: And where all these are best preserved and advanced, the Government is best administered; and where they are not, the Government is impotent, wicked, or unfortunate; and where the Government is so, the People will be so, there being always and every where a certain Sympathy and Analogy between the Nature of the Government and the Nature of the People. This holds true in every Instance. Public Men are the Patterns of Private; and the Virtues and Vices of the Governors become quickly the Virtues and Vices of the Governed.

Regis ad exemplum totus componitur orbis.[2]

Nor is it Example alone that does it. Ill Governments, subsisting by Vice and Rapine, are jealous of private Virtue, and Enemies to private Property. *Opes pro crimine; & ob virtutes certissimum exitium.*[3] They must be wicked and mischievous to be what they are; nor are they secure while any Thing good

---

[2] The quotation is a slight variation on a line from Claudius Claudianus, *Panegyric on the Fourth Consulship of the Emperor Honorius*, 299-301: "*Componitur orbis regis ad exemplum. . . .*" ("The world shapes itself after its ruler's pattern. . . .") Claudianus lived in Rome and Milan about the year A.D. 400. His panegyrics, invectives, and short poems provide information on Roman politics at the end of the fourth century.

[3] The line is probably a variant from Tacitus, *Histories* I. 2: ". . . *Nobilitas, opes, omissi gestique honores pro crimine et ob virtutes certissimum exitium.*" ("High birth, wealth, the refusal or acceptance of office—all gave ground for accusations, and virtues caused the surest ruin.")

or valuable is secure. Hence it is, that to drain, worry, and debauch their Subjects, are the steady Maxims of their Politicks, their favourite Arts of Reigning. In this wretched Situation the People, to be safe, must be poor and lewd: There will be but little Industry where Property is precarious; small Honesty where Virtue is dangerous.

Profuseness or Frugality, and the like Virtues or Vices, which affect the Publick, will be practised in the City, if they be practised in the Court; and in the Country, if they be in the City. Even *Nero* (that Royal Monster in Man's Shape) was adored by the common Herd at *Rome*, as much as he was flattered by the Great; and both the Little and the Great admired, or pretended to admire, his Manners, and many to imitate them. *Tacitus* tells us, that those Sort of People long lamented him, and rejoiced in the Choice of a Successor that resembled him, even the profligate *Otho*.[4]

Good Government does, on the contrary, produce great Virtue, much Happiness, and many People. *Greece* and *Italy*, while they continued free, were each of them, for the Number of Inhabitants, like one continued City; for Virtue, Knowledge, and Great Men, they were the Standards of the World; and that Age and Country that could come nearest to them, has ever since been reckoned the happiest. Their Government, their Free Government, was the Root of all these Advantages, and of all this Felicity and Renown; and in these great and fortunate States the People were the Principals in the Government; Laws were made by their Judgment and Authority, and by their Voice and Commands were Magistrates created and

---

[4] Nero Claudius Caesar (A.D. 37–68) was Emperor of Rome from A.D. 54 to his assassination. The judgment of Trenchard and Gordon reflected their familiarity with Suetonius and with Tacitus, who sums up his views of Nero in the words of a tribune about to be executed for treason: "murderer of mother and wife—a chariot-driver, an actor, a fire-raiser" (*Annals* XV. 67). The description of those who lamented the passing of Nero and hailed a succcssor, Otho, as a new "Nero" may be found in Suetonius, *Twelve Caesars*, "Nero" LVII and "Otho" VII.

condemned. The City of *Rome* could conquer the World; nor could the great *Persian* Monarch, the greatest then upon Earth, stand before the Face of one *Greek* City.

But what are *Greece* and *Italy* now? *Rome* has in it a Herd of pampered Monks, and a few starving Lay Inhabitants; the *Campania* of *Rome*,[5] the finest spot of Earth in *Europe,* is a Desart. And for the modern *Greeks,* they are a few abject contemptible Slaves, kept under Ignorance, Chains, and Vileness, by the *Turkish* Monarch, who keeps a great Part of the Globe intensely miserable, that he may seem great without being so.

Such is the Difference between one Government and another, and of such important Concernment is the Nature and Administration of Government to a People. And to say that private Men have nothing to do with Government, is to say that private Men have nothing to do with their own Happiness and Misery.

What is the Publick, but the collective Body of private Men, as every private Man is a Member of the Publick? And as the Whole ought to be concerned for the Preservation of every private Individual, it is the Duty of every Individual to be concerned for the Whole, in which himself is included.

One Man, or a few Men, have often pretended the Publick, and meant themselves, and consulted their own personal Interest, in Instances essential to its Well-being; but the whole People, by consulting their own Interest, consult the Publick, and act for the Publick by acting for themselves: This is particularly the Spirit of our Constitution, in which the whole Nation is represented; and our Records afford Instances, where the House of Commons have declined entering upon a Question of Importance, till they had gone into the Country, and consulted their Principals, the People: So far were they from thinking that private Men had no Right to meddle with Gov-

---

[5] The term designates the region of Italy immediately surrounding the city of Rome. Here it is used to suggest the manner in which misrule leads to an impoverished country.

ernment. In Truth, our whole worldly Happiness and Misery (abating for Accidents and Diseases) are owing to the Order or Mismanagement of Government; and he who says that private Men have no Concern with Government, does wisely and modestly tell us, that Men have no Concern in that which concerns them most; it is saying that People ought not to concern themselves whether they be naked or clothed, fed or starved, deceived or instructed, and whether they be protected or destroyed: What Nonsense and Servitude in a free and wise Nation!

For myself, who have thought pretty much of these Matters, I am of Opinion, that a whole Nation are like to be as much attached to themselves, as one Man or a few Men are like to be, who may by many Means be detached from the Interest of a Nation. It is certain that one Man, and several Men, may be bribed into an Interest opposite to that of the Publick; but it is as certain that a whole Country can never find an Equivalent for itself, and consequently a whole Country can never be bribed. It is the eternal Interest of every Nation, that their Government should be good; but they who direct it frequently reason a contrary Way, and find their own Account in Plunder and Oppression; and while the publick Voice is pretended to be declared, by one or a few, for vile and private Ends, the Publick know nothing of what is done, till they feel the terrible Effects of it.

By the Bill of Rights, and the Act of Settlement, at the *Revolution,* a Right is asserted to the People of applying to the King and to the Parliament, by Petition and Address, for a Redress of publick Grievances and Mismanagements, when such there are, of which They are left to judge; And the Difference between free and enslaved Countries lies principally here, that in the former, their Magistrates must consult the Voice and Interest of the People; but in the latter, the private Will, Interest, and Pleasure of the Governors, are the sole End and Motives of their Administration.

Such is the Difference between *England* and *Turkey;* which Difference they who say that private Men have no Right to concern themselves with Government, would absolutely destroy; they would convert Magistrates into Bashaws, and introduce Popery into Politicks. The late Revolution stands upon the very opposite Maxim; and that any Man dares to contradict it since the *Revolution,* would be amazing, did we not know that there are, in every Country, Hirelings who would betray it for a Sop.

G   *I am, &c.*

SATURDAY, SEPTEMBER 16, 1721.

Of the Equality and Inequality of Men.

SIR,

Men are naturally equal, and none ever rose above the rest but by Force or Consent: No Man was ever born above all the rest, nor below them all; and therefore there never was any Man in the World so good or so bad, so high or so low, but he had his Fellow. Nature is a kind and benevolent Parent; she constitutes no particular Favourites with Endowments and Privileges above the rest; but for the most part sends all her Offspring into the World furnished with the Elements of Understanding and Strength, to provide for themselves: She gives them Heads to consult their own Security, and Hands to execute their own Counsels; and according to the Use that they make of their Faculties, and of the Opportunities that they find, Degrees of Power and Names of Distinction grow amongst them, and their natural Equality is lost.

Thus Nature, who is their Parent, deals with Men: But Fortune, who is their Nurse, is not so benevolent and impartial; she acts wantonly and capriciously, often cruelly; and counterplotting Justice as well as Nature, frequently sets the Fool above the wise Man, and the Best below the Worst.

And from hence it is, that the most Part of the World, attending much more to the noisy Conduct and glaring Effects of Fortune, than to the quiet and regular Proceedings of Nature, are misled in their Judgment upon this Subject: They confound Fortune with Nature, and too often ascribe to natural Merit and Excellency the Works of Contrivance or Chance. This however, shews that Reason and Equity run in our Heads, while we endeavour to find a just Cause for Things that are not just; and this is the Source of the Reverence which we pay to Men whom Fortune sometimes lifts on high, though Nature had placed them below. The Populace rarely see any Creature rise, but they find a Reason for it in his Parts; when probably the true one will be found in his own Baseness, or another Man's Folly.

From the same Reasoning may be seen why it is, that, let who will be at the Head of a Party, he is always extolled by his Party as superior to the rest of Mankind; and let who will be the first Man of his Country, he will never fail being complimented by many as the first of his Species. But the Issue and their own Behaviour constantly shew, that the highest are upon a Level with the rest, and often with the lowest. Men that are high are almost ever seen in a false Light; the most Part see them at a great Distance, and through a magnifying Medium; some are dazzled with their Splendor, many are awed by their Power. Whatever appears shining or terrible, appears great, and is magnified by the Eye and the Imagination.

That Nature has made Men equal, we know and feel; and when People come to think otherwise, there is no Excess of Folly and Superstition which they may not be brought to practise. Thus they have made Gods of dead Men, and paid divine Honours to many while they were yet living: They saw them to be but Men, yet they worshipped them as Gods. And even they who have not gone quite so far, have yet, by their wild Notions of Inequality, done as much Mischief; they have made Men, and often wicked Men, to be Vice-Gods; and then made God's Power (falsly so called) as irresistible in the Hands of Men as in his own, and much more frightful.

It is evident to common Sense, that there ought to be no Inequality in Society, but for the Sake of Society; but these Men have made one Man's Power and Will the Cause of all Men's Misery. They gave him as far as they could the Power of God, without obliging him to practise the Mercy and Goodness of God.

Those that think themselves furthest above the rest, are generally by their Education below them all. They are debased by a Conceit of their Greatness: They trust to their Blood; which, speaking naturally, gives them no Advantage; and neglect their Mind, which alone, by proper Improvements, sets one Man above another. It is not Blood or Nature, but Art or Accident, which makes one Man excel others. *Aristotle*, therefore, must either have been in Jest, when he said, that he, who naturally excelled all others, ought to govern all; or said it to flatter his Pupil and Prince, *Alexander* the Great. It is certain, that such a Man never yet was found in the World, and never will be found till the End of it. *Alexander* himself, notwithstanding the Greatness of his Spirit, and his Conquests, had in his own Army, and perhaps among the common Soldiers, Men naturally as great and brave as himself, and many more wise.

Whoever pretends to be naturally superior to other Men, claims from Nature what she never gave to any Man. He sets up for being more than a Man; a Character with which Nature has nothing to do. She has thrown her Gifts in common amongst us; and as the highest Offices of Nature fall to the Share of the Mean as well as of the Great, her vilest Offices are performed by the Great as well as by the Mean: Death and Diseases are the Portion of Kings as well as of Clowns; and the Corpse of a Monarch is no more exempted from Stench and Putrefaction, than the Corpse of a Slave.

Mors aequo pulsat pede.[1]

All the Arts and Endowments of Men to acquire Pre-eminence and Advantages over one another, are so many Proofs and Confessions that they have not such Pre-eminence and Advantages from Nature; and all their Pomp, Titles, and Wealth, are Means and Devices to make the World think that they who possess them are superior in Merit to those that want them. But it is not much to the Glory of the upper Part of Mankind, that their boasted and superior Merit is often the Work of Heralds, Artificers, and Money; and that many derive their whole Stock of Fame from Ancestors, who lived an Age or many Ages ago.

The first Founders of great Families were not always Men of Virtue or Parts; and where they were so, those that came after them did frequently, and almost generally, by trusting to their Blood, disgrace their Name. Such is the Folly of the World, and the Inconvenience of Society, to allow Men to be great by Proxy! An Evil that can scarce ever be cured. The Race of *French* Kings, called by their Historians in Contempt, *Les Rois faineants* and the Succession of the *Roman Caesars,* (in both which, for one good Prince they had ten that were intolerable, either for Folly, or Cruelty, and often for both) might be mentioned as known Proofs of the above Truth; and every Reader will find in his own Memory many more.

I have been told of a Prince, who, while yet under Age, being reproved by his Governor for doing Things ill or indecent, used to answer, *Je suis Roy; I am King;* as if his Quality had altered the Nature of Things, and he himself had been better

---

[1] The line comes from Horace (*Odes* I. 4. 13–14):
Pallida Mors aequo pulsat pede pauperum tabernas
　　regumque turris. . . .
Pale Death with foot impartial knocks at the poor
man's cottage and at prince's palaces.

than other Men, while he acted worse. But he spoke from that Spirit which had been instilled into him from his Cradle. *I am King!* What then, Sir? The Office of a King is not to do Evil, but to prevent it. You have Royal Blood in your Veins: But the Blood of your Page is, without being Royal, as good as yours; or, if you doubt, try the Difference in a Couple of Porringers next Time you are ill; and learn from this Consideration and Experiment, that by Nature you are no better than your People, though subject from your Fortune to be worse, as many of your Ancestors have been.

If my Father got an Estate and Title by Law or the Sword, I may by Virtue of his Will or his Patent enjoy his Acquisition; but if I understand neither Law nor the Sword, I can derive Honour from neither: My Honour therefore is, in the Reason of Things purely nominal; and I am still by Nature a *Plebeian*, as all Men are.

There is nothing moral in Blood, or in Title, or in Place: Actions only, and the Causes that produce them, are moral. He therefore is best that does best. Noble Blood prevents neither Folly, nor Lunacy, nor Crimes: but frequently begets or promotes them: And Noblemen, who act infamously, derive no Honour from virtuous Ancestors, whom they dishonour. A Man who does base Things, is not noble; nor great, if he do little Things: A sober Villager is a better Man than a debauched Lord; an honest Mechanick than a Knavish Courtier.

- - - *Nobilitas sola est atque unica virtus.*

- -

Prima mihi debes animi bona; sanctus haberi
Justitiaeque tenax factis, dictisque mereris?[2]

Juv. Sat. 8.

---

[2] The quotation comes from Juvenal, *Satire* VIII. 20, 24–25:
        Virtue is the only and sole real nobility. . . .
        You owe first the virtues of the mind—
        do you deserve to be accounted honest, and
        tenacious of justice, in word and deed?

We cannot bring more natural Advantages into the World than other Men do; but we can acquire more Virtue in it than we generally acquire. To be great is not in every Man's Power; but to be good is in the Power of all: Thus far every Man may be [u]pon a Level with another, the Lowest with the Highest: and Men might thus come to be morally as well as naturally equal.

G   *I am, &c.*

[With the publication of Letter Number 59 on January 6, 1721, Trenchard and Gordon began a significant series of comments on the origin of government, the contrasting effects of liberty and of tyranny, and the problems of preserving free government. The two authors repeated their ideas in other places, but, in this Letter and the eight which followed, they presented perhaps the clearest statement of their own general position. Since the arguments have a logical coherence, they are presented here at length. Only illustrative material, similar to that included in earlier Letters, has been removed from the following numbers.]

Number 59.

SATURDAY, DECEMBER 30, 1721.

Liberty proved to be the unalienable Right of all Mankind.

SIR,
I Intend to entertain my Readers with Dissertations upon *Liberty,* in some of my succeeding Letters; and shall, as a Preface to that Design, endeavour to prove in this, that Liberty is the unalienable Right of all Mankind.

All Governments, under whatsoever Form they are administered, ought to be administered for the Good of the Society; when they are otherwise administered, they cease to be government, and become Usurpation. This being the End of all Government, even the most despotick have this Limitation to their Authority: In this Respect, the only Difference between the most absolute Princes and limited Magistrates, is, that in free Governments there are Checks and Restraints appointed and expressed in the Constitution itself: In despotick Governments, the People submit themselves to the Prudence and Discretion of the Prince alone: But there is still this tacit Condition annexed to his Power, that he must act by the unwritten Laws of Discretion and Prudence, and employ it for the sole Interest of the People, who give it to him, or suffer him to enjoy it, which they ever do for their own Sakes.

Even in the most free Governments, single Men are often trusted with discretionary Power: But they must answer for that Discretion to those that trust them. Generals of Armies and Admirals of Fleets have often unlimited Commissions; and yet are they not answerable for the prudent Execution of those Commissions? The Council of Ten, in *Venice*, have absolute Power over the Liberty and Life of every Man in the State: But if they should make use of that Power to slaughter, abolish, or enslave the Senate; and, like the *Decemviri* of *Rome*, to set up themselves; would it not be lawful for those, who gave them that Authority for other Ends, to put those Ten unlimited Traytors to Death, any Way that they could? The Crown of *England* has been for the most part entrusted with the sole Disposal of the Money given for the Civil List, often with the Application of great Sums raised for other publick Uses; yet, if the Lord-Treasurer had applied this Money to the Dishonour of the King, and Ruin of the People (though by the private Direction of the Crown itself) will any Man say that he ought not to have compensated for his Crime, by the Loss of his Head and his Estate?

I have said thus much, to shew that no Government can be absolute in the Sense, or rather Nonsense, of our modern Dogmatizers, and indeed in the Sense too commonly practised. No barbarous Conquest; no extorted Consent of miserable People, submitting to the Chain to escape the Sword; no repeated and hereditary Acts of Cruelty, though called Succession, no Continuation of Violence, though named Prescription; can alter, much less abrogate, these fundamental Principles of Government itself, or make the Means of Preservation the Means of Destruction, and render the Condition of Mankind infinitely more miserable than that of the Beasts of the Field, by the sole Privilege of that Reason which distinguishes them from the Brute Creation.

Force can give no Title but to Revenge, and to the Use of Force again; nor could it ever enter into the Heart of any Man, to give another Power over him, for any other End but to be exercised for his own Advantage: And if there are any Men mad or foolish enough to pretend to do otherwise, they ought to be treated as Idiots or Lunaticks; and the Reason of their Conduct must be derived from their Folly and Frenzy.

All Men are born free; Liberty is a Gift which they receive from God himself; nor can they alienate the same by Consent, though possibly they may forfeit it by Crimes. No Man has Power over his own Life, or to dispose of his own Religion; and cannot consequently transfer the Power of either to any body else: Much less can he give away the Lives and Liberties, Religion or acquired Property of his Posterity, who will be born as free as he himself was born, and can never be bound by his wicked and ridiculous Bargain.

The Right of the Magistrate arises only from the Right of private Men to defend themselves, to repel Injuries, and to punish those who commit them: That Right being conveyed by the Society to their publick Representative, he can execute the same no further than the Benefit and Security of that Society requires he should. When he exceeds his Commission, his

Acts are as extrajudicial as are those of any private Officer usurping an unlawful Authority, that is, they are void; and every Man is answerable for the Wrong which he does. A Power to do Good can never become a Warrant for doing Evil.

But here arises a grand Question, which has perplexed and puzzled the greatest Part of Mankind: Yet, I think, the Answer to it easy and obvious. The Question is, who shall be Judge whether the Magistrate acts justly, and pursues his Trust? To this it is justly said, That if those who complain of him are to judge him, then there is a settled Authority above the Chief Magistrate, which Authority must be itself the Chief Magistrate; which is contrary to the Supposition; and the same Question and Difficulty will recur again upon this new Magistracy. All this I own to be absurd; and I aver it to be at least as absurd to affirm, That the Person accused is to be the decisive Judge of his own Actions, when it is certain that he will always judge and determine in his own Favour; and thus the whole Race of Mankind will be left helpless under the heaviest Injustice, Oppression, and Misery, that can afflict human Nature.

But if neither Magistrates, nor they who complain of Magistrates, and are aggrieved by them, have a Right to determine decisively, the one for the other; and if there be no common established Power, to which both are subject; then every Man interested in the Success of the Contest, must act according to the Light and Dictates of his own Conscience, and inform it as well as he can. Where no Judge is nor can be appointed, every Man must be his own; that is, when there is no stated Judge upon Earth, we must have Recourse to Heaven, and obey the Will of Heaven, by declaring ourselves on that which we think the juster Side.

If the Senate and People of *Rome* had differed irreconcileably, there could have been no common Judge in the World between them; and consequently no Remedy but the last: For that Government consisting in the Union of the Nobles and the People, when they differed, no Man could determine between them; and therefore every Man must have been at Liberty to provide for his own Security, and the general Good, in the best Manner he was able. In that Case the common Judge ceasing, every one was his own: The Government becoming incapable of acting, suffered a political Demise: The Constitution was dissolved; and there being no Government in Being, the People were in the State of Nature again.

The same must be true, where two absolute Princes, governing a Country, come to quarrel, as sometimes two *Caesars* in Partnership did, especially towards the latter End of the *Roman* Empire; or where a Sovereign Council govern a Country, and their Votes come equally to be divided. In such a Circumstance, every Man must take that Side which he thinks most for the publick Good, or choose any proper Measures for his own Security: For, if I owe my Allegiance to two Princes agreeing, or to the Majority of a Council; when between these Princes there is no longer any Union, nor in that Council any Majority, no Submission can be due to that which is not; and the Laws of Nature and Self-Preservation must take place, where there are no other.

The Case is still the same, when there is any Dispute about the Titles of absolute Princes, who govern independently on the States of a Country, and call none. Here too every Man must judge for himself what Party he will take, to which of the Titles he will adhere; and the like private Judgment must guide him, whenever a Question arises whether the said Prince be an Idiot or a Lunatick, and consequently whether he be capable or incapable of Government. Where there are no States, there can be no other way of judging; but by the Judgment of private Men the Capacity of the Prince must be judged, and his Fate determined. Lunacy and Idiotism are, I think, allowed by all to be certain Disqualifications for Government; indeed they are as much so, as if he were deaf, blind, and dumb, or even dead. He who can neither execute an Office, nor appoint a Deputy, is not fit for one.

Now I would fain know, why private Men may not as well use their Judgment in an Instance that concerns them more; I mean that of a tyrannical Government, of which they hourly feel the sad Effects, and sorrowful Proofs; whereas they have not by far the equal Means of coming to a Certainty about the natural Incapacity of their Governor. The Persons of great Princes are known but to few of their Subjects, and their Parts to much fewer; and several Princes have, by the Management of their Wives, or Ministers, or Murderers, reigned a good while after they were dead. In Truth, I think it is as much the Business and Right of the People to judge whether their Prince be good or bad, whether a Father or an Enemy, as to judge whether he be dead or alive; unless it be said (as many such wise Things have been said) that they may judge whether he can govern them, but not whether he does; and that it behoves them to put the Administration in wiser Hands, if he be a harmless Fool, but it is impious to do it, if he be only a destructive Tyrant; that Want of Speech is a Disqualification, but Want of Humanity, none.

That Subjects were not to judge of their Governors, or rather for themselves in the Business of Government, which of all human Things concerns them most, was an Absurdity that never entered into the Imagination of the wise and honest Ancients: Who, following for their Guide that everlasting Reason, which is the best and only Guide in human Affairs, carried Liberty, and human Happiness, the legitimate Offspring and Work of Liberty, to the highest Pitch that they were capable of arriving at. But the above Absurdity, with many others as monstrous and mischievous, were reserved for the Discovery of a few wretched and dreaming *Mahometan* and Christian Monks, who, ignorant of all Things, were made, or made themselves, the Directors of all Things; and bewitching the World with holy Lies and unaccountable Ravings, dressed up in barbarous Words and uncouth Phrases, bent all their Fairy Force against common Sense and common Liberty and Truth, and founded a pernicious, absurd, and visionary Empire upon their Ruins. Systems without Sense, Propositions without Truth, Religion without Reason, a rampant Church without Charity, Severity without Justice, and Government without Liberty or Mercy, were all the blessed Handy-works of these religious Mad-men, and godly Pedants; who, by pretending to know the other World, cheated and confounded this. Their Enmity to common Sense, and Want of it, were their Warrants for governing the Sense of all Mankind: By Lying, they were thought the Champions of the Truth; and by their Fooleries, Impieties, and Cruelty, were esteemed the Favourites and Confidents of the God of Wisdom, Mercy, and Peace.

These were the Men, who, having demolished all Sense and human Judgment, first made it a Principle, that People were not to judge of their Governor and Government, nor to meddle with it; nor to preserve themselves from publick Destroyers, falsly calling themselves Governors: Yet these Men, who thus set up for the Support and Defenders of Government, without the common Honesty of distinguishing the Good from the Bad, and Protection from Murder and Depredation, were at the same Time themselves the constant and avowed Troublers of every Government which they could not direct and command; and every Government, however excellent, which did not make their Reveries its own Rules, and themselves alone its peculiar Care, has been honoured with their professed Hatred; whilst Tyrants and publick Butchers, who flattered them, have been deified. This was the poor State of *Christendom* before the *Reformation;* and I wish I could say, of no Parts of its since.

This barbarous Anarchy in Reasoning and Politicks, has made it necessary to prove Propositions which the Light of Nature had demonstrated. And, as the Apostles were forced to prove to the misled *Gentiles,* that they were no Gods which were made with Hands; I am put to prove, that the People have a Right to judge, whether their Governors were made for them, or they for their Governors? Whether their Governors have necessary and natural Qualifications? Whether they have any Governors or no? And whether, when they have none, every Man must not be his own? I therefore return to Instances and Illustrations from Facts which cannot be denied; though Propositions as true as Facts may, by those especially who are defective in Point of Modesty or Discernment.

In *Poland*, according to the Constitution of that Country, it is necessary, we are told, that, in their Diets, the Consent of every Man present must be had to make a Resolve effectual: And therefore, to prevent the cutting of People's Throats, they have no Remedy but to cut the Throats of one another; that is, they must pull out their Sabres, and force the refractory Members (who are always the Minority) to submit. And amongst us in *England*, where a Jury cannot agree, there can be no Verdict; and so they must fast till they do, or till one of them is dead, and then the Jury is dissolved.

This, from the Nature of Things themselves, must be the constant Case in all Disputes between Dominion and Property. Where the Interest of the Governors and that of the Governed clash, there can be no stated Judge between them: To appeal to a foreign Power, is to give up the Sovereignty; for either Side to submit, is to give up the Question: And therefore, if they themselves do not amicably determine the Dispute between themselves, Heaven alone must. In such case, Recourse must be had to the first Principles of Government itself; which being a Departure from the State of Nature, and a Union of many Families forming themselves into a political Machine for mutual Protection and Defence, it is evident, that this formed Relation can continue no longer than the Machine subsists and can act; and when it does not, the Individuals must return to their former State again. No Constitution can provide against what will happen, when that Constitution is dissolved. Government is only an Appointment of one or more Persons, to do certain Actions for the Good and Emolument of the Society; and if the Persons thus interested will not act at all, or act contrary to their Trust, their Power must return of Course to those who gave it.

Suppose, for Example, the Grand Monarch, as he was called, had bought a neighbouring Kingdom, and all the Lands in it, from the Courtiers, and the Majority of the People's Deputies; and amongst the rest, the Church-Lands, into the Bargain, with the Consent of their Convocation or Synod, or by what other Name that Assembly was called; would the People and Clergy have thought themselves obliged to have made good this Bargain, if they could have helped it? I dare say that neither would; but, on the contrary, that the People would have had the Countenance of these reverend Patriots to have told their Representatives in round Terms, that they were chosen to act for the Interest of those that sent them, and not for their own; that their Power was given them to protect and defend their Country, and not to sell and enslave it.

This Supposition, as wild as it seems, yet is not absolutely and universally impossible. King *John* actually sold the Kingdom of *England* to his Holiness: And there are People in all Nations ready to sell their Country at Home; and such can never have any Principles to with-hold them from selling it Abroad.

It is foolish to say, that this Doctrine can be mischievous to Society, at least in any Proportion to the wild Ruin and fatal Calamities which must befal, and do befal the World, where the contrary Doctrine is maintained: For, all Bodies of Men subsisting upon their own Substance, or upon the Profits of their Trade and Industry, find their Account so much in Ease and Peace, and have justly such terrible Apprehensions of Civil Disorders, which destroy every thing that they enjoy; that they always bear a Thousand Injuries before they return One, and stand under the Burthens as long as they can bear them; as I have in another Letter observed.

What with the Force of Education, and the Reverence which

People are taught, and have been always used to pay to Princes; what with the perpetual Harangues of Flatterers, the gaudy Pageantry and Outside of Power, and its gilded Ensigns, always glittering in their Eyes; what with the Execution of the Laws in the sole Power of the Prince; what with all the regular Magistrates, pompous Guards and standing Troops, with the fortified Towns, the Artillery, and all the Magazines of War, at his Disposal; besides large Revenues, and Multitudes of Followers and Dependants, to support and abet all that he does: Obedience to Authority is so well secured, that it is wild to imagine, that any Number of Men, formidable enough to disturb a settled State, can unite together and hope to over-turn it, till the publick Grievances are so enormous, the Op-pression so great, and the Disaffection so universal, that there can be no Question remaining, whether their Calamities be real or imaginary, and whether the Magistrate has protected or endeavoured to destroy his People.

This was the Case of *Richard* II. *Edward* II. and *James* II. and will ever be the Case under the same Circumstances. No Society of Men will groan under Oppressions longer than they know how to throw them off; whatever unnatural Whimsies and Fairy Notions idle and sedentary Babblers may utter from Colleges and Cloisters; and teach to others, for vile Self-Ends, Doctrines, which they themselves are famous for not practising.

Upon this Principle of People's judging for themselves, and resisting lawless Force, stands our late happy *Revolution,* and with it the just and rightful Title of our most excellent Sover-eign King *George,* to the Scepter of these Realms; a Scepter which he has, and I doubt not will ever sway, to his own Honour, and the Honour, Protection, and Prosperity of us his People.

T   *I am, &c.*

Number 60.

SATURDAY, JANUARY 6, 1721.

All Government proved to be instituted by Men, and only to intend the general Good of Men.

SIR,

There is no Government now upon Earth, which owes its Formation or Beginning to the immediate Revelation of God, or can derive its Existence from such Revelation: It is certain, on the contrary, that the Rise and Institution or Variation of Government, from Time to Time, is within the Memory of Men or of Histories; and that every Government, which we know at this Day in the World, was established by the Wisdom and Force of mere Men, and by the Concurrence of Means and Causes evidently human. Government therefore can have no Power, but such as Men can give, and such as they actually did give, or permit for their own Sakes: Nor can any Government be in Fact framed but by Consent, if not of every Subject, yet of as many as can compel the rest; since no Man, or Council of Men, can have personal Strength enough to govern Multitudes by Force, or can claim to themselves and their Families any Superiority, or natural Sovereignty over their Fellow-Creatures naturally as good as them. Such Strength, therefore, where-ever it is, is civil and accumulative Strength, derived from the Laws and Constitutions of the Society, of which the Governors themselves are but Members.

So that to know the Jurisdiction of Governors, and its Limits, we must have Recourse to the Institution of Government, and ascertain those Limits by the Measure of Power, which Men in the State of Nature have over themselves and one another: And as no Man can take from many, who are stronger than him, what they have no Mind to give him; and he who has not Consent must have Force, which is itself the Consent of the Stronger; so no Man can give to another either what is none of his own, or what in its own Nature is inseparable from himself; as his Religion particularly is.

Every Man's Religion is his own; nor can the Religion of any Man, of what Nature or Figure soever, be the Religion of another Man, unless he also chooses it; which Action utterly excludes all Force, Power, or Government. Religion can never come without Conviction, nor can Conviction come from Civil Authority; Religion, which is the Fear of God, cannot be subject to Power, which is the Fear of Man. It is a Relation between God and our own Souls only, and consists in a Disposition of Mind to obey the Will of our great Creator, in the Manner which we think most acceptable to him. It is independent upon all human Directions, and superior to them; and consequently uncontroulable by external Force, which cannot reach the free Faculties of the Mind, or inform the Understanding, much less convince it. Religion therefore, which can never be subject to the Jurisdiction of another, can never be alienated to another, or put in his Power.

Nor has any Man in the State of Nature Power over his own Life, or to take away the Life of another, unless to defend his own, or what is as much his own, namely, his Property. This Power therefore, which no Man has, no Man can transfer to another.

Nor could any Man in the State of Nature, have a Right to violate the Property of another; that is, what another had acquired by his Act or Labour; or to interrupt him in his Industry and Enjoyments, as long as he himself was not injured by that Industry and those Enjoyments. No Man therefore could transfer to the Magistrate that Right which he had not himself.

No Man in his Senses was ever so wild as to give an unlimited Power to another to take away his Life, or the Means of Living, according to the Caprice, Passion, and unreasonable

Pleasure of that other: But if any Man restrained himself from any Part of his Pleasures, or parted with any Portion of his Acquisitions, he did it with the honest Purpose of enjoying the rest with the greater Security, and always in Subserviency to his own Happiness, which no Man will or can willingly and intentionally give away to any other whatsoever.

And if any one, through his own Inadvertence, or by the Fraud or Violence of another, can be drawn into so foolish a Contract, he is relievable by the eternal Laws of God and Reason. No Engagement that is wicked and unjust can be executed without Injustice and Wickedness: This is so true, that I question whether there be a Constitution in the World which does not afford, or pretend to afford, a Remedy for relieving ignorant, distressed, and unwary Men, trepanned into such Engagements by artful Knaves, or frightened into them by imperious ones. So that here the Laws of Nature and general Reason supersede the municipal and positive Laws of Nations; and no where oftner than in *England*. What else was the Design, and ought to be the Business, of our Courts of Equity? And I hope whole Countries and Societies are no more exempted from the Privileges and Protection of Reason and Equity, than are private Particulars.

Here then is the natural Limitation of the Magistrate's Authority: He ought not to take what no Man ought to give; nor exact what no Man ought to perform: All he has is given him, and those that gave it must judge of the Application. In Government there is no such Relation as Lord and Slave, lawless Will and blind Submission; nor ought to be amongst Men: But the only Relation is that of Father and Children, Patron and Client, Protection and Allegiance, Benefaction and Gratitude, mutual Affection and mutual Assistance.

So that the Nature of Government does not alter the natural Right of Men to Liberty, which in all political Societies is alike their Due: But some Governments provide better than others for the Security and impartial Distribution of that Right. There has been always such a constant and certain Fund of

Corruption and Malignity in human Nature, that it has been rare to find that Man, whose Views and Happiness did not center in the Gratification of his Appetites, and worst Appetites, his Luxury, his Pride, his Avarice, and Lust of Power; and who considered any publick Trust reposed in him, with any other View, than as the Means to satiate such unruly and dangerous Desires! And this has been most eminently true of Great Men, and those who aspired to Dominion. They were first made Great for the Sake of the Publick, and afterwards at its Expence. And if they had been content to have been moderate Traytors, Mankind would have been still moderately happy; but their Ambition and Treason observing no Degrees, there was no Degree of Vileness and Misery which the poor People did not often feel.

The Appetites therefore of Men, especially of Great Men, are carefully to be observed and stayed, or else they will never stay themselves. The Experience of every Age convinces us, that we must not judge of Men by what they ought to do, but by what they will do; and all History affords but few Instances of Men trusted with great Power without abusing it, when with Security they could. The Servants of Society, that is to say, its Magistrates, did almost universally serve it by seizing it, selling it, or plundering it; especially when they were left by the Society unlimited as to their Duty and Wages. In that Case these faithful Stewards generally took all; and, being Servants, made Slaves of their Masters.

For these Reasons, and convinced by woful and eternal Experience, Societies found it necessary to lay Restraints upon their Magistrates or publick Servants, and to put Checks upon those who would otherwise put Chains upon them; and therefore these Societies set themselves to model and form national Constitutions with such Wisdom and Art, that the publick Interest should be consulted and carried at the same Time, when those entrusted with the Administration of it were consulting and pursuing their own.

Hence grew the Distinction between Arbitrary and Free

Governments: Not that more or less Power was vested in the one than in the other; nor that either of them lay under less or more Obligations, in Justice, to protect their Subjects, and study their Ease, Prosperity, and Security, and to watch for the same. But the Power and Sovereignty of Magistrates in free Countries was so qualified, and so divided into different Channels, and committed to the Direction of so many different Men, with different Interests and Views, that the Majority of them could seldom or never find their Account in betraying their Trust in fundamental Instances. Their Emulation, Envy, Fear, or Interest, always made them Spies and Checks upon one another. By all which Means the People have often come at the Heads of those who forfeited their Heads, by betraying the People.

In despotick Governments Things went far otherwise, those Governments having been framed otherwise; if the same could be called Governments, where the Rules of publick Power were dictated by private and lawless Lust; where Folly and Madness often swayed the Scepter, and blind Rage weilded the Sword. The whole Wea[l]th of the State, with its Civil or Military Power, being in the Prince, the People could have no Remedy but Death and Patience, while he oppressed them by the Lump, and butchered them by Thousands: Unless perhaps the Ambition or personal Resentments of some of the Instruments of his Tyranny procured a Revolt, which rarely mended their Condition.

The only Secret therefore in forming a Free Government, is to make the Interests of the Governors and of the Governed the same, as far as human Policy can contrive. Liberty cannot be preserved any other Way. Men have long found, from the Weakness and Depravity of themselves and one another, that most Men will act for Interest against Duty, as often as they dare. So that to engage them to their Duty, Interest must be linked to the Observance of it, and Danger to the Breach of it. Personal Advantages and Security, must be the rewards of

Duty and Obedience; and Disgrace, Torture, and Death, the Punishment of Treachery and Corruption.

Human Wisdom has yet found out but one certain Expedient to effect this; and that is, to have the Concerns of all directed by all, as far as possibly can be: And where the Persons interested are too numerous, or live too distant to meet together on all Emergencies, they must moderate Necessity by Prudence, and act by Deputies, whose Interest is the same with their own, and whose Property is so intermingled with theirs, and so engaged upon the same Bottom, that Principals and Deputies must stand and fall together. When the Deputies thus act for their own Interest, by acting for the Interest of their Principals; when they can make no Law but what they themselves, and their Posterity, must be subject to; when they can give no Money, but what they must pay their Share of; when they can do no Mischief, but what must fall upon their own Heads in common with their Countrymen; their Principals may then expect good Laws, little Mischief, and much Frugality.

Here therefore lies the great Point of Nicety and Care in forming the Constitution, that the Persons entrusted and representing, shall either never have any Interest detached from the Persons entrusting and represented, or never the Means to pursue it. Now to compass this great Point effectually, no other Way is left, but one of these two, or rather both; namely, to make the Deputies so numerous, that there may be no Possibility of corrupting the Majority; or, by changing them so often, that there is no sufficient Time to corrupt them, and to carry the Ends of that Corruption. The People may be very sure, that the major Part of their Deputies being honest, will keep the rest so; and that they will all be honest, when they have no Temptations to be Knaves.

We have some Sketch of this Policy in the Constitution of our several great Companies, where the General Court, composed of all its Members, constitutes the Legislature, and the

Consent of that Court is the Sanction of their Laws; and where the Administration of their Affairs is put under the Conduct of a certain Number chosen by the Whole. Here every Man con[c]erned saw the Necessity of securing Part of their Property, by putting the Persons entrusted under proper Regulations; however remiss they may be in takeing Care of the Whole. And if Provision had been made, That, as a Third Part of the Directors are to go out every Year, so none should stay in above Three, (as I am told was as first promised) all Juggling with Courtiers, and raising great Estates by Confederacy, at the Expence of the Company, had, in a great Measure, been prevented; though there were still wanting other Limitations, which might have effectually obviated all those Evils.

This was the ancient Constitution of *England:* Our Kings had neither Revenues large enough, nor Offices gainful and numerous enough in their Disposal, to corrupt any considerable Number of Members; nor any Force to frighten them. Besides, the same Parliament seldom or never met twice: For, the serving in it being found an Office of Burthen, and not of Profit, it was thought reasonable that all Men qualified should, in their Turns, leave their Families and domestick Concerns, to serve the Publick; and their Borough bore their Charges. The only Grievance then was, that they were not called together often enough, to redress the Grievances which the People suffered from the Court during their Intermission: And therefore a Law was made in *Edward* the IIId's Time, That Parliaments should be holden once a Year.

But this Law, like the late Queen's Peace, did not execute itself; and therefore the Court seldom convened them, but when they wanted Money, or had other Purposes of their own to serve; and sometimes raised Money without them: Which arbitrary proceeding brought upon the Publick numerous Mischiefs; and, in the Reign of King *Charles* the Ist, a long and bloody Civil War. In that Reign an Act was passed, That they should meet of themselves, if they were not called according to the Direction of that Law; which was worthily repealed upon the Restoration of King *Charles* the IId: And in the same kind Fit, a great Revenue was given him for Life, and continued to his Brother. By which Means these Princes were enabled to keep standing Troops, to corrupt Parliaments, or to live without them; and to commit such Acts of Power as brought about, and indeed forced the People upon the late happy *Revolution*. Soon after which a new Act was passed, That Parliaments should be rechosen once in three Years: Which Law was also repealed, upon his Majesty's Accesssion to the Throne, that the present Parliament might have Time to rectify those Abuses which we labour under, and to make Regulations proper to prevent them *All* for the future. *All* which has since been happily effected; and, I bless God, we are told, that the People will have the Opportunity to thank them, in another Election, for their great Services to their Country. I shall be always ready, on my Part, to do them Honour, and pay them my Acknowledgments, in the most effectual Manner in my Power.——But more of this in the succeeding Papers.

T   *I am, &c.*

SATURDAY, JANUARY 13, 1721.

How free Governments are to be framed so as to last, and how they differ from such as are arbitrary.

SIR,

The most reasonable Meaning that can be put upon this Apothegm, that *Virtue is its own Reward,* is, that it seldom meets with any other. God himself, who having made us, best knows our Natures, does not trust to the intrinsick Excellence and native Beauty of Holiness alone, to engage us in its Interests and Pursuits, but recommends it to us by the stronger and more affecting Motives of Rewards and Punishments. No wise Man, therefore, will in any Instance of Moment trust to the mere Integrity of another. The Experience of all Ages may convince us, that Men, when they are above Fear, grow for the most part above Honesty and Shame: And this is particularly and certainly true of Societies of Men, when they are numerous enough to keep one another in Countenance; for when the Weight of Infamy is divided amongst many, no one sinks under his own Burthen.

Great Bodies of Men have seldom judged what they ought to do, by any other Rule than what they could do. What Nation is there that has not oppressed any other, when the same could be done with Advantage and Security? What Party has ever had Regard to the Principles which they professed, or ever reformed the Errors which they condemned? What Company, or particular Society of Merchants or Tradesmen, has ever acted for the Interest of general Trade, though it always filled their Mouths in private Conversation?

And yet Men, thus formed and qualified, are the Materials for Government. For the Sake of Men it is instituted, by the Prudence of Men it must be conducted; and the Art of political Mechanism is, to erect a firm Building with such crazy and corrupt Materials. The strongest Cables are made out of loose Hemp and Flax; the World itself may, with the Help of proper Machines, be moved by the Force of a single Hair; and so may the Government of the World, as well as the World itself. But whatever Discourses I shall hereafter make upon this great and useful Subject, I shall confine myself in this Letter to free monarchical Constitutions alone,[1] and to the Application of some of the Principles laid down in my last.

---

[1] An example, for Trenchard and Gordon, would be that of Great Britain after the Glorious Revolution, when the royal prerogative was very clearly limited by constitutional law. France would be regarded as an unfree monarchy, where the personal whim of the monarchs had overwhelmed such restraints as might once have been placed upon it by the Estates-General.

It is there said, that when the Society consists of too many, or when they live too far apart to be able to meet together, to take Care of their own Affairs, they can no otherwise preserve their Liberties, than by choosing Deputies to represent them, and to act for them; and that these Deputies must be either so numerous, that there can be no Means of corrupting the Majority; or so often changed, that there shall be no Time to do it so as to answer any End by doing it. Without one of these Regulations, or both, I lay it down as a certain Maxim in Politicks, that it is impossible to preserve a free Government long.

I think I may with great Modesty affirm, that in former Reigns the People of *England* found no sufficient Security in the Number of their Representatives. What with the Crowd of Offices in the Gift of the Crown, which were possessed by Men of no other Merit, nor held by any other Tenure, but merely a Capacity to get into the House of Commons, and the Disservice which they could and would do their Country there: What with the Promises and Expectations given to others, who by Court-Influence, and often by Court-Money, carried their Elections: What by artful Caresses, and the familiar and deceitful Addresses of great Men to weak Men: What with luxurious Dinners, and Rivers of *Burgundy, Champaign,* and *Tokay,* thrown down the Throats of Gluttons; and what with Pensions, and other personal Gratifications, bestowed where Wind and Smoke would not pass for current Coin: What with Party Watch-Words and imaginary Terrors, spread amongst the drunken 'Squires, and the deluded and enthusiastick Bigots, of dreadful Designs in *Embrio,* to blow up the Church, and the Protestant Interest; and sometimes with the Dread of mighty Invasions just ready to break upon us from the Man in the Moon: I say, by all these corrupt Arts, the Representatives of the *English* People, in former Reigns, have been brought to betray the People, and to join with their Oppressors. So much are Men governed by artful Applications to their private Passions and Interest. And it is evident to me, that if ever we have a weak or an ambitious Prince, with a

Ministry like him, we must find out some other Resources, or acquiesce in the Loss of our Liberties. The Course and Transiency of human Affairs will not suffer us to live always under the present righteous Administration.

So that I can see no Means in human Policy to preserve the publick Liberty and a monarchical Form of Government together, but by the frequent fresh Elections of the People's Deputies: This is what the Writers in Politicks call Rotation of Magistracy. Men, when they first enter into Magistracy, have often their former Condition before their Eyes: They remember what they themselves suffered, with their Fellow-Subjects, from the Abuse of Power, and how much they blamed it; and so their first Purposes are to be humble, modest, and just; and probably, for some Time, they continue so. But the Possession of Power soon alters and viciates their Hearts, which are at the same time sure to be leavened, and puffed up to an unnatural Size, by the deceitful Incense of false Friends, and by the prostrate Submission of Parasites. First, they grow indifferent to all their good Designs, then drop them: Next, they lose their Moderation; afterwards, they renounce all Measures with their old Acquaintance and old Principles; and seeing themselves in magnifying Glasses, grow, in Conceit, a different Species from their Fellow-Subjects; and so by too sudden Degrees become insolent, rapacious and tyrannical, ready to catch at all Means, often the vilest and most oppressive, to raise their Fortunes as high as their imaginary Greatness. So that the only Way to put them in mind of their former Condition, and consequently of the Condition of other People, is often to reduce them to it; and to let others of equal Capacities share of Power in their Turn: This also is the only Way to qualify Men, and make them equally fit for Dominion and Subjection.

A Rotation therefore, in Power and Magistracy, is essentially necessary to a free Government: It is indeed the Thing itself; and constitutes, animates, and informs it, as much as the

Soul constitutes the Man. It is a Thing sacred and inviolable, where-ever Liberty is thought sacred; nor can it ever be committed to the Disposal of those who are trusted with the Preservation of National Constitutions: For though they may have the Power to model it for the publick Advantage, and for the more effectual Security of that Right; yet they can have none to give it up, or, which is the same Thing, to make it useless.

The Constitution of a limited Monarchy, is the joint Concurrence of the Crown and of the Nobles (without whom it cannot subsist) and of the Body of the People, to make Laws for the common Benefit of the Subject; and where the People, through Number or Distance, cannot meet, they must send Deputies to speak in their Names, and to attend upon their Interest: These Deputies therefore act by, under, and in Subserviency to the Constitution, and have not a Power above it and over it. . . .

T   *I am, &c.*

Number 62.

Saturday, January 20, 1721.

An Enquiry into the Nature and Extent of Liberty; with its Loveliness and Advantages, and the vile Effects of Slavery.

SIR,

I Have shewn, in a late Paper, wherein consists the Difference between Free and Arbitrary Governments, as to their frame and Constitution; and in this and the following I shall show their different Spirit and Effects. But first I shall shew wherein Liberty itself consists.

By Liberty, I understand the Power which every Man has over his own Actions, and his Right to enjoy the Fruit of his

Labour, Art, and Industry, as far as by it he hurts not the
Society, or any Members of it, by taking from any Member,
or by hindering him from enjoying what he himself enjoys.
The Fruits of a Man's honest Industry are the just Rewards
of it, ascertained to him by natural and eternal Equity, as is
his Title to use them in the Manner which he thinks fit: And
thus, with the above Limitations, every Man is sole Lord and
Arbiter of his own private Actions and Property. —A Character
of which no Man living can divest him but by Usurpation, or
his own Consent.

The entering into political Society, is so far from a Departure
from his natural Right, that to preserve it was the sole Reason
why Men did so; and mutual Protection and Assistance is the
only reasonable Purpose of all reasonable Societies. To make
such Protection practicable, Magistracy was formed, with
Power to defend the Innocent from Violence, and to punish
those that offered it; nor can there be any other Pretence for
Magistracy in the World. In order to this good End, the Magistrate is intrusted with conducting and applying the united
Force of the Community; and with exacting such a Share of
every Man's Property, as is necessary to preserve the Whole,
and to defend every Man and his Property from foreign and
domestick Injuries. These are the Boundaries of the Power
of the Magistrate, who deserts his Function whenever he
breaks them. By the Laws of Society, he is more limited and
restrained than any Man amongst them; since, while they are
absolutely free in all their Actions, which purely concern
themselves; all his Actions, as a publick Person, being for the
Sake of Society, must refer to it, and answer the Ends of it.

It is a mistaken Notion in Government, that the Interest of
the Majority is only to be consulted, since in Society every Man
has a Right to every Man's Assistance in the Enjoyment and
Defence of his private Property; otherwise the greater Number may sell the lesser, and divide their Estates amongst themselves; and so, instead of a Society, where all peaceable Men

are protected, become a Conspiracy of the Many against the Minority. With as much Equity may one Man wantonly dispose of all, and Violence may be sanctified by mere Power.

And it is as foolish to say, that Government is concerned to meddle with the private Thoughts and Actions of Men, while they injure neither the Society, nor any of its Members. Every Man is, in Nature and Reason, the Judge and Disposer of his own domestick Affairs; and, according to the Rules of Religion and Equity, every Man must carry his own Conscience. So that neither has the Magistrate a Right to direct the private Behaviour of Men; nor has the Magistrate, or any body else, any manner of Power to model People's Speculations, no more than their Dreams. Government being intended to protect Men from the Injuries of one another, and not to direct them in their own Affairs, in which no one is interested but themselves; it is plain, that their Thoughts and domestick Concerns are exempted intirely from its Jurisdiction: In Truth, Mens Thoughts are not subject to their own Jurisdiction.

Idiots a[n]d Lunaticks indeed, who cannot take Care of themselves, must be taken Care of by others: But whilst Men have their five Senses, I cannot see what the Magistrate has to do with Actions by which the Society cannot be affected; and where he meddles with such, he meddles impertinently or tyrannically. Must the Magistrate tie up every Man's Legs, because some Men fall into Ditches? Or, must he put out their Eyes, because with them they see lying Vanities? Or, would it become the Wisdom and Care of Governors to establish a travelling Society, to prevent People, by a proper Confinement, from throwing themselves into Wells, or over Precipices; Or to endow a Fraternity of Physicians and Surgeons all over the Nation, to take Care of their Subjects Health, without being consulted; and to vomit, bleed, purge, and scarify them at Pleasure, whether they would or no, just as these established Judges of Health should think fit? If this were the Case, what a Stir and Hubbub should we soon see kept about the established Potions and Lancets? Every Man, Woman, or Child, though ever so healthy, must be a Patient, or woe be to them! The best Diet and Medicines would soon grow pernicious from any other Hand; and their Pills alone, however ridiculous, insufficient, or distasteful, would be attended with a Blessing.

Let People alone, and they will take Care of themselves, and do it best; and if they do not, a sufficient Punishment will follow their Neglect, without the Magistrate's Interposition and Penalties. It is plain, that such busy Care and officious Intrusion into the personal Affairs, or private Actions, Thoughts, and Imaginations of Men, has in it more Craft than Kindness; and is only a Device to mislead People, and pick their Pockets, under the false Pretence of the publick and their private God. To quarrel with any Man for his Opinions, Humours, or the Fashion of his Clothes, is an Offence taken without being given. What is it to a Magistrate how I wash my Hands, or cut my Corns; what Fashion or Colours I wear, or what Notions I entertain, or what Gestures I use, or what Words I pronounce, when they please me, and do him and my Neighbour no Hurt? As well may he determine the Colour of my Hair, and controul my Shape and Features.

True and impartial Liberty is therefore the Right of every Man to pursue the natural, reasonable, and religious Dictates of his own Mind; to think what he will, and act as he thinks, provided he acts not to the Prejudice of another; to spend his own Money himself, and lay out the Produce of his Labour his own Way; and to labour for his own Pleasure and Profit, and not for others who are idle, and would live and riot by pillaging and oppressing him, and those that are like him.

So that Civil Government is only a partial Restraint put by the Laws of Agreement and Society upon natural and absolute Liberty, which might otherwise grow licentious: And Tyranny is an unlimited Restraint put upon natural Liberty, by the Will of one or a few. Magistracy, amongst a free People, is the Exercise of Power for the Sake of the People; and Tyrants abuse the People, for the Sake of Power. Free Government is the protecting the People in their Liberties by stated Rules: Tyranny is a brutish Struggle for unlimited Liberty to one or a few, who would rob all others of their Liberty, and act by no Rule but lawless Lust.

So much for an Idea of Civil Liberty. I will now add a Word or two, to shew how much it is the Delight and Passion of Mankind; and then shew its Advantages.

The Love of Liberty is an Appetite so strongly implanted in the Nature of all Living Creatures, that even the Appetite of Self-preservation, which is allowed to be the strongest, seems to be contained in it; since by the Means of Liberty they enjoy the Means of preserving themselves, and of satisfying their Desires in the Manner which they themselves choose and like best. Many Animals can never be tamed, but feel the Bitterness of Restraint in the midst of the kindest Usage; and rather than bear it, grieve and starve themselves to Death; and some beat out their Brains against their Prisons.

Where Liberty is lost, Life grows precarious, always miserable, often intolerable. Liberty is, to live upon one's own Terms; Slavery is, to live at the mere Mercy of another; and a Life of Slavery is, to those who can bear it, a continual State of Uncertainty and Wretchedness, often an Apprehension of Violence, often the lingering Dread of a violent Death: But by others, when no other Remedy is to be had, Death is reckoned a good one. And thus, to many Men, and to many other Creatures, as well as Men, the Love of Liberty is beyond the Love of Life.

This Passion for Liberty in Men, and their Possession of it, is of that Efficacy and Importance, that it seems the Parent of all the Virtues: And therefore in free Countries there seems to be another Species of Mankind, than is to be found under Tyrants. Small Armies of *Greeks* and *Romans* despised the greatest Hosts of Slaves; and a Million of Slaves have been

sometimes beaten and conquered by a few Thousand Freemen. Insomuch that the Difference seemed greater between
them than between Men and Sheep. It was therefore well said
by *Lucullus*,[1] when, being about to engage the great King
Tigranes's Army, he was told by some of his Officers, how
prodigious great the same was, consisting of between Three
and Four Hundred Thousand Men: *No matter*, said that brave
Roman, drawing up his little Army of Fourteen Thousand, but
Fourteen Thousand *Romans: No matter; the Lion never en-
quires into the Number of the Sheep.* And these Royal Troops
proved no better; for the *Romans* had little else to do but to
kill and pursue; which yet they could scarce do for laughing;
so much more were they diverted than animated by the ridiculous Dread and sudden Flight of these Imperial Slaves and
Royal Cowards.

Men eternally cowed and oppressed by haughty and insolent
Governors, made base themselves by the Baseness of that Sort
of Government, and become Slaves by ruling over Slaves, want
Spirit and Souls to meet in the Field Freemen, who scorn
Oppressors, and are their own Governors, or at least measure
and direct the Power of their Governors.

Education alters Nature, and becomes stronger. Slavery,
while it continues being a perpetual Awe upon the Spirits,
depresses them, and sinks natural Courage; and Want and
Fear, the Concomitants of Bondage, always produce Despond-
ency and Baseness; nor will Men in Bonds ever fight bravely,
but to be free. Indeed, what else should they fight for; since
every Victory that they gain for a Tyrant, makes them poorer
and fewer; and, increasing his Pride, increases his Cruelty,
with their own Misery and Chains?

---

[1] Trenchard and Gordon refer to the triumph of the Roman Lucullus
over a vastly superior army under Tigranes at Tigranocerta in 69 B.C. Plu-
tarch (*Lives*, "Lucullus," XXVIII. 7) quotes a fragment of Livy as a summary of the battle: "The Romans were never in such inferior numbers
when they faced an enemy; for the victors were hardly even a twentieth
part of the vanquished, but less than this."

Those, who, from Terror and Delusion, the frequent Causes and certain Effects of Servitude, come to think their Governors greater than Men, as they find them worse, will be as apt to think themselves less: And when the Head and the Heart are thus both gone, the Hands will signify little. They who are used like Beasts, will be apt to degenerate into Beasts. But those, on the contrary, who, by the Freedom of their Government and Education, are taught and accustomed to think freely of Men and Things, find, by comparing one Man with another, that all Men are naturally alike; and that their Governors, as they have the same Face, Constitution, and Shape with themselves, and are subject to the same Sickness, Accidents, and Death, with the meanest of their People; so they possess the same Passions and Faculties of the Mind which their Subjects possess, and not better. They therefore scorn to degrade and prostrate themselves, to adore those of their own Species, however covered with Titles, and disguised by Power: They consider them as their own Creatures; and, as far as they surmount themselves, the Work of their own Hands, and only the chief Servants of the State, who have no more Power to do Evil than one of themselves, and are void of every Privilege and Superiority, but to serve them and the State. They know it to be a Contradiction in Religion and Reason, for any Man to have a Right to do Evil; that not to resist any Man's Wickedness, is to encourage it; and that they have the least Reason to bear Evil and Oppression from their Governors, who of all Men are the most obliged to do them Good. They therefore detest Slavery, and despise or pity Slaves; and, adoring Liberty alone, as they who see its Beauty and feel its Advantages always will, it is no Wonder that they are brave for it.

Indeed Liberty is the divine Source of all human Happiness. To possess, in Security, the Effects of our Industry, is the most powerful and reasonable Incitement t[o] be industrious: And to be able to provide for our Children, and to leave them all that we have, is the best Motive to beget them. But where

Property is precarious, Labour will languish. The Privileges of thinking, saying, and doing what we please, and of growing as rich as we can, without any other Restriction, than that by all this we hurt not the Publick, nor one another, are the glorious Privileges of Liberty; and its Effects, to live in Freedom, Plenty, and Safety.

These are Privileges that increase Mankind, and the H[a]ppiness of Mankind. And therefore Countries are generally peopled in Proportion as they are free, and are certainly happy in that Proportion: And upon the same Tract of Land that would maintain a Hundred Thousand Freemen in Plenty, Five Thousand Slaves would starve. In *Italy*, fertile *Italy*, Men die sometimes of Hunger amongst the Sheaves, and in a plentiful Harvest; for what they sow and reap is none of their own; and their cruel and greedy Governors, who live by the Labour of their wretched Vassals, do not suffer them to eat the Bread of their own Earning, nor to sustain their Lives with their own Hands.

Liberty naturally draws new People to it, as well as increases the old Stock; and Men as naturally run when they dare from Slavery and Wretchedness, whithersoever they can help themselves. Hence great Cities losing their Liberty become Desarts, and little Towns by Liberty grow great Cities; as will be fully proved before I have gone through this Argument. I will not deny, but that there are some great Cities of Slaves: But such are only Imperial Cities, and the Seats of great Princes, who draw the Wealth of a Continent to their Capital, the Center of their Treasure and Luxury. *Babylon, Antioch, Seleucia,* and *Alexandria,* were great Cities peopled by Tyrants; but peopled partly by Force, partly by the above Reason, and partly by Grants and Indulgencies. Their Power, great and boundless as it was, could not alone people their Cities; but they were forced to soften Authority by Kindness; and having brought the Inhabitants together by Force, and by driving them Captive like Cattle, could not keep them together, without bestowing on them many Privileges, to encourage the first Inhabitants to stay, and to invite more to come.

This was a Confession in those Tyrants, that their Power was mischievous and unjust; since they could not erect one great City, and make it flourish, without renouncing in a great measure their Power over it; which, by granting it these Privileges, in Effect they did. These Privileges were fixed Laws, by which the Trade and Industry of the Citizens were encouraged, and their Lives and Properties ascertained and protected, and no longer subjected to the Laws of mere Will and Pleasure: And therefore, while these free Cities, enjoying their own Liberties and Laws, flourished under them, the Provinces were miserably harrassed, pillaged, dispeopled, and impoverished, and the Inhabitants exhausted, starved, butchered, and carried away captive.

This shews that all Civil Happiness and Prosperity is inseparable from Liberty; and that Tyranny cannot make Men, or Societies of Men, happy, without departing from its Nature, and giving them Privileges inconsistent with Tyranny. And here is an unanswerable Argument, amongst a Thousand others, against absolute Power in a single Man. Nor is there one Way in the World to give Happiness to Communities, but by sheltering them under certain and express Laws, irrevocable at any Man's Pleasure.

There is not, nor can be, any Security for a People to trust to the mere Will of one, who, while his Will is his Law, cannot protect them if he would. The Number of Sycophants and wicked Counsellors, that he will always and necessarily have about him, will defeat all his good Intentions, by representing Things falsly, and Persons maliciously; by suggesting Danger where it is not, and urging Necessity where there is none; by filling their own Coffers, under Colour of filling his, and by raising Money for themselves, pretending the publick Exigencies of the State; by sacrificing particular Men to their own Revenge, under Pretence of publick Security; and by engaging him and his People in dangerous and destructive Wars, for their own Profit or Fame; by throwing publick Affairs into perpetual Confusion, to prevent an Enquiry into their own Behaviour; and by making him jealous of his People, and his People of him, on purpose to manage and mislead both Sides.

By all these, and many more wicked Arts, they will be constantly leading him into cruel and oppressive Measures, destructive to his People, scandalous and dangerous to himself; but entirely agreeable to their own Spirit and Designs. Thus will they commit all Wickedness by their Master's Authority, against his Inclinations, and grow rich by the People's Poverty, without his Knowledge; and the Royal Authority will be first a Warrant for Oppression, afterwards a Protection from the Punishment due to it. For, in short, the Power of Princes is often little else but a Stalking-Horse to the Intrigues and Ambition of their Minister.

But if the Disposition of such a Prince be evil, what must be the forlorn Condition of his People, and what Door of Hope can remain for common Protection! The best Princes have often evil Counsello[r]s, the Bad will have no other: And in such a Case, what Bounds can be set to their Fury, and to the Havock they will make? The Instruments and Advisers of Tyranny and Depredation always thrive best and are nearest their Ends, when Depredation and Tyranny run highest: When most is plundered from the People, their Share is greatest; we may therefore suppose every Evil will befal such a People, without supposing extravagantly. No Happiness, no Security, but certain Misery, and a vile and precarious Life, are the blessed Terms of such a Government—A Government which necessarily introduces all Evils, and from the same Necessity neither must nor can redress any.

The Nature of his Education, bred up as he ever is in perpetual Flattery, makes him haughty and ignorant; and the Nature of his Government, which subsists by brutish Severity and Oppression, makes him cruel. He is inaccessible, but by his Ministers, whose Study and Interest will be to keep him from knowing or helping the State of his miserable People. Their Master's Knowledge in his own Affairs, would break in upon their Scheme and Power; they are not likely to lay before him Representations of Grievances caused by themselves; nor, if they be the Effects of his own Barbarity and Command, will he hear them.

Even where absolute Princes are not Tyrants, there Ministers will be Tyrants. But it is indeed impossible for an arbitrary Prince to be otherwise, since Oppression is absolutely necessary to his being so. Without giving his People Liberty, he cannot make them happy; and by giving them Liberty, he gives up his own Power. So that to be and continue arbitrary, he is doomed to be a Tyrant in his own Defence. The Oppression of the People, Corruption, wicked Counsellors, and pernicious Maxims in the Court, and every where Baseness, Ignorance, and Chains, must support Tyranny, or it cannot be supported. So that in such Governments there are inevitable Grievances, without possible Redress; Misery, without Mitigation or Remedy; whatever is good for the People, is bad for their Governors; and what is good for the Governors, is pernicious to the People.

G   *I am, &c.*

SATURDAY, JANUARY 27, 1721.

Civil Liberty produces all Civil Blessings, and how; with the baneful Nature of Tyranny.

SIR,

I Go on with my Considerations upon Liberty, to shew that all Civil Virtue and Happiness, every moral Excellency, all Politeness, all good Arts and Sciences, are produced by

nd that all Wickedness, Baseness, and Misery, are
ely and necessarily produced by Tyranny; which be-
ded upon the Destruction of every thing that is valu-
a~   sireable, and noble, must subsist upon Means suitable
to its Nature, and remain in everlasting Enmity to all Goodness
and every human Blessing.

By the Establishment of Liberty, a due Distribution of Property and an equal Dist[r]ibution of Justice is established and
secured. As Rapine is the Child of Oppression, Justice is the
Offspring of Liberty, and her Handmaid; it is the Guardian
of Innocence, and the Terror of Vice: And when Fame, Honour,
and Advantages, are the Rewards of Virtue, she will be courted
for the Dower which she brings; otherwise, like Beauty without
Wealth, she may be praised, but more probably will be
calumniated, envied, and very often persecuted; while Vice,
when it is gainful, like rich Deformity and prosperous Folly,
will be admired and pursued. Where Virtue is all its own
Reward, she will be seldom thought any; and few will buy
That for a great Price, which will sell for none. So that Virtue,
to be followed, must be endowed, and her Credit is best secured by her Interest; that is, she must be strengthened and
recommended by the publick Laws, and embellished by publick Encouragements, or else she will be slighted and shunned.

Now the Laws which encourage and increase Virtue, are
the fixed Laws of general and impartial Liberty; Laws, which
being the Rule of every Man's Actions, and the Measures of
every Man's Power, make Honesty and Equity their Interest.
Where Liberty is thoroughly established, and its Laws equally
executed, every Man will find his Account in doing as he would
be done unto, and no Man will take from another what he
would not part with himself: Honour and Advantage will follow the Upright, Punishment overtake the Oppressor. The
Property of the Poor will be as sacred as the Privileges of the
Prince, and the Law will be the only Bulwark of both. Every
Man's honest Industry and useful Talents, while they are em-

ployed for the Publick, will be employed for himself; and while he serves himself, he will serve the P[u]blick: Publick and private Interest will secure each other; all will chearfully give a Part to secure the Whole, and be brave to defend it.

These certain Laws therefore are the only certain Beginnings and Causes of Honesty and Virtue amongst Men. There may be other Motives, I own; but such as only sway particular Men, few enough, God knows: And universal Experience has shewn us, that they are not generally prevailing, and never to be depended upon. Now these Laws are to be produced by Liberty alone, and only by such Laws can Liberty be secured and increased: And to make Laws certainly good, they must be made by mutual Agreement, and have for their End the general Interest.

But Tyranny must stand upon Force; and the Laws of Tyranny being only the fickle Will and unsteady Appetite of one Man, which may vary every Hour; there can be no settled Rule of Right or Wrong in the variable Humours and sudden Passions of a Tyrant, who, though he may sometimes punish Crimes, perhaps more out of Rage than Justice, will be much more likely to persecute and oppress Innocence, and to destroy Thousands cruelly, for one that he protects justly. There are Instances of Princes, who, being out of Humour with a Favourite, have put to Death all that spoke well of him, and afterwards all that did not: Of Princes, who put some of their Ministers to Death, for using one or two of their Barbers and Buffoons ill; as they did others of their Ministers, for using a whole Country well: Of Princes, who have destroyed, a whole People, for the Crimes or Virtues of one Man; and who, having killed a Minion in a Passion, have, to revenge themselves upon those who had not provoked them, destroyed in the same unreasonable Fury, a Hundred of their Servants who had no Hand in it, as well as all that had; who yet would have been destroyed, had they not done it: Of Princes, who have destroyed Millions in single mad Projects and Expeditions: Of Princes, who have given up Cities and Provinces to the Revenge or Avarice of a vile Woman or Eunuch, to be plundered, or massacred, or burned, as he or she thought fit to direct: Of Princes, who, to gratify the Ambition and Rapine of a few sorry Servants, have lost the Hearts of their whole People, and detached themselves from their good Subjects, to protect these Men in their Iniquity, who yet had done them no other Service, but that of destroying their Reputation, and shaking their Throne.

Such are arbitrary Princes, whose Laws are nothing but sudden Fury, or lasting Folly and Wickedness in uncertain Shapes. —Hopeful Rules these, for the governing of Mankind, and making them happy! Rules which are none, since they cannot be depended upon for a Moment; and generally change for the worse, if that can be. A Subject worth Twenty Thousand Pounds to Day, may, by a sudden Edict issued by the dark Counsel of a Traytor, be a Beggar to Morrow, and lose his Life without forfeiting the same. The Property of the whole Kingdom shall be great, or little, or none, just at the Mercy of a Secretary's Pen, guided by a Child, or a Dotard, or a foolish Woman, or a favourite Buffoon, or a Gamester, or whoever is uppermost for the Day; the next Day shall alter entirely the Yesterday's Scheme, though not for the better; and the same Men, in different Humours, shall be the Authors of both. Thus in arbitrary Countries, a Law aged Two Days i[s] an old Law; and no Law is suffered to be a standing Law, but such as are found by long Experience to be so very bad, and so thoroughly destructive, that human Malice, and all the A[r]ts of a Tyrant's Court, cannot make them worse.—A Court which never ceaseth to squeeze, kill, and oppress, till it has wound up human Misery so high, that it will go no further. This is so much Fact, that I appeal to all History and Travels, and to those that read them, whether in arbitrary Countries, both in *Europe* and out of it, the People do not grow daily thinner, and their Misery greater; and whether Countries are not peopled and rich, in Proportion to the Liberty which they enjoy and allow.

It has been long my Opinion, and is more and more so, that in slavish Countries the People must either throw off their cruel and destroying Government, and set up another in its Room, or in some Ages the Race of Mankind there will be extinct. Indeed, if it had not been for free States, that have repaired and prevented in many Places the Mischiefs done by Tyrants, the Earth had been long since a Desart, as the finest Countries in it are at this Day by that Means. The Gardens of the World, the fruitful and lovely Countries of the lower *Asia*, filled formerly by Liberty with People, Politeness, and Plenty, are now gloriously peopled with Owls and Grashoppers; and perhaps here and there, at vast Distances, with Inhabitants not more valuable, and less happy; a few dirty Huts of Slaves groaning, starving, and perishing, under the fatherly Protection of the *Sultan,* a Prince of the most Orthodox Standard.[1]

The Laws therefore of Tyrants are not Laws, but wild Acts of Will, counselled by Rage or Folly, and executed by Dragoons. And as these Laws are evil, all Sorts of Evil must concur to support them. While the People have Common-Sense left, they will easily see whether they are justly governed, and well or ill used; whether they are protected or plundered: They will know that no Man ought to be the Director of the Affairs of All, without their Consent; that no Consent can give him unlimited Power over their Bodies and Minds; and that the Laws of Nature can never be entirely abrogated by positive Laws; but that, on the contrary, the entering into Society, and becoming subject to Goverment, is only the parting with natural Liberty, in some Instances, to be protected in the Enjoyment of it in others.

So that for any Man to have arbitrary Power, he must have it without Consent; or if it be unadvisedly given at first, they who gave it soon repent when they find its Effects. In Truth,

---

[1] Trenchard and Gordon here once again indicate their dislike for the Ottoman Sultan and the Moslem faith.

all those Princes that have such Power, by keeping up great Armies in Time of Peace, effectually confess that they rule without Consent, and dread their People, whose worst Enemies they undoubtedly are. An arbitrary Prince therefore must preserve and execute his Power by Force and Terror; which yet will not do, without calling in the auxiliary Aids and strict Allies of Tyranny, Imposture, and constant Oppression. Let this People be ever so low and miserable, if they be not also blind, he is not safe. He must have established Deceivers to mislead them with Lyes, to terrify them with the Wrath of God, in case they stir Hand or Foot, or so much as a Thought, to mend their doleful Condition; as if the good God was the Sanctifier of all Villainy, the Patron of the worst of all Villains! He must have a Band of standing Cut-throats to murder all Men who would sacrilegiously defend their own. And both his Cut-throats and his Deceivers must go Shares with him in his Tyranny.

Men will naturally see their Interests, feel their Condition; will quickly find that the Sword, the Rack, and the Spunge, are not Government, but the Height of Cruelty and Robbery; and will never submit to them, but by the united Powers of Violence and Delusion: Their Bodies must be chained, their Minds enchanted and deceived; the Sword kept constantly over their Heads, and their Spirits kept low with Poverty, before they can be brought to be used at the wanton and brutish Pleasure of the most dignified and lofty Oppressor. So that God must be belied, his Creatures must be fettered, frightened, deceived, and starved, and Mankind made base and undone, that one of the worst of them may live riotously and safely amongst his Whores, Butchers, and Buffoons.

Men, therefore, must cease to be Men, and in Stupidity and Tameness grow Cattle, before they can become quiet Subjects to such a Government; which is a Complication of all the Villainies, Falshood, Oppression, Cruelty, and Depredation, upon the Face of the Earth: Nor can there be a more provoking, impudent, shocking, and blasp[h]emous Position, than to assert all this *Groupe* of Horrors, or the Author of them, to be of God's Appointment.

> *If such Kings are by God appointed,*
> *Satan may be the Lord's Anointed.*

And whoever scatters such Doctrine, ought, by all the Laws of God, Reason, and Self-preservation, to be put to Death as a general Poisoner, and Advocate for publick Destruction.

All Men own, that it is the Duty of a Prince to protect his People: And some have said, that it is their Duty to obey him, when he butchers them.—An admirable Consequence, and full of sweet Consolation! His whole Business and Office is to defend them, and to do them Good; therefore they are bound to let him destroy them.—Was ever such Impudence in an enlightened Country? It is perfectly agreeable to the Doctrines and Followers of *Mahomet:* But shall *Englishmen,* who make their own Laws, be told, that they have no Right to the common Air, to the Life and Fortune which God has given them, but by the Permission of an Officer of their own making; who is what he is only for their Sakes and Security, and has no more Right to these Blessings, nor to do Evil, than one of themselves? And shall we be told this by Men, who are eternally the first to violate their own Doctrines? Or shall they after this have the Front to teach us any Doctrine, or to recommend to us any one Virtue, when they have thus given up all Virtue and Truth, and every Blessing that Life affords? For there is no Evil, Misery, and Wickedness, which arbitrary Monarchies do not produce, and must produce; nor do they, nor can they, produce any certain, general, or diffusive Good.

I have shewn, in my last, that an arbitrary Prince cannot protect his People if he would; and I add here, that he dares not. It would disgust the Instruments of his Power, and the Sharers in his Oppression, who will consider the Property of the People as the Perquisites of their Office, and claim a Privilege of being little Tyrants, for making him a great one: So that every Kindness to his Subjects will be a Grievance to his Servants; and he must assert and exercise his Tyranny to the Height for their sakes, or they will do it for him. And the Instances are rare, if any, of any absolute Monarch's protecting in earnest his People against the Depredations of his Ministers and Soldiers, but it has cost him his Life; as may be shewn by many Examples in the *Roman* History: For this the Emperor *Pertinax* was murdered, and so was *Galba*.[2]

Machiavel has told us, that it is impossible for such a Prince to please both the People and his Soldiers: The one will not be satisfied without Protection, nor the other without Rapine: To comply with the People, he must give up his Power; to comply with his Soldiers, he must give up his People. So that to continue what he is, and to preserve himself from the Violence of his Followers, he must countenance all their Villainies and Oppression, and be himself no more than an Imperial Thief at the Head of a Band of Thieves; for which Character he is generally well qualified by the base and cruel Maxims of that Sort of Power, and by the vile Education always given to such a Prince by the worst and most infamous of all Men, their supple and lying Sycophants.

Even the Christian Religion can do but little or no Good in Lands of Tyranny, since Miracles have ceased; but is made to do infinite Harm, by being corrupted and perverted into a deadly Engine in the Hands of a Tyrant and his Impostors, to rivet his Subjects Chains, and to confirm them thorough Wretches, Slaves, and Ignorants. I cannot indeed say, that they have the Christian Religion at all amongst them, but only use

---

[2] The two were Roman Emperors. Galba took part in the uprising which overthrew Nero. He made the mistake of being thrifty in his gifts to the army and was overthrown himself and slain by the Praetorian Guard after a very brief reign in A.D. 68–69. Pertinax suffered the same fate after three months of rule (A.D. 193) and for much the same reason, his failure to make sufficient gifts to the soldiers, and, in addition, for his hints of reforms to come.

its amiable Name to countenance abominable Falshoods, Non-sense, and heavy Oppression; to defend furious and implacable Bigotry, which is the direct Characteristick and Spirit of *Mahometism,* and destroys the very Genius and first Principles of Christianity. All this will be further shewn hereafter. I shall conclude with observing, that arbitrary Monarchy is a constant War upon Heaven and Earth, against the Souls as well as Bodies and Properties of Men.

G   *I am, &c.*

SATURDAY, FEBRUARY 3, 1721.

Trade and Naval Power the Offspring of Civil Liberty only, and cannot subsist without it.

SIR,

I Have in former Letters begun to shew, by an Induction of Particulars, and shall hereafter more fully shew, that Population, Riches, true Religion, Virtue, Magnanimity, Arts, Sciences, and Learning, are the necessary Effects and Productions of Liberty; and shall spend this Paper in proving, that an extensive Trade, Navigation, and Naval Power, entirely flow from the same Source: In this Case, if natural Advantage and Encouragements be wanting, Art, Expence, and Violence, are lost and thrown away. Nothing is more certain, than that Trade cannot be forced; she is a coy and humorous Dame, who must be won by Flattery and Allurements, and always flies Force and Power; she is not confined to Nations, Sects, or Climates, but travels and wanders about the Earth, till she fixes her Residence where she finds the best Welcome and kindest Reception; her Contexture is so nice and delicate, that she cannot breathe in a tyrannical Air; Will and Pleasure are so opposite to her Nature, that but touch her with the Sword, and she dies: But if you give her gentle and kind Entertainment, she is a grateful and beneficent Mistress; she will turn Deserts into fruitful Fields, Villages into great Cities, Cottages into Palaces, Beggars into Princes, convert Cowards into Heroes, Blockheads into Philosophers; will change the Coverings of little Worms into the richest Brocades, the Fleeces of harmless Sheep into the Pride and Ornaments of Kings, and by a further Metamorphosis will transmute them again into armed Hosts and haughty Fleets.

Now it is absolutely impossible, from the Nature of an arbitrary Government, that she should enjoy Security and Protection, or indeed be free from Violence, under it. There is not One Man in a Thousand that has the Endowments and Abilities necessary to govern a State, and much fewer yet that have just Notions how to make Trade and Commerce useful and advantageous to it; and, amongst these, it is rare to find one who will forego all personal Advantages, and devote himself and his Labours wholly to his Country's Interest: But if such a Phoenix should arise in any Country, he will find it hard to get Access to an arbitrary Court, and much harder yet to grapple with and stem the raging Corruptions in it, where Virtue has nothing to do, and Vice rides triumphant; where Bribery, servile Flattery, blind Submission, riotous Expence, and very often Lust and unnatural Prostitutions, are the Ladders to Greatness; which will certainly be supported by the same Methods by which it is obtained.

What has a virtuous Man to do, or what can he do, in such Company? If he pity the People's Calamities, he shall be called seditious; if he recommend any publick Good, he shall be called preaching Fool; if he should live soberly and virtuously himself, they will think him fit only to be sent to a Cloyster; if he do not flatter the Prince and his Superiors, he will be thought to envy their Prosperity; if he presume to advise his Prince to pursue his true Interest, he will be esteemed a formidable Enemy to the whole Court, who will unite to destroy him: In fine, his Virtues will be Crimes, Reproaches, and of dangerous Consequence to those who have none. As Jails pick up all the little pilfering Rogues of a Country, so such Courts engross all the great Ones; who have no Business there but to grow rich, and to riot upon the publick Calamities, to use all the Means of Oppression and Rapine, to make hasty Fortunes before the Bow-string overtakes them, or a sudden Favourite supplants them.

Now what Encouragement or Security can Trade and Industry receive from such a Crew of Banditti? No Privileges and Immunities, or even Protection, can be obtained but for Money, and are always granted to such who give most; and these again shall be curtailed, altered, abrogated, and cancelled, upon the Change of a Minister, or of his Inclinations, Interest, and Caprices: Monopolies, exclusive Companies, Liberties of Pre-emption, &c. shall be obtained for Bribes or Favour, or in Trust for Great Men, or vile and worthless Women. Some Merchants shall be openly encouraged and protected, and get Exemptions from Searches and Duties, or shall be connived at in escaping them; others shall be burthened, oppressed, manacled, stopped, and delayed, to extort Presents, to wreak Revenge, or to give Preference of Markets to Favourites. Governors of Port-Towns, or of Colonies, who have purchased their Employments at Court, shall be indulged and countenanced in making Reprisals upon the Traders, and to enable them to satisfy the yearly Presents due to Minions: Admirals and Commanders of Men of War shall press their Sailors, to be paid for not doing it; and Military Officers and Soldiers shall molest and interrupt them in the Course of their Commerce and honest Industry.

Nor shall it be in the Power of the most vigilant, active and virtuous Prince, to prevent these and a Thousand other daily

Oppressions; he must see with his Ministers Eyes, and hear with their Ears; nor can there be any Access to him but by their Means, and by their Leave: Constant Spies shall watch and observe the first Intentions, or least Approaches to a Complaint; and the Person injured shall be threatened, way-laid, imprisoned, perhaps murdered; but if he escape all their Treacheries, and can get to the Ear of his Prince, it is great odds but he will be treated and punished as a Calumniator, a false Accuser, and a seditious Disturber of his Majesty's Government: No Witness will dare to appear for him, many false ones will be suborned against him; and the whole Posse of Ministers, Officers, Favourites, Parasites, Pathicks, Strumpets, Buffoons, Fidlers, and Pimps, will conspire to ruin him, as a common Enemy to their common Interests.

But if all these Mischiefs could be avoided, the Necessities of such a Prince, arising from the Profusion and vast Expence of his Court, from his foolish Wars, and the Depredations, Embezzlements, and various Thefts of his Ministers and Servants, will be always calling for new Supplies, for new Extortions, which must be raised by all the Means by which they can be raised: New and sudden Impositions shall be put upon Trade, new Loans be exacted from Merchants; Commodities of general use shall be bought up by the Prince's Order, perhaps upon Trust, and afterwards retailed again at extravagant Advantages: Merchants shall be encouraged to import their Goods, upon Promises of easy and gentle Usage; these Goods when imported shall be subjected to exorbitant Impositions and Customs, perhaps confiscated upon frivolous Pretences. But if these, and infinite other Oppressions, could be prevented for some time, by the Vigilance of a wise Prince, or the Care of an able Minister; yet there can be no probable Security, or even Hopes of the Continuance of honest and prudent Measures in such a Government: For One wise Prince so educated, there will be Twenty foolish ones; and for One honest Minister, there will be a Thousand corrupt ones.

Under such natural Disadvantages, perpetual Uncertainties, or rather certain Oppressions, no Men will embark large Stocks and extensive Talents for Business, breed up their Children to precarious Employments, build Forts, or plant Colonies, when the Breath of a weak Prince, or the Caprice of a corrupt Favourite, shall dash at once all their Labours and their Hopes; and therefore it is impossible that any Trade can subsist long in such a Government, but what is necessary to support the Luxury and Vices of a Court; and even such Trade is, for the most part, carried on by the Stocks, and for the Advantage of free Countries, and their own petty Merchants are only Factors to the others. True Merchants are Citizens of the World, and that is their Country where they can live best and most secure; and whatever they can pick up and gather together in tyrannical Governments, they remove to free ones. *Tavernier*[1] invested all the Riches he had amassed by his long Ramble over the World, in the barren Rocks of *Switzerland:* And being asked by the last King of *France*, how it came to pass that he, who had seen the finest Countries on the Globe, came to lay out his Fortune in the worst? He gave his haughty Majesty this short Answer, That he was willing to have something which he could call his own.

As I think it is evident, by what I have said before, that Trade cannot long subsist, much less flourish, in arbitrary Governments; so there is so close and inseparable a Connexion between that and Naval Power, that I dare boldly affirm, that the latter can never arrive to any formidable Height, and continue long in that Situation, under such a State. Where there is an extensive Trade; great Numbers of able-bodied and courageous Sailors, Men bred up to Fatigues, Hardships, and Hazards, and consequently Soldiers by Profession, are kept in constant Pay; not only without any Charge to the Publick, but

---

[1] Jean Baptiste Tavernier (1605–1689) was a French merchant, whose business carried him through Turkey, Persia, central Asia, and the East Indies. His *Voyages* were first published in 1676–1679.

greatly to its Benefit; not only by daily adding to its Wealth and Power, but by venting and employing Abroad, to their Country's Honour and Safety, those turbulent and unruly Spirits that would be Fuel for Factions, and the Tools and Instruments of ambitious or discontented Great Men at Home. These Men are always ready at their Country's Call, to defend the Profession which they live by, and with it the publick Happiness: They are, and ever must be, in the publick Interest, with which their own is so closely united; for they subsist by exporting the Productions of the People's Industry, which they constantly increase by so doing: They receive their Pay from the Merchants, a Sort of Men always in the Interests of Liberty, from which alone they can receive Protection and Encouragement. And as this Race of Men contribute vastly to the publick Security and Wealth, so they take nothing from it: They are not quartered up and down their native Country, like the Bands of despotick Princes, to oppress their Subjects, interrupt their Industry, debauch their Wives and Daughters, insult their Persons, to be Examples of Lewdness and Prodigality, and to be always ready at Hand to execute the bloody Commands of a Tyrant.

No Monarch was ever yet powerful enough to keep as many Seamen in constant Pay at his own Expence, as single Cities have been able to do without any at all: The Pay of a Sailor, with his Provision, is equal to that of a Trooper in arbitrary Governments; nor can they learn their Trade, by taking the Sea-Air for a few Summer Months, and wafting about the Coasts of their own Country: They gain Experience and Boldness, by various and difficult Voyages, by being constantly inured to Hardships and Dangers. Nor is it possible for single Princes, with all their Power and Vigilance, to have such regular Supplies of Naval Provisions, as trading Countries must have always in Store. There must be a regular and constant Intercourse with the Nations from whom these Supplies come; a certain and regular Method of paying for them; and constant

Demands will produce constant Supplies. There are always numerous Magazines in the Hands of private Merchants, ready for their own Use or Sale. There must be great Numbers of Shipwrights, Anchor Smiths, Rope and Sail-Makers, and infinite other Artificers, sure always of constant Employment; and who, if they are oppressed by one Master, may go to another. There must be Numbers of Ships used for Trade, that, upon Occasions, may be employed for Men of War, for Transports, for Fireships, and Tenders. Now all these Things, or scarce any of them, can ever be brought about by arbitrary Courts; Stores will be embezzled, exhausted, and worn out, before new ones are supplied; Payments will not be punctually made; Artificers will be discouraged, oppressed, and often left without Employ: Every thing will be done at an exorbitant Expence, and often not done when it is paid for; and when Payments are made, the greatest Part shall go in Fees, or for Bribes, or in secret Trusts.

For these Reasons, and many others, despotick Monarchs, though infinitely powerful at Land, yet could never rival *Neptune,* and extend their Empire over the liquid World; for though great and vigorous Efforts have been often made by these haughty Tyrants of Mankind, to subject that Element to their Ambition and their Power, being taught by woful Experience, arising from perpetual Losses and Disappointments, of what vast Importance that Dominion was to unlimited and universal Sovereignty; yet all their Riches, Application, and Pride, have never been able, in one Instance, to effect it. Sometimes, indeed, Trade, like a Phantom, has made a faint Appearance at an arbitrary Court, but disappeared again at the first Approach of the Morning Light: She is the Portion of free States, is married to Liberty, and ever flies the foul and polluted Embraces of a Tyrant. . . .

T   *I am, &c.*

Number 65.

SATURDAY, FEBRUARY 10, 1721.

Military Virtue produced and supported by Civil Liberty only.

SIR,

I Have shewn in my last, that Trade and Naval Power are produced by Liberty only; and shall shew in this, that Military Virtue can proceed from nothing else, as I have in a good measure shewn already.

In free Countries, as People work for themselves, so they fight for themselves: But in arbitrary Countries, it is all one to the People, in Point of Interest, who conquers them; they cannot be worse used; and when a Tyrant's Army is beaten, his Country is conquered: He has no Resource; his Subjects having neither Arms, nor Courage, nor Reason to fight for him: He has no Support but his standing Forces; who, for enabling him to oppress, are Sharers in his Oppression; and fighting for themselves while they fight for him, do sometimes fight well: But his poor People, who are oppressed by him, can have no other Concern for his Fate, than to wish him the worst.

In Attacks upon a free State, every Man will fight to defend it, because every Man has something to defend in it. He is in love with his Condition, his Ease, and Property, and will venture his Life rather than lose them; because with them he loses all the Blessings of Life. When these Blessings are gone, it is Madness to think that any Man will spill his Blood for him who took them away, and is doubtless his Enemy, though he may call himself his Prince. It is much more natural to wish his Destruction, and help to procure it.

For these Reasons, small free States have conquered the greatest Princes; and the greatest Princes have never been able to conquer free States, but either by surprizing them basely, or by corrupting them, or by Forces almost infinitely superior, or when they were distracted and weakened by domestick Divisions and Treachery. . . .

The only dreadful Foes which the *Romans* ever found, were People as free as themselves; and the most dreadful of all were the *Carthaginians. Hannibal* alone beat them oftener, and slew more of their Men in Battle, than all the Kings in the World ever did, or could do. But for all the great and repeated Defeats which he gave them; though he had destroyed Two Hundred Thousand of their Men, and many of their excellent Commanders; though, at the same Time, their Armies were cut off in *Spain,* and with them the two brave *Scipios;* and though they had suffered great Losses in Sicily, and at Sea, yet they never sunk nor wanted Soldiers, nor their Soldiers Courage; and as to great Commanders, they had more and better than ever they had before: And having conquered *Hannibal,* they quickly conquered the World.

This vast Virtue of theirs, and this unconquerable Spirit, was not owing to Climate or Complexion, but to Liberty alone, and to the Equality of their Government, in which every *Roman* had a Share: They were nursed up in the Principles of Liberty; in their Infancy they were instructed to love it; Experience afterwards confirmed their Affections, and shewed them its glorious Advantages: Their own happy Condition taught them a Contempt and Indignation for those wretched and barbarous Governments, which could neither afford their Subjects Happiness nor Protection: And when they attacked such Governments and their wretched People, they found themselves like Lions amongst Sheep.

It is therefore Government alone that makes Men cowardly or brave: And *Boccalini*[1] well ridicules the absurd Complaint

---

[1] Traiano Boccalini (1556–1613) was an Italian satirist. His *The New Found Politicke,* which discussed, among other subjects, relations of Protestants and Papists, appeared in English in 1626; his *Advertisements from Parnassus* were translated and published at least three times in the period of Trenchard and Gordon's activity.

of the Princes of his Time, that their Subjects wanted that
Love for their Country which was found in free States, when
he makes *Apollo* tell them, that no People were ever in Love
with Rapine, Fraud, and Oppression; that they must mend
their own Administration, and their People's Condition; and
that People will then love their Country, when they live happily in it. The old *Romans* were Masters of Mankind; but the
present Race of People in *Rome* are not a Match for one of
the *Swiss* Cantons; nor could these Cantons ever be conquered,
even by the united Forces of the House of *Austria. Charles*
Duke of *Burgundy* was the last that durst invade them; but
though he had been long a Terror and constant Rival to *Louis*
the Eleventh of *France*, a crafty, politick, and powerful Monarch, and often too hard for him; he paid dear for his Bravery
in attacking the *Switzers*, and lost by doing it Three Armies,
and his own Life.[2] They were a free People, and fought in their
own Quarrel; the greatest Incitement upon Earth to Boldness
and Magnanimity. The *Switzers* had a Property, though in
Rocks; and were Freemen, though amongst Mountains. This
gives them the Figure which they make in *Europe;* such a
Figure, that they are courted by the greatest Princes in it, and
have supported some of them in their Wars, when their own
native Slaves could not support them.

The *Dutch*, having revolted from the greatest Potentate then
in *Europe*,[3] defended themselves against all his Power for near

---

[2] Charles the Bold (1433–1477), Duke of Burgundy, was the bitter enemy of Louis XI of France (1423–1483). Charles's defeat and death led to
the later lapsing of the title to Burgundy to the King of France. Charles was
twice badly defeated by the Swiss in 1476.

[3] Trenchard and Gordon here describe the long and ultimately successful effort of the Netherlands to gain independence from Spain. The Dutch
began their uprising against Phillip II in 1567. While their independence
was virtually recognized by the Twelve Years' Truce with Spain in 1609, it
was not officially established until the Treaty of Westphalia in 1648. This
late recognition is the basis for Trenchard and Gordon's references to "near
a Hundred Years" of Dutch resistance to the Spanish.

a Hundred Years, and grew rich all the Time, while he grew poor; so poor, that *Spain* has never yet recovered its Losses in that War: A[n]d though they are in their Constitution more formed for Trade than War, yet their own Bravery in their own Defence is astonishing to those that know not what the Spirit of Liberty can do in any People: Even their Women joined to defend their Walls; as the Women of *Sparta* once did, and as the Women of *Barcelona* more lately did, though the united Force of the Two Monarchies of *France* and *Spain* had at last the Honour to take that City, especially when We, who had engaged them in the War, had also given them up.[4]

These same *Dutch* in that War, when they were closely besieged in one of their Towns by the *Spanish* Army, let in the Sea upon their Country, trusting rather to the Mercy of that Element, than to the Mercy of an invading Tyrant; and the Sea saved them. It must be remembered too, that they had the Power of the Emperor, as well as that of *Spain,* to contend with; both these mighty Monarchs having joined their Counsels and Arms to subdue Seven little Provinces, which yet they never were able to subdue: The City of *Ostend* alone cost them a Three Years Siege, and an Hundred and Thirty Thousand Men; and when they took it, they only took a Heap of Rubbish, to which it was reduced before it was surrendered.

In free States, every Man being a Soldier, or quickly made so, they improve in a War, and every Campaign fight better and better. Whereas the Armies of an absolute Prince grow every Campaign worse; especially if they be composed of his own Subjects, who, being Slaves, are with great Difficulty and long Discipline made Soldiers, and scarce ever made good ones;

---

[4] The incident at Barcelona occurred during the War of the Spanish Succession (1701–1714), in which the English opposed the succession of a member of the Bourbon family to the throne of Spain. England and Holland made peace with the new Bourbon monarch in 1713, leaving Austria to carry on the conflict. Thus deserted, the Austrians continued the war until May of 1714, and Barcelona continued its opposition even longer, until it was finally forced to capitulate in September of that year.

and when his old Troops are gone, his new ones signify little. This was eminently shewn in the late War with *France,* which degenerated in Arms every Year; while the *English* and *Dutch* did as evidently mend.[5] And doubtless, if the *French* Barrier of fortified Towns had been quite broken through, as it was very near, One Battle would have completed the Conquest of *France,* and perhaps it would not have cost a Battle.

And if free States support themselves better in a War than an absolute Prince, they do likewise much sooner retrieve their Losses by it. The *Dutch,* when they had been beaten twice at Sea by *Cromwell's* Admirals and *English* Seamen, with great Slaughter and Loss of ships, did nothwithstanding, in Two Months Time, after the second great Defeat, fit out a Third Fleet of a Hundred and Forty Men of War, under the famous *Van Trump:* Upon this Lord *Clarendon* observes, that "there cannot be a greater Instance of the Opulency of that People, than that they should be able, after so many Losses, and so late a great Defeat, in so short a Time, to set out a Fleet strong enough to visit those who had so lately overcome them."[6] This is what no arbitrary Prince in *Europe,* or upon the Face of the Earth, could have done; nor do I believe, that all the arbitrary Monarchs in *Europe, Africa,* and *Asia,* with all their united Powers together, could do it at this Day. The whole Strength of the *Spanish* Monarchy could not fit out their famous *Armada,* without the Assistance of Money from the little free State of *Genoa;* and that invincible *Armada,* being beaten by

---

[5] Trenchard and Gordon again describe the War of the Spanish Succession, in which the English armies enjoyed notable successes under the leadership of the Duke of Marlborough.

[6] Edward Hyde, First Earl of Clarendon (1609–1674), served as Lord Chancellor under Charles II from 1660 to 1667. He was then impeached and banished by Parliament. His name was somewhat inaccurately attached to the Clarendon Code, a series of enactments designed to suppress Protestant dissent and firmly re-establish the Church of England. His writings include the famous *History of the Rebellion* and the *Life of Edward, Earl of Clarendon.* The quotation refers to the events of 1653 during the First Anglo-Dutch War and may be found in the *History,* Book XIV, 29.

the *English*, and quite destroyed, *Spain* has never been able, with all her *Indies*, and her Mountains of Silver and Gold, to make any Figure at Sea since, nor been able to pay that very Money which equipped that its last great Fleet. . . .

From the Moment that the *Romans* lost their Liberty, their Spirit was gone, and their Valour scarce ever after appeared. In the Beginning of *Augustus*'s Reign, the best and bravest of them perished by the Sword, either in the Civil War, where, *Romans* fighting against *Romans*, Multitudes were slain, with *Brutus* and *Cassius*, the last brave Men that ever drew a Sword for the Commonwealth; or in the bloody Proscriptions that followed, in which all the excellent Men and Assertors of Liberty, who escaped the Battle, were gleaned up and murdered by Soldiers and Informers, and, amongst the rest, the divine *Cicero*.[7] Afterwards, when *Augustus* had got the World to himself, *jura omnium in se traxit;*[8] Flatterers were his only Favourites, and none were preferred to Magistracy, but the servile Creatures of his Power; Liberty was extinct, and its Spirit gone; and though there was a universal Peace, yet the Power of the Empire continually decayed. *Augustus* himself was so sensible of this, that the Loss of two or three Legions under *Varus* in *Germany*,[9] frightened him, and had almost broke his Heart; not from any Tenderness in it, for he had butchered Myriads, and enslaved all; but he knew that now *Roman* Legions were hard to be got, and scarce worth getting. Having destroyed so many brave *Romans*, and made

---

[7] The adjective attached to the name of Cicero indicated once again the feeling of Trenchard and Gordon toward the heroes of the Roman Republic, those who had resisted the overthrow of the constitution by Caesar and his successors. As Cato himself had died after his resistance to Caesar, so Cicero was slain because of his opposition to Antony and Octavius.

[8] The phrase may be roughly translated, when "he had drawn all authority to himself."

[9] Publius Quinctilius Varus was attacked by surprise in a German forest in A.D. 9. His three legions were exterminated and he committed suicide in the course of the battle.

the rest base by Slavery, and by the Corruptions which support it, he knew the Difficulty of forming a *Roman* Army.

His Successors were worse; they went on in a perpetual Series of Slaughters, dreading and destroying every Thing that had the Appearance of Virtue or Goodness; and even so early as *Tiberius*'s Reign, That Emperor, says *Tacitus*, knew *magis fama quam vi stare res suas*,[10] that his Empire was supported more by the Reputation of *Roman* Greatness, than by the real Strength of the *Romans*, who grew every Day more and more weak and wretched; and though they had now and then a little Sun-shine in the Reign of a good Emperor, yet the Root of the Evil remained: They were no longer Freemen, and for far the most part, their Government was nothing else but a constant State of Oppression, and a continual Succession of Massacres. Tyrants governed them, and Soldiers created and governed the Tyrants, or butchered them if they would not be Butchers.

As to Military Virtue, it was no more: The Praetorian Bands were only a Band of Hangmen with an Emperor at their Head; *Italy* and the Provinces were exhausted; the *Roman* People were nothing but an idle and debauched Mob, that cared not who was uppermost, so they had but a little Victuals, and saw Shews: The provincial Armies were foreign Hirelings, and there was not a *Roman* Army in the *Roman* Empire. *Inops Italia, plebs urbana imbellis nihil in exercitibus validum praeter externum.*[11] This was said not long after the Death of *Augustus;* nor

[10] The phrase comes from Tacitus, *Annals* VI. 30, and may be rendered: "His fortunes stood more by prestige than by real strength." In context, the phrase refers more to the fortunes of Tiberius than those of the Empire and it serves as an example of the relatively loose way in which Gordon, in particular, borrowed Latin quotations.

[11] This is another very free rendering of Tacitus. In *Annals* III. 40, there appears the following line: "*Egregium resumendae libertati tempus, si ipsi florentes quam inops Italia, quam inbellis urbana plebes, nihil validum in exercitibus nisi quod externum, cogitarent.*" ("... It was an unequaled opportunity for regaining their independence; they had only to look from their own resources to the poverty of Italy, the unwarlike city population, the feebleness of the armies except for the leavening of foreigners.") Tacitus thus describes the background of a rebellion which occurred in Gaul in A.D. 21, just seven years after the death of Augustus.

do I remember an Instance of one great *Roman* Captain after *Germanicus* and *Corbulo;*[12] the first murdered by *Tiberius,* his Uncle and Father by Adoption; and the other by *Nero,* for whom he reconquered and settled the *East;* and after *Vespasian* and *Titus,*[13] every *Roman* Emperor of remarkable Bravery was a Foreigner, and every Victory gained by them, was gained by Foreigners; who, being all Mercenaries, were perpetually setting up and pulling down their own Monarchs. At length, being possessed of the whole Power of the Empire, they took it to themselves; and thus it ended, and became dismembered by several Nations, and into several Governments, according to their Fortune; and it is remarkable, that though those Nations had frequent Wars amongst themselves about the Countries which they invaded, yet they had nothing to apprehend from the *Romans* while they were seizing *Roman* Provinces.

Tyrants are so sensible, that when they have lost their Army, they have lost all, that amongst their other destructive Expedients to preserve themselves, whatever becomes of their People, one of their Methods is, to lay whole Countries waste, and to keep them waste, to prevent an Invader from subsisting; and their best Provinces are by this Means turned often into Wildernesses. For this Reason a March to *Constantinople* is scarce practicable to an Enemy from any Quarter.

I will conclude with answering an Objection: It may be said, that the Armies of Tyrants often fight bravely, and are brave; and I own it to be true in many instances; But I desire it may be remembered, that in arbitrary Countries nothing flourishes

[12] Germanicus Julius Caesar (15 B.C.–A.D. 19) was a successful general and adopted son of the Emperor Tiberius. He died under mysterious circumstances, convinced that he had been poisoned by the Governor of Syria. Gnaeus Domitius Corbulo (d. A.D. 67), a successful and popular general, was ordered to commit suicide by the Emperor Nero.

[13] On Titus, see *Letter* 24, note 6, p. 67. Titus Flavius Vespasianus (Vespasian) was Emperor from A.D. 69 to 79, and father of the Emperor Titus. He led the Empire in a period of recovery from the excesses of Nero and helped to rebuild the economy and the fiscal structure of the Roman administration. He also brought temporary peace to the borders of his realm.

except the Court and the Army. A Tyrant must give his Spoilers Part of the Spoil, or else they will fight but faintly for it, or perhaps put him to Death if he do not. The most absolute Princes must therefore use their Soldiers like Freemen, as they tender their own Power and their Lives; and under the greatest Tyrants the Men of War enjoy great Privileges, even greater than in free States. The Privileges and Immunities which they enjoy, constitute a Sort of Liberty, dear to themselves, but terrible always to the Subject, and often pernicious to the Prince: It being the certain Condition of a Tyrant, that to be able to oppress his People, or plague his Neighbours, he must empower his Soldiers to destroy himself.

The chief Forces therefore of an arbitrary Prince consist of Freemen: Such were the Praetorian Bands of the *Roman* Emperors, and such are the *Turkish* Janizaries; and both of them, though they maintained the Tyranny, have frequently killed the Tyrants; and such are the Grand Seignior's *Zaims, Timariots*,[14] or Horsemen, who have Lands given them in the Provinces, and are the only Nobility and Gentry there: And such too were the *Mamalukes* of *Egypt*, which Country at last they usurped for themselves, haveing put the King their Master to Death. I might mention here the *Swiss* Guards, and *Gens d'Armes* of a neighbouring Prince, which are his Janizaries. As to the *Turkish* Janizaries, I own the Sultan may put particular Men of them to Death, but no Sultan dares touch their Privileges as a Body; and two or three of their greatest Emperors were deposed and destroyed by them for attempting it.

Mere Slaves can defend no Prince, nor enable him even to rule over Slaves: So that by giving Liberty, or rather Licentiousness, to a Few, the Slavery of All is maintained.

All this does, I think, fully prove, that where there is no

---

[14] Gordon refers here to the Turkish feudal system of dividing conquered lands. The lands were held on the basis of military service and classified as "Ziamets" or "Timars." A "Zaim" was master of a Ziamet.

Liberty, there can be no Magnanimity. It is true, Enthusiasm has inspired Armies, and most remarkably of all the *Saracen* Armies, with amazing Resolution and Fury; but even that was Fierceness for Liberty of Opinion to themselves, and for subduing all Men to it; and besides, this Courage of Enthusiasm is rarely eminent, except in the first Rise of States and Empires.

G   *I am, &c.*

Number 66.

SATURDAY, FEBRUARY 17, 1721.

Arbitrary Government proved incompatible with true Religion, whether Natural or Revealed.

SIR,

I SHALL shew, in this Paper, that neither the Christian Religion, nor Natural Religion, nor any Thing else that ought to be called Religion, can subsist under tyrannical Governments, now that Miracles are ceased. I readily confess, that such Governments are fertile in Superstition, in wild Whimsies, delusive Phantoms, and ridiculous Dreams; proper to terrify the human Soul, degrade its Dignity, deface its Beauty, and fetter it with slavish and unmanly Fears, to render it a proper Object of Fraud, Grimace, and Imposition; and to make Mankind the ready Dupes of gloomy Impostors, and the tame Slaves of raging Tyrants. For, Servitude established in the Mind, is best established.

But all these bewildered Imaginations, these dark and dreadful Horrors, which banish Reason, and contract and imbitter the Heart, what have they to do with true Religion, unless to destroy it? —That Religion, which improves and enlarges the Faculties of Men, exalts their Spirits, and makes them brave for God and themselves; that Religion, which gives them great and worthy Conceptions of the Deity; and that Religion which inspires them with generous and beneficent Affections to one another, and with universal Love and Benevolence to the whole Creation? No Man can love God, if he love not his Neighbour; and whoever loves his Neighbour, will neither injure, revile, nor oppress him: Nor can we otherwise shew our Love to God, than by kind, humane, and affectionate Actions to his Creatures: *A new Commandment,* says our blessed Saviour, *I give unto you, that ye love one another.*

Almighty God, the great Author of our Nature, and of all Things, who has the Heavens for his Throne, and the Earth for his Footstool, is raised far above the Reach of our Kindness, our Malice, or our Flattery. He derives infinite Happiness from his own infinite Perfections; nor can any frail power or Actions of ours lessen or improve it: Religion therefore, from which he can reap no Advantage, was instituted by him for the Sake of Men, as the best Means and the strongest Motive to their own Happiness, and mutual Happiness; and by it Men are taught and animated to be useful, assisting, forgiving, kind and merciful one to another. But to hurt, calumniate, or hate one another, for his Sake, and in Defence of any Religion, is a flat Contradiction to *his* Religion, and an open Defiance to the Author of Religion: And to quarrel about Belief and Opinions, which do not immediately and necessarily produce practical Virtue and social Duties, is equally wicked and absurd. This is to be wicked in behalf of Righteousness, and to be cruel out of Piety. A Religion which begets Selfishness and Partiality only to a few, and its own Followers, and which inspires Hatred and Outrage towards all the rest of the World, can never be the Religion of the merciful and impartial Maker and Judge of the World. Speculations are only so far a Part of Religion, as they produce the moral Duties of Religion, general Peace, and unlimited

Charity, publick Spirit, Equity, Forbearance, and good Deeds
to all Men: And the Worship of God is no longer the Worship
of God, than as it warms our Minds with the Remembrance of
his gracious Condescensions, his indulgent Care, Bounty, and
Providence, exercised towards us; and as it raises and forms
our Affections to an Imitation of such his divine and unrestrained Goodness, and to use one another kindly by his great
Example, who uses us all so. So that our worthy, tender, and
beneficent Behaviour to one another, is the best Way to
acknowledge his to us: It is the most acceptable Way that we
can worship him, and the Way which he will best accept our
Worship: And whatever Devotion has not this Effect, or a contrary Effect, is the dry or mad Freaks of an Enthusiast, and
ought to be called by another and a properer Name.

This is a General Idea of true Religion; these are the certain
and only Marks of it: All which, as they are opposite to the
Essence and Spirit of an arbitrary Government; so every arbitrary Government is an Enemy to the Spirit of true Religion,
and defeats its Ends. In these Governments, in Defiance of
Religion, Humanity, and common Sense, Millions must be
miserable to exalt and embellish One or a Few, and to make
them proud, arrogant, and great: Protection and Security are
no more; the Spirit of the People is sunk, their Industry discouraged and lost, or only employed to feed Luxury and Pride;
and Multitudes starve, that a few may riot and abound. All
Love to Mankind is extinct, and Virtue and publick Spirit are
dangerous or unknown; while Vice, Falshood, and servile
Sycophancy, become necessary to maintain precarious Safety
and an ignominious Life: And, in fine, Men live upon the Spoils
of one another, like ravenous Fishes and Beasts of Prey: They
become rapacious, brutish, and savage to one another, as their
cruel Governors are to them all; and, as a further Imitation of
such Masters, their Souls are abject, mean, and villainous. To
live upon Prey, and worry human Race, is the Genius and
Support of Tyrants, as well as of Wolves and Tygers; and it is

the Spirit and Practice of Men to resemble their Governors, and to act like them. Virtue and Vice, in Courts, run like Water in a continual Descent, and quickly overflow the inferior Soil.

Torva Leaena lupum, &c.[1]

Now, what can be found here to answer the Spirit and Precepts of the Christian Religion, which is all Love, Charity, Meekness, mutual Assistance, and mutual Indulgence; and must either destroy Tyranny, which destroys all these, or be destroyed by it? A Religion given by God, to inspire Men with every social Virtue, and to furnish them with every Argument for social Happiness, will never find Quarter, much less Protection, from a Government, which subsists by an unrelenting War against every Virtue, and all human Felicity. On the contrary, all its divine Doctrines shall be perverted, all its divine Principles mangled, and both its Principles and its Precepts corrupted, disguised, and wrested, to be made free of the Court: Truth will be made to patronize Imposture, and Meekness to support Tyranny: Obedience to equal Laws, and Submission to just Authority, shall be turned into a servile and crouching Subjection to blind Rage and inhuman Fury; complaisant and respective Behaviour into slavish Flattery, and supple Homage to Power; Meekness and Humility into Dejection, Poorness of Spirit, and bodily Prostrations; Charity, Benevolence, and Humanity, into a fiery and outrageous Zeal to propagate fashionable and gainful Opinions: Christian Courage shall be changed into Cruelty and brutish Violence; impartial Justice into savage Severity; Protection into Oppression and Plundering; the Fear of God into the Fear of Man; and the Worship of the Deity into an idolatrous Adoration of a Tyrant.

---

[1] The quotation comes from Virgil, *Ecloga* II. 63–64:
Torva leaena lupum sequitur; lupus ipse capillam;
Florentam cytisum sequitur lasciva capella. . . .
("The lioness follows the wolf, the wolf the she-goat, the capering goat herself the blossoming clover. . . .")

Though God Almighty sent his only Son into the World to teach his Will to Men, and to confirm his Mission by Wonders and Miracles; yet, having once fully manifested himself and his Law, he has left it to be propagated and carried on by human Means only, according to the Holy Writings inspired by Him; and if the Powers of the World will not submit to those Directions, and will neither pursue them themselves, nor suffer their Subjects to pursue them, nor leave them the Means of doing it; then the Christian Religion must take the Fate of all sublunary Things, and be lost from amongst Men, unless Heaven interpose again miraculously in its Favour. Now the Experience of all Ages will convince us, that all tyrannical Princes will be against the Religion which is against them; and either abolish it, or, which is much worse, pervert it into a deadly and unnatural Engine, to increase and defend that Pride and Power, which Christianity abhors; and to promote those Evils and Miseries, which Christianity forbids, and, were it left to itself, would prevent or relieve. A Religion modelled by usurped Power, to countenance Usurpation and Oppression, is as opposite to the Christian Religion, as Tyranny is to Liberty, and Wickedness to Virtue. When Religion is taught to speak Court-Language, and none are suffered to preach it, but such as speak the same Dialect; when those who are Ministers of the Gospel, must be also the Ministers of Ambition, and either sanctify Falsehood and Violence, by the Word of Mercy and Truth, or hold their Tongues; when Preferments and worldly Honours are on the Side of Imposture, and Galleys, Racks and Dungeons, are the Rewards of Conscience and Piety; the Good and Efficacy of Christianity will be as effectually gone, as if it were formally exchanged for *Mahometanism;* and under those Circumstances, if its Name be retained, it is only retained to do Evil, and might be as innocently banished with the Thing.

The Christian Religion has as rarely gained by Courts, as Courts have improved by the Christian Religion; and arbitrary Courts have seldom meddled with it, but either to persecute it, or debase and corrupt it; nor could the Power and Fury of Tyrants ever hurt or weaken it so much, as their pretended Favours and Countenance have done: By appearing for it, they turn their Power most effectually against it. Their avowed Persecution of Christianity, did only destroy Christians; but afterwards, while they set up for protecting none but the true Christians, that is, those that were as bad as themselves, and having no Religion of their own, adopted blindly the Religion of their Prince; and whilst they were for punishing all who were not true Christians, that is, all that were better than themselves, and would take their Religion from no Man's Word, but only from the Word of God; they listed Christians against Christians, and disfigured, and undermined, and banished Christianity itself, by false Friendship to its Professors: And these Professors thus corrupted, joining a holy Title to an impious Cause, concurred in the Conspiracy, and contended fiercely in the Name of Christ for secular Advantages, which Christ never gave nor took, and for a secular Sovereignty, which he rejected, and his Gospel forbids. Thus one Sort of Tyranny was artfully made to support another, and both by a Union of Interests maintained a War against Religion, under Colour of defending it, and fought the Author of it under his own Banner; that is, as Dr. *Tillotson* finely says, *They lied for the Truth, and killed for God's Sake.*[2]

The many various and contradictory Opinions of Weak Enthusiasts, or of designing Men, and all the different and repugnant Interpretations of Scripture, published and contended for by them, could have done but small Prejudice to Religion and Society, if human Authority had not interposed with its Penalties and Rewards annexed to the believing or not believing fortuitous Speculations, useless Notions, dry Ideas, and the inconsistent Reveries of disordered Brains; or the

---

[2] John Tillotson (1630–1694) was a noted English theologian and Archbishop of Canterbury.

selfish Inventions of usurping Popes, ambitious Synods, and turbulent and aspiring Doctors, or the crafty Schemes of discontented or oppressive Statesmen: For all these have been the important Causes, and the wicked Fuel, of religious Wars and Persecutions.

It is so much the general Interest of Society to perform and to encourage all its Members to perform the practical Duties of Religion, that if a stronger and more prevailing Interest were not thrown by Power into the contrary Scale, there would be no Difference amongst Men about the Nature and Extent of their Duties to Magistrates, to Parents, Children, and to Friends and Neighbours: And if these social Duties (the only Duties which human Society, as such, is concerned to promote) were agreed upon and practised, the Magistrate would have no more to do with their Opinions than with their Shape and Complexion; nor could he know, if he would, by what Method to alter them. No Man's Belief is in his own Power, or can be in the Power of another.

The utmost Length that the Power of the Magistrate can in this Matter extend, beyond that of Exhortation, which is in every Man's Power, can be only to make Hypocrites, Slaves, Fools, or Atheists. When he has forced his Subjects to belye their Consciences, or to act against them, he has in effect driven them out of all Religion, to bring them into his own; and when they thus see and feel the professed Defender of Religion overturning all its Precepts, exhorting by Bribes, rebuking by Stripes, Confiscations and Dungeons, and making Christianity the Instrument of Fury, Ambition, Rapine, and Tyranny; what can they think, but either that he is no Christian, or that Christianity is not true? If they come to suspect it of Imposture, they grow Infidels; if they grow into a Belief that Religion countenances Bitterness, Outrage, and Severities, nay, commands all these, they become Bigots; the worst and most mischievous Character of the Two: For, Unbelievers, guided by the Rules of Prudence or Good Nature, may be good Neighbours and inoffensive Men; but Bigotry, standing upon the Ruins of Reason, and being conducted by no Light but that of an inflamed Imagination, and a sour, bitter, and narrow Spirit, there is no Violence nor Barbarity which it is not capable of wishing or acting.

Happiness is the chief End of Man, and the saving of his Soul is his chief Happiness; so that every Man is most concerned for his own Soul, and more than any other can be: And if no Obstruction be thrown in his Way, he will for the most part do all in his Power for his own Salvation, and will certainly do it best; and when he has done all that he can, he has done all that he ought: People cannot be saved by Force; nor can all the Powers in the World together make one true Christian, or convince one Man. Conviction is the Province and Effect of Reason; when that fails, nothing but the Grace of God can supply it: And what has the Power and Penalties of Men to do either with Reason or Grace; which being both the Gifts of God, are not to be conquered by Chains, though they may be weakened, and even banished, by worldly Allurements blended with Christianity, and by the worldly Pride of its Professors?

The Methods of Power are repugnant to the Nature of Conviction, which must either be promoted by Exhortation, Kindness, Example, and Arguments, or can never be promoted at all: Violence does, on the contrary, but provoke Men, and confirm them in Error; nor will they ever be brought to believe, that those who barbarously rob them of their present Happiness, can be charitably concerned for their future.

It is evident in Fact, that most of the different religious Institutions now subsisting in the World, have been founded upon Ambition and Pride; and were advanced, propagated, and established, by Usurpation, Faction, and Oppression: They were begun for the most part by Enthusiasts, or by designing and unpreferred Churchmen; or at least occasioned by the continued Usurpations and Insults of cruel and oppressive ones, and always in Times of Faction and general Discontent. Turbulent and aspiring Men, discarded and discontented Courtiers, or ambitious and designing Statesmen, have taken Advantage from these general Disorders, or from the hot and giddy Spirits of an enthusiastical or oppressed People, and from thence have formed Parties; and setting themselves at the Head, formed National Establishments, with the Concurrence of weak Princes, sometimes in Opposition to them, by the Assistance of factious Clergymen and factious Assemblies, often by Tumults and popular Insurrections; and at last, under Pretence of saving Mens Souls, they seized their Property. A small Acquaintance with Ecclesiastical History, and the History of the *Turks* and *Saracens,* will shew such Causes as these to have given Rise to most of the National Religious Establishments upon Earth: Nor can I see how any future one can arise by other Means, whilst Violence and worldly Interest have any thing to do with them.

Such therefore as is the Government of a Country, such will be made its Religion; and no body, I hope, is now to learn what is, and ever will be, the Religion of most Statesmen; even a Religion of Power, to do as little Good and as much Mischief as they please. Nor have Churchmen, when they ruled States, had ever any other View; but having double Authority, had generally double Insolence, and remarkably less Mercy and Regard to Conscience or Property, than others who had fewer Ties to be merciful and just: And therefore the sorest Tyrants have been they, who united in one Person the Royalty and Priesthood. The Pope's Yoke is more grievous than that of any Christian Prince upon Earth; nor is there a Trace of Property, or Felicity, or of the Religion of *Jesus Christ,* found in the Dominions of this Father of *Christendom;* all is Ignorance, Bigotry, Idolatry, Barbarity, Hunger, Chains, and every Species of Misery. The *Caliphs* of *Egypt,* who founded the *Saracen* Empire there, and maintained it for a great while, were at once

Kings and Priests; and there never lived more raging Bigots, or more furious and oppressive Barbarians. The Monarchy of *Persia,* which is also a severe Tyranny, has the Priesthood annexed to it; and the *Sophy* is at the same time the *Caliph.* The *Turkish* Religion is founded on Imposture, blended with outrageous and avowed Violence; and by their Religion, the Imperial Executioner is, next to their *Alcoran,* the most sacred Thing amongst them: And though he be not himself Chief Priest, yet he creates and uncreates him at Pleasure, and is, without the Name of *Mufti,* the Chief Doctor, or rather Author of their Religion; and we all know what Sort of a Religion it is.

In Fact, as arbitrary Princes want a Religion suited to the Genius of their Power, they model their Religion so as to serve all the Purposes of Tyranny; and debase, corrupt, discourage, or persecute all Religion which is against Tyranny, as all true Religion is: For this Reason, not one of the great absolute Princes in *Europe* embraced the *Reformation,* nor would suffer his People to embrace it, but they were all bitter and professed Enemies to it: Whereas all the great free States, except *Poland,* and most of the small free States, became *Protestants.* Thus the *English, Scotch,* the *Dutch,* the *Bohemians,* and *Sweden* and *Denmark,* (which were then free Kingdoms) the greatest Part of *Swisserland,* with *Geneva,* and all the *Hans-Towns,* which were not awed by the Emperor, threw off the *Popish* Yoke: And not one of the free *Popish* States, out of *Italy,* could be ever brought to receive the *Inquisition;* and the State of *Venice,* the greatest free State there, to shew that they received it against their Will, have taken wise Care to render it ineffectual: And many of the *Popish* free States would never come into Persecution, which they knew would impoverish and dispeople them; and therefore the States of *Arragon, Valencia,* and *Catalonia,* opposed, as much as they were able, the Expulsion of the *Moors,* which was a pure Act of Regal Power, to the Undoing of *Spain;* and therefore a destructive and barbarous Act of Tyranny. As to the *Protestant* Countries, which have since lost their Liberties, there is much miserable Ignorance, and much bitter and implacable Bigotry, but little Religion, and no Charity, amongst them.

We look upon *Montezuma*, and other Tyrants, who worshipped God with human Sacrifice, as so many Monsters, and hug ourselves that we have no such Sons of *Moloch* here in *Europe;* not considering, that every Man put to Death for his Religion, by the *Inquisition* and elsewhere, is a real human Sacrifice, as it is burning and butchering Men for God's Sake.

I think no body will deny, but that in King *James*'s Time, we owed the Preservation of our Religion to our Liberties, which both our Clergy and People almost unanimously concurred to defend, with a Resolution and Boldness worthy of *Britons* and Freemen.[3] And as the Cause and Blessings of Liberty are still better understood, its Spirit and Interest daily increase. Most of the Bishops, and many of the inferior Clergy, are professedly in the Principles of Civil and Religious Liberty, notwithstanding the strong and early Prejudices of Education. And I hope soon to see them all as thorough Advocates for publick Liberty, as their Predecessors were, upon Grounds less just, in the Times of *Popery;* and then there will be an End of the pernicious and knavish Distinction of *Whig* and *Tory;* and all the World will unite in paying them that Respect which is due to their holy Office.

I shall conclude with this short Application; That as we love Religion, and the Author of it, we ought to love and preserve our Liberties.

G   *I am, &c.*

---

[3] The reference here is obviously to the brief reign of King James II (1685–1688) and to the fears raised among all Protestants by his Catholicism.

Number 67.

SATURDAY, FEBRUARY 24, 1721.

Arts and Sciences the Effects of Civil Liberty only, and ever destroyed or oppressed by Tyranny.

SIR,

Having already shewn, that Naval Trade and Power cannot subsist but in free Countries alone, I will now shew, that the same is true of domestic Arts and Sciences; and that both these, and Population, which is their constant Concomitant, and their chief Cause as well as their certain Effect, are born of Liberty, and nursed, educated, encouraged, and endowed, by Liberty alone.

Men will not spontaneously toil and labour but for their own Advantage, for their Pleasure or their Profit, and to obtain something which they want or desire, and which, for the most part, is not to be obtained but by Force or Consent. Force is often dangerous; and when employed to acquire what is not ours, it is always unjust; and therefore Men, to procure from others what they had not before, must gain their Consent; which is not to be gained, but by giving them in lieu of the Thing desired, something which they want and value more than what they part with. This is what we call Trade; which is the Exchange of one Commodity for another, or for that which purchases all Commodities, Silver and Gold.

Men, in their first State, content themselves with the spontaneous Productions of Nature, the Fruits of the Field and the liquid Stream, and such occasional Supplies as they now and then receive from the Destruction of other Animals. But when those Supplies become insufficient to support their Numbers, their next Resource is to open the Bosom of the Earth, and, by proper Application and Culture, to extort her hidden Stores:

And thus were invented Tillage and Planting. And an Hundred Men thus employed can fetch from the Bowels of our common Mother, Food and Sustenance enough for Ten Times their own Number; and one Tenth part more may possibly be able to supply all the Instruments of Husbandry, and whatever is barely necessary to support these Husbandmen: So that all the rest of the People must rob or starve, unless either the Proprietors of the Land will give them the Produce of their Estates for nothing, or they can find something wherewithal to purchase it.

Now in Countries where no other Arts are in Use, but only Husbandry and the Professions necessary to it, and to support those who are employed about it; all the other Inhabitants have no Means of purchasing Food and Raiment, but by selling their Persons, and becoming vile Slaves and Vassals to their Princes, Lords, or other Proprietors of the Land; and are obliged, for necessary Sustenance, to follow them in their wild Wars, and their personal and factious Quarrels, and to become the base Instruments of their Ambition and Pride. Great Men will rather throw their Estates into Forests and Chaces, for the Support of wild Beasts, and for their own Pleasure in hunting them, than into Farms, Gardens, and fruitful Fields, if they can get nothing from the Productions of them.

This is the forlorn Condition of Mankind, in most of the wild Empires of the *East;* this was their Condition in all the *Gothick* Governments; and this is the Condition of *Poland* and of the *Highlands* of *Scotland;* where a few have Liberty, and all the rest are Slaves. And nothing can free Mankind from this abject and forlorn Condition, but the Invention of Arts and Sciences; that is, the finding out of more Materials and Expedients to make Life easy and pleasant; and the inducing People to believe, what they will readily believe, that other Things are necessary to their Happiness, besides those which Nature has made necessary. Thus the Luxury of the Rich becomes the Bread of the Poor.

As soon as Men are freed from the Importunities of Hunger and Cold; the Thoughts and Desire of Conveniency, Plenty, Ornament, and Politeness, do presently succeed: And then follow after, in very quick Progression, Emulation, Ambition, Profusion, and the Love of Power: And all these, under proper Regulations, contribute to the Happiness, Wealth, and Security of Societies. It is natural to Men and Societies, to be setting their Wits and their Hands to work, to find out all Means to satisfy their Wants and Desires, and to enable them to live in Credit and Comfort, and to make suitable Provision that their Posterity may live so after them.

Necessity is the Mother of Invention; and so is the Opinion of Necessity. Whilst Things are in their own Nature necessary to us, or, from Custom and Fancy, made necessary; we will be turning every Thought, and trying every Method, how to come at them; and where they cannot be got by Violence and Rapine, Recourse will be had to Invention and Industry. And here is the Source of Arts and Sciences; which alone can support Multitudes of People, who will never be wanting to the Means which bring them Support.

Where-ever there is Employment for People, there will be People; and People, in most Countries, are forced, for want of other Employment, to cut the Throats of one another, or of their Neighbours; and to ramble after their Princes in all their mad Conquests, ridiculous Contentions, and other mischievous Maggots; and all to get, with great Labour, Hazard, and often with great Hunger and Slaughter, a poor, precarious, and momentary Subsistence.

And therefore whatever State gives more Encouragement to its Subjects than the neighbouring States do, and finds them more Work, and gives them greater Rewards for that Work; and by all these laudable Ways makes human Condition easier than it is elsewhere, and secures Life and Property better; that State will draw the Inhabitants from the neighbouring Countries to its own; and when they are there, they will, by being richer and safer, multiply faster. Men will naturally fly from

Danger to Security, from Poverty to Plenty, and from a Life of Misery to a Life of Felicity.

And as there will be always Industry where-ever there is Protection; so where-ever there is Industry and Labour, there will be the Silver, the Gold, the Jewels, the Power, and the Empire. It does not import who they are that have conquered, or inhabit the Countries where Silver and Gold are Natives, or who they are that toil for them in the Mines; since they will be the Possessors of the Coin, who can purchase it afterwards with the Goods and Manufactures which the Proprietors of the Mine and their People want. One Artificer in *England*, or *Holland*, can make Manufacture enough in a Week to buy as much Silver and Gold at the Mine, as a Labourer there can dig and prepare in a Month, or perhaps Two; and all the while that *Spain* and *Portugal* lessen their Inhabitants, we encrease ours: They lose their People by sending them away to dig in the Mines; and we, by making the Manufactures which they want, and the Instruments which they use, multiply ours. By this Means every Man that they send out of their Country is a Loss to it, because the Reason and Produce of their Labour goes to enrich rival Nations; whereas every Man that we send to our Plantations, adds to the Number of our Inhabitants here at Home, by maintaining so many of them employed in so many Manufactures which they take off there; besides so many Artificers in Shipping, and all the numerous Traders and Agents concerned in managing and venting the Produce of the Plantations, when it is brought hither, and in bringing it hither: So that the *English* Planters in *America*, besides maintaining themselves and Ten times as many *Negroes*, maintain likewise great Numbers of their Countrymen in *England*.[1]

---

1 This favorable reference to the American colonists should be compared with Trenchard and Gordon's fuller statements about the colonies in *Cato's Letters,* Number 106. The notion of "Ten times as many Negroes" presumably refers to the Southern and West Indian colonies and suggests the relative favor of even enlightened theorists toward the staple-producing areas.

Such are the Blessings of Liberty, and such is the Difference which it makes between Country and Country! The *Spanish* Nation lost much more by the Loss of their Liberties, followed with the Expulsion of the *Moors*, than ever they got by the Gold and Silver Mountains of *Mexico* and *Peru*, or could get by all the Mines of Gold, Silver, and Diamonds upon Earth.

Where there is Liberty, there are Encouragements to Labour, be[c]ause People labour for themselves; and no one can take from them the Acquisitions which they make by their Labour: There will be the greatest Numbers of People, because they find Employment and Protection; there will be the greatest Stocks, because most is to be got, and easiest to be got, and safest when it is got; and those Stocks will be always encreasing by a new Ac[c]ession of Money acquired elsewhere, where there is no Security of enjoying it; there People will be able to work cheapest, because less Taxes will be put upon their Work, and upon the Necessaries which must support them whilst they are about it: There People will dare to own their being rich; there will be most People bred up to Trade, and Trade and Traders will be most respected; and there the Interest of Money will be lower, and the Security of possessing it greater, than it ever can be in tyrannical Governments, where Life and Property and all Things must depend upon the Humour of a Prince, the Caprice of a Minister, or the Demand of a Harlot. Under those Governments few People can have Money, and they that have must lock it up, or bury it to keep it; and dare not engage in large Designs, when the Advantages may be reaped by their rapacious Governors, or given up by them in a senseless and wicked Treaty: Besides, such Governors contemn Trade and Artificers; and only Men of the Sword, who have an Interest incompatible with Trade, are encouraged by them.

For these Reasons, Trade cannot be carried on so cheap as in free Countries; and whoever supplies the Commodity cheapest, will command the Market. In free Countries, Men bring out their Money for their Use, Pleasure, and Profit, and think of all Ways to employ it for their Interest and Advantage. New Projects are every Day invented, new Trades searched after, new Manufactures set up; and when Tradesmen have nothing to fear but from those whom they trust, Credit will run high, and they will venture in Trade for many times as much as they are worth: But in arbitrary Countries, Men in Trade are every Moment liable to be undone, without the Guilt of Sea or Wind, without the Folly or Treachery of their Correspondents, or their own want of Care or Industry: Their Wealth shall be their Snare; and their Abilities, Vigilance, and their Success, shall either be their undoing, or nothing to their Advantage: Nor can they trust any one else, or any one else them, when Payment and Performance must depend upon the Honesty and Wisdom of those who often have none. . . .

T   *I am, &c.*

Number 68.

SATURDAY, MARCH 3, 1721.

Property and Commerce secure in a free Government only; with the consuming Miseries under simple Monarchies.

SIR,
I Here send you what I have to say further upon Arts, Industry, and Population. To live securely, happily, and independently, is the End and Effect of Liberty; and it is the Ambition of all Men to live agreeably to their own Humours and Discretion. Nor did ever any Man that could live satisfactorily without a Master, desire to live under one; and real or fancied Necessity alone makes Men the Servants, Followers, and Creatures of one another. And therefore all Men are animated by

the Passion of acquiring and defending Property, because Property is the best Support of that Independency, so passionately desired by all Men. Even Men the most dependent have it constantly in their Heads and their Wishes, to become independent one Time or other; and the Property which they are acquiring, or mean to acquire by that Dependency, is intended to bring them out of it, and to procure them an agreeable Independency. And as Happiness is the Effect of Independency, and Independency the Effect of Property; so certain Property is the Effect of Liberty alone, and can only be secured by the Laws of Liberty; Laws which are made by Consent, and cannot be repealed without it.[1]

All these Blessings, therefore, are only the Gifts and Consequences of Liberty, and only to be found in free Countries, where Power is fixed on one Side, and Property secured on the other; where the one cannot break Bounds without Check, Penalties or Forfeiture, nor the other suffer Diminution without Redress; where the People have no Masters but the Laws, and such as the Laws appoint; where both Laws and Magistracy are formed by the People or their Deputies; and no Demands are made upon them, but what are made by the Law, and they know to a Penny what to pay before it is asked; where they that exact from them more than the Law allows, are punishable by the Law; and where the Legislators are equally bound by their own Acts, equally involved in the Consequences.

There can be no Good, where there are none of the Causes of Good; and consequently all the Advantages of Liberty must be lost with Liberty, and all the Evils of Tyranny must accompany Tyranny. I have in my last taken a View of the *Eastern* Monarchies, with regard to the miserable Decay of their

---

[1] The notion of Trenchard and Gordon that happiness was an end of government and was in turn promoted by the secure enjoyment of property suggests the obvious way in which eighteenth-century Whigs came to link security, property, and happiness and indicates the transition from Locke's "property" to Jefferson's "pursuit of happiness."

People and Arts; I shall in this confine myself, for Instances, to
Europe, and begin with *Muscovy*, by far the gre[a]test Empire
for Territory in *Christendom:* And because the best short Ac-
count that I have seen of that Government, is given by *Giles
Fletcher*, who was there in the latter End of Queen *Elizabeth's*
Time, I shall here recite Part of that Account.[2]

Talking of the many wicked and barbarous Arts used by the
late *Czars* of *Russia*, to drain and oppress their People, he says;
"They would suffer their People to give freely to the Monasteries, (as many do, especially in their last Wills) and this
they do, because they may have the Money of the Realm more
ready at Hand, when they list to take it, which is many Times
done; the Friars parting freely with some, rather than lose all.

"*John Basilowitz* pretended to resign the Crown to the Prince
of *Cazan*, and to retire for the rest of his Life to a Monastery:
He then caused this new King to call in all the Ecclesiastical
Charters, and to cancel them.[3] Then pretending to dislike this
Fact, and the Misrule of the new King, he resumed the Sceptre,
possessed as he was of all the Church Lands; of which he kept
what he would, and gave new Charters for the rest. By this he
wrung from the Ecclesiasticks a vast Sum; and yet hoped to
abate the ill Opinion of his Government, by shewing a worse.

"When they want to levy a new Tax, they make a Shew of
Want, as was done by Duke *Theodore;* who, though left very
rich by his Father, yet sold most of his Plate, and coined the
rest, that he might seem in Necessity: Whereupon presently
came out a new Tax upon his People.

---

[2] Giles Fletcher (1549–1611) was an Elizabethan diplomat and writer.
In 1591 he wrote an account of his embassy to Russia, an account so un-
favorable that it was suppressed on the fear of the Russia Company that it
might upset trade with Muscovy. It was subsequently published in an
abridged edition.

[3] "John Basilowitz" was Trenchard and Gordon's version of Ivan Vasil-
ievich, Ivan IV, commonly known as Ivan the Terrible (1530–1584). The
"Theodore" mentioned in the next paragraph was Feodor I (1557–1598),
the son of Ivan and the last member of the Rurik dynasty to rule Muscovy.

"They would sometimes send their Messengers into the Provinces to forestall and engross the Commodities of the Country, taking them at small Prices, what they themselves listed, and selling them again at excessive Prices to their own Merchants, or to Strangers. If they refuse to buy them, then they force them into it: The like they do, when any Commodity thus engrossed, Foreign or Native, such as Cloth of Gold, Broad Cloth, and the like, happens to decay, by lying upon Hand; it is forced upon the Merchants at the Emperor's Price, whether they will or no.

"Besides the engrossing of foreign Commodities, and forcing them upon the Merchants, they make a Monopoly for a Season of all such Commodities as are paid the Prince for Rent or Custom; and this they do to enhance the Price of them: Thus they monopolize Furs, Corn, Wood, &c. during all which Time none must sell of the same Commodity, till the Emperor's be all sold.

"The above-mentioned *John Basilowitz* sent into *Permia* (a Country of the poor *Samoides*) for certain Loads of *Cedar,* though he well knew that none grew there; and the Inhabitants returned Answer, that they could find none. Whereupon he taxed the Country in Twelve Thousand Rubles.——Again, he sent to the City of *Moscow* to provide for him a Measure full of Fleas, for a Medicine. They answered, that the Thing was impossible; and if they could get them, yet they could not measure them, because of their leaping out. Upon which he set a Mulct upon them of Seven Thousand Rubles.

"To these may be added, their Seizures and Confiscations upon such as are under Displeasure, and the Connivance at the Oppression and Extortions of the Governors of the Provinces, till their Time be expired; and then turning all their wicked Plunder into the Emperor's Treasury, but never a Penny back again to the right Owner, how great or evident so-ever the Injury be.

"As to the People, they are of no Rank or Account, and

esteemed no better than Villains; and so they subscribe themselves in all their Writings to any of the Nobility, as they of the Nobility do to the Emperor: And indeed, no Bond Slaves are kept more in Awe and Subjection, than the common People are, by the Nobility, Officers, and Soldiers; so that when a poor *Mousick* (one of the Commonalty) meets any of them upon the Highway, he must turn himself about, as not daring to look them in the Face, and fall down with his Head to the very Ground.

"And as to the Lands and Goods of these miserable People, they are so exposed to the Rapine of the Nobility and Soldiers, besides the Taxes, Customs, and Seizures, and other publick Exactions laid upon them by the Emperor, that they are utterly discouraged from following their Trades and Professions; because the more they have, the more Danger they are in, not only of their Goods, but even of their Lives: And if they happen to have any thing, they convey it into Monasteries, or hide it in Woods or under Ground, as Men do when they are in Fear of a Foreign I[n]vasion. So that many Villages and Towns are intirely without Inhabitants; and in the Way towards *Moscow*, betwixt *Volaghda* and *Yareslave*, for about an Hundred *English* Miles, there are at least Fifty Villages, some half a Mile long, some a whole Mile long, that stand wholly desolate, without a single Inhabitant. The like Desolation is seen in all other Places of the Realm, as I have been told by those that travelled the Country.

"In every great Town the Emperor hath a Drinking-House, which he rents out: Here the Labouring Man and Artificer many Times spends all from his Wife and Children. Some drink away all that they wear about them, to their very Shirts, and so walk naked; and all for the Honour of the Emperor. Nay, while they are thus drinking themselves naked, and starving their Families, no body must call them away, upon any Account, because he would hinder the Emperor's Revenue.

"The capital Punishments upon the People are very cruel;

but if Theft or Murder be committed upon them by one of the Nobility, he is seldom punished, or so much as called to Account for it, because the People are the Slaves of the Nobility: Or if these Crimes are committed by a Gentleman Soldier, perhaps he may be imprisoned at the Emperor's Pleasure, or perhaps fined——and that is all."

I make this Quotation chiefly upon Memory, having only taken down some Hints when I read it; but I can assert it to be a just one, and almost wholly in the Doctor's Words.

I know much has been said of the Improvements made by the present *Czar,* and of his many Projects in Favour of Arts and Trade: And it is very true, that he is a Prince of a very active and inquisitive Genius.[4] But though he has made himself a more powerful Prince than any of his Predecessors were, I do not find that the Numbers of his People are increased, or their general wretched Condition much mended. He has a vast Army constantly on Foot; he keeps vast Numbers of his poor Subjects constantly employed in making Havens and Canals; great Taxes are raised, great and daily Waste is made of his People, who are likewise miserably oppressed by his *Boyars,*[5] to whom he still leaves the raising of Money, and the Direction of Trade: So that the general Oppression remains; Trade is dead[e]ned and distressed; the People burdened beyond Measure; sudden and arbitrary Duties are laid upon Commodities imported; the old Way of Monopolies is continued; the State of the Exchange, and the Allay and uncertain Value of the current Coin, are as bad as they can be; Arts and Ingenuity are really discouraged, and those who have Skill in any Art must conceal it, to avoid working for nothing; there are Grievances without Number, and like to be, for he who

---

[4] The ruling Czar was Peter the Great (reigned from 1682 to 1725), whose Westernizing activities were obviously known to Trenchard and Gordon.

[5] The merchant class of Russia.

complains is certainly undone, and Petitions are answered with Stripes, sometimes with Death itself. In short, the Condition of the *Russian* People is much upon the same Foot as it was in Dr. *Fletcher's* Time; and whoever doubts it, may find full Conviction from Captain *Perry's* State of *Russia*, under the present *Czar*.[6]

In *Poland*, nothing can be more miserable than the Condition of the Peasants, who are subject to the mere Mercy of the great Lords, as to Life and Death and Property; and must labour Five Days in a Week, nay sometimes Six, for these Lords; and if they cannot subsist themselves and their Families upon One Day's Labour in Seven, they must famish. The State of the other Northern Kingdoms is, with respect to the People, as wretched as any yet named: They have many Soldiers, endless Taxes, dreadful Poverty, few People, and gaudy Courts. It is indeed said of some arbitrary Princes in some Parts of *Europe*, that they are merciful to their Subjects, and do not use them barbarously; that is, they do not deliberately butcher them, but only take all that they have, and leave them to starve peaceably upon the rest: All the Riches of the Country are to be seen at Court, and the People are wretchedly poor. . . .

[Gordon continues his tour of Europe. He discusses at length the conditions in the various Italian states, contrasting the areas of freedom with those, such as the Papal States in particular, which he regards as being under arbitrary government. Finally, he passes on to Switzerland and France and again presents a picture of the results of freedom as opposed to those of absolutism.]

"The People in *France*," (says the Author of the Supplement

---

[6] John Perry was in Russia from 1698 to 1712. He had been hired by Peter the Great when the latter had visited England. Perry worked as an engineer in Russia, quarreled with Peter when the Czar failed to pay the agreed-upon fees for work, and returned to England in a fit of anger. Perry published a critical account, *The State of Russia under the Present Tsar* (London: Benjamin Tooke), in 1716.

to.Dr. *Burnet's* Travels)[7] "especially the Peasants, are very poor, and most of them reduced to great Want and Misery; and yet *France* is an extraordinary good Country. The People of *Switzerland (which is a Country of Mountains)* cannot be said to be very rich, but there are very few, even of the Peasants, that are miserably poor.——The most Part of them have enough to live on. Every where in *France*, even in the best Cities, there are Swarms of Beggars; and yet scarce any to be seen throughout all *Switzerland*. The Houses of the Country People in *France* are extremely mean; and in them no other Furniture is to be found, but poor nasty Beds, Straw Chairs, with Plates and Dishes of Wood and Earth. In *Switzerland*, the Peasants have their Houses furnished with good Feather-Beds, good Chairs, and other convenient Household-Stuffs; their Windows are all of Glass, always kept mended and whole; and their Linnen, both for Bedding and their Tables, is very neat and white."

This was written above Thirty Years ago, when *France* was in a much better Condition than it has been since. The Glory of their late Grand Monarch cost them much Misery, and many Myriads of People.[8] And yet even Thirty Years ago their Miseries were great and affecting! "As I came from *Paris* to *Lyons*," (says Dr. *Burnet*) "I was amazed to see so much Misery as appeared not only in Villages, but even in big Towns; where

---

[7] Gilbert Burnet (1643–1715) was the politically active and important Bishop of Salisbury. A sometime friend of Charles II and the Duke of York, the future James II, he was vigorously anti-Catholic, while favoring toleration and moderation within the Protestant community. Under the Stuarts, he spent considerable time in exile and returned to England as an accomplice of William III. His exile led to his writing *Some Letters, Containing an Account of What Seemed Most Remarkable in Switzerland, Italy, etc.* This was published in Amsterdam by A. Acher in 1686(7), and a Supplement appeared in Rotterdam in the following year. The supplement bore the inscription "Written by a nobleman of Italy, and communicated to the author," who was presumably Burnet himself.

[8] The grand monarch was, of course, Louis XIV, King of France from 1643 to 1714, a figure heartily detested by Trenchard and Gordon.

all the Marks of an extreme Poverty shewed themselves, both in the Buildings, the Clothes, and almost in the Looks of the Inhabitants. And a general dispeopling in all the Towns, was a very visible Effect of the Hardships under which they lay." What blessed Circumstances that great Kingdom is in now, Mr. *Law*, who is amongst us, can best tell; though we all pretty well know.[9] It is really a Science, and no easy one, to know the Names, Numbers, and Quality of their Taxes; which are so many, so various, and so heavy, that one of their own Writers calls them, *Inventions proper to impoverish the People, and to enrich the Dictionaries.*[10] *Bulion*,[11] Treasurer to *Lewis* the Thirteenth, told his Master, that *his Subjects were too happy, they were not yet reduced to eat Grass.* And the cruel Spirit and Politicks of that Minister were afterwards so well improved, that I am apt to think their present Felicity is no Part of their Misfortunes.

Such Instances shew what hopeful Methods such Governors take to increase People, Trade, and Riches.

As to the politer Arts, I own several of them have flourished under some of the Popes themselves, and some other arbitrary Princes; such as Painting, Architecture, Sculpture, and Musick. But these Arts, and the Improvements of them, were so far from owing any Thing to that Sort of Government, that by Liberty alone, and the Privileges given to the Professors of them, they came to excel in them; nor would they ever have excelled upon the common Foot and Condition of their other Subjects: So that to make them Excellent, they made them

---

[9] John Law of Lauriston (1671–1729) was a Scottish financier who became involved in the Mississippi scheme in France.

[10] The editor has been unable to trace the exact source of this quotation.

[11] Claude de Bullion (1580–1640) was a confidant of Richelieu and financial adviser under Louis XIII. The *Dictionnaire de Biographie Française* (Paris: Libraire Letouzey et Ané, 1956), VII, 660, notes tactfully that after his death: *"Il fut, comme tous les collecteurs d'impôts, peu regretté."* ("He was, like all tax collectors, little mourned.") Thus grew the numerous apocryphal stories about his grasping character.

Free. And thus even Tyrants, the Enemies of Liberty, were, for their Furniture, Luxury, Pomp, Pleasure, and Entertainment, forced to be beholden to Liberty; and for those particular Purposes, they gave it to particular Men. But for the rest of their Subjects, they were left by them in the Condition of Brutes, both in Point of Livelihood and Knowledge: For it is Liberty more than Shape, that makes the Difference; since Reason without Liberty proves little better, and sometimes worse, than none. Servitude mars all Genius; nor is either a Pen or a Pencil of any Use in a Hand that is manacled.

G   *I am, &c.*

Number 71.

SATURDAY, MARCH 31, 1722.

Polite Arts and Learning naturally produced in Free States, and marred by such as are not free.

SIR,

In the First Rise and Beginning of States, a rough and unhewn Virtue, a rude and savage Fierceness, and an unpolished Passion for Liberty, are the Qualities chiefly in Repute. To these succeed military Accomplishments, domestick Arts and Sciences, and such political Knowledge and Acquirements, as are necessary to make States great and formidable Abroad, and to preserve Equality, and domestick Happin[e]ss, and Security, at Home. And lastly, when these are attained, follow Politeness, speculative Knowledge, moral and experimental Philosophy, with other Branches of Learning and the whole Train of the Muses. . . .

But neither will the single Invitations of Leisure and Ease

prove sufficient to engage Men in the Pursuits of Knowledge as far as it may be pursued. Other Motives must be thrown in; they must find certain Protection and Encouragements in such Pursuits, and proper Rewards at the End of them. The Laurel is often the chief Cause of the Victory. The *Greeks* who encouraged Learning and the Sciences more, and preserved them longer than any People ever did, kept stated, publick and general Assemblies, on Purpose for the Trial and Encouragement of Wit and Arts, and for the distinguishing of those who professed them. Thither resorted all who had any Pretensions that Way, or had engaged in Performances of that Kind: All the most illustrious Men in *Greece,* the Nobility, the Magistracy, the Ambassadors of Princes, sometimes Princes themselves, were the Auditors and Judges: By these Merit was distinguished, the Contention for Glory decided, the Victory declared, and by these the Rewards of it were bestowed. Thus glorious was the Price of Excelling; thus equitable, publick, and loud was the Fame of it. It is therefore no Wonder that it was courted by the *Greeks* with as much Ardour and Application, as the chief Dignities in a State are courted by others. And, considering how strong were the Stimulations of the *Greeks* to study, *Horace* might well say,

> *Graiis ingenium, Graiis dedit ore rotundo*
> *Musa loqui - - -*[1]

Before this august Assembly, *Herodotus* repeated his History with great Applause; which so animated *Thucydides,* then very young, that, in Emulation of *Herodotus,* he wrote a better History than that of *Herodotus.* Here *Cleomenes* recommended himself, by only repeating some Verses skilfully collected out of *Empedocles;* and here *Euripides* and *Xenocles* contended for Preference in the *Drama.*

---

[1] The lines come from Horace's "Epistula ad Pisones" ("Ars Poetica"), 323: "It was the Greeks, aye the Greeks, covetous of praise alone, that the Muse endowed with quick wit and rounded utterance."

Indeed, the Honours attending a Victory upon these Occasions were excessive, and, according to *Cicero,* did almost equal those of a *Roman* triumph. The Victors were reckoned to have arrived to the highest human Felicity, to have entailed Glory upon all that belonged to them, upon their Families, Friends, their native City, and the Place of their Education. Elogiums were made upon them, Statues were erected to them, and, ever after, they met every-where the same Preference, which they had met at the *Olympick* Assemblies. —A Preference which so fired the Emperor *Nero,* that, when he had ridiculously stood Competitor at a Singing-match, and taken a Journey to *Greece* on purpose, he first declared himself Victor, and then, to destroy all Marks and Memory of those who had been so before him, he commanded all their Pictures and Statues to be pulled down, and thrown into the Privies.

The *Romans,* as soon as they had Leisure from their long and many Wars, fell quickly into the same Studies, and into the same Emulation to excel in them. They no sooner had any Acquaintance with *Greece,* but they were possessed with a Fondness for all her Refinements.

> *Graecia capta ferum victorem cepit, & artes*
> *Intulit agresti Latio - - - -*[2]

The fierce *Romans* subdued *Greece* by their Arms; and *Greece* made rustick *Italy* a Captive to her Arts. All the Youth of *Rome* were charmed with the Beauties of Learning, and eager to possess them: Many of the Senators were caught by the same Passions; even the elder *Cato,* who was at first against these Improvements, which, he feared, would soften too much the rough *Roman* Genius, yet changed his Opinion so far afterwards, as to learn *Greek* in his old Age.

---

[2] The passage is from Horace, *Epistulae* II. 1. 156, "The Epistle to Augustus, Explaining the Modern Literary Attitude towards the Ancient Greeks":

> Greece captive captured her rough conqueror,
> And gave her arts to Latium, rude before.

This prodigious Progress of the *Romans* in Learning had no other Cause than the Freedom and Equality of their Government. The Spirit of the People, like that of their State, breathed nothing but Liberty, which no Power sought to controul, or could controul. The Improvement of Knowledge, by bringing no Terror to the Magistrates, brought no Danger to the People. Nothing is too hard for Liberty; that Liberty which made the *Greeks* and *Romans* Masters of the World, made them Masters of all the Learning in it: And, when their Liberties perished, so did their Learning. That Eloquence, and those other Abilities and Acquirements, which raised those who had them to the highest Dignities in a free State, became under Tyranny a certain Train to Ruin, unless they were prostituted to the Service of the Tyrant.

That Knowledge, and those Accomplishments, which create Jealousy instead of Applause, and Danger instead of Reward, will be but rarely and faintly pursued; and for the most part not at all. No man will take great Pains, spend his Youth, and lose his Pleasures, to purchase Infamy or Punishment: And therefore when such Obstacles are thrown in his Way, he will take Counsel of Self-love, acquiesce in the fashionable Stupidity, and prefer gilded and thriving Folly to dangerous and forbidden Wisdom.

Ignorance accompanies Slavery, and is introduced by it. People who live in Freedom will think with Freedom; but when the Mind is enslaved by Fear, and the Body by Chains, Inquiry and Study will be at an End. Men will not pursue dangerous Knowledge, nor venture their Heads, to improve their Understandings. Besides, their Spirits, dejected with Servitude and Poverty, will want Vigour as well as Leisure to cultivate Arts, and propagate Truth; which is ever High-Treason against Tyranny. Neither the Titles nor the Deeds of Tyrants will bear Examination; and their Power is concerned to stupify and destroy the very Faculties of Reason and Thinking: Nor can Reason travel far, when Force and Dread are in the Way; and when Men dare not see, their Eyes will soon grow useless.

In *Turkey*, Printing is forbid, lest by its Means common Sense might get the better of Violence, and be too hard for the Imperial Butcher. It is even Capital, and certain Death there, only to reason freely upon their *Alcoran*.—A sure Sign of Imposture? But by Imposture, Stupidity, and Janizaries, his Throne is supported; and his vast, but thin Dominions, know no Inhabitants but barbarous, ignorant, and miserable Slaves.

Nor is Printing in other arbitrary Countries of much Use but to rivet their Chains: It is permitted only on one Side, and made the further Means of Servitude. Even in Christian Countries, under arbitrary Princes, the People are for the most part as ignorant and implacable Bigots as the *Turks* are. And as it is rare to find a Slave who is not a Bigot, no Man can shew me a Bigot who is not an ignorant Slave; for Bigotry is a Slavery of the Soul to certain religious Opinions, Fancies, or Stories, of which the Bigot knows little or nothing, and damns all that do.

The least Cramp or Restraint upon Reasoning and Inquiry of any Kind, will prove soon a mighty Bar in the Way to Learning. It is very true, that all sorts of Knowledge, at least all sorts of sublime and important Knowledge, are so complicated and interwoven together, that it is impossible to search into any Part of it, and to trace the same with Freedom to its first Principles, without borrowing and taking in the Help of most, if not all, of the other Parts. Religion and Government, particularly, are at the Beginning and End of every Thing, and are the Sciences in the World the most necessary and important to be known; and as these are more or less known, other Knowledge will be proportionably greater or smaller, or none: But, where these cannot be freely examined, and their Excellencies searched into, and understood, all other Wisdom will be maimed and ineffectual, indeed scarce worth having.

Now, in all arbitrary Governments, and under all created

and imposing Religions, nothing must be found true in Philosophy, which thwarts the received Scheme, and the uppermost Opinions: The most evident mathematical Demonstrations must not disprove orthodox Dogma's, and established Ideas; the finest poetical Flights must be restrained and discouraged, when they would fly over the narrow Inclosures and Prison-walls of Bigots: Nor must the best, the strongest, and the most beautiful Reasoning dare to break through popular Prejudices, or attempt to contend with powerful and lucrative Usurpation. A Bishop was burned before the *Reformation,* for discovering the World to be round; and, even in the last Century, the excellent *Galileo* was put into the dismal Prison of the *Inquisition,* for maintaining the Motion of the Earth round the Sun, as her Centre. This proposition of his, which he had demonstrated, he was forced to recant, to save his Life, and satisfy the Church.

Where Religion and Government are most deformed, as Religion ever is where it is supported by Craft and Force, and Government ever is when it is maintained by Whips and Chains, there all Examination into either, and all Reasoning about them, is most strictly forbid and discouraged: And as one sort of Inquiry and Knowledge begets another; and as, when the Wits of Men are suffered to exert themselves freely, no body knows where their Pursuits may end; so no Tyranny of any kind is safe, where general, impartial, and useful Knowledge is pursued. Inhuman Violence, and stupid Ignorance, are the certain and necessary Stay of Tyrants; and every thing that is good or valuable in the World is against them.

In the *East* (if we except *China*) there is not a Glimmering of Knowledge; though the Eastern People are, from their natural Climate and Genius, vastly capable of all Knowledge. *Bernier,*[3] mentioning the Cruelty of the Government, and the

---

[3] François Bernier (d. 1688) was a French doctor, traveler, and philosopher. He published the first part of his travels to the Middle East in 1670 and later added to it. Versions appeared in English as early as 1671 and 1675.

great Misery of the People there, says, "From the same Cause, a gross and profound Ignorance reigns in those States: Nor is it possible there should be Academies and Colleges well founded in them. Where are there such Founders to be met with? And, if they were, where are the Scholars to be had? Where are those who have Means sufficient to maintain their Children in Colleges? And, if there were, who durst appear to be rich? And if they would, where are those Benefices, Preferments, and Dignities, which require Knowledge and Abilities, and animate young Men to Study?"

I will not deny, but that, in arbitrary Countries, there are sometimes found Men of great Parts and Learning. But these are either Ecclesiasticks, who, even in the greatest Tyrannies, at least in *Europe,* are blessed with great Liberty, and many independent Privileges, and are Freemen in the Midst of Slaves, and have suitable Leisure and Revenues to support them in their Studies; or they are Men invited and encouraged by the Prince to flatter his Pride, and administer to his Pomp and Pleasures, and to recommend his Person and Power. For these Reasons alone they are caressed, protected, and rewarded. They are endowed with the Advantages of Freemen, merely to be the Instruments of Servitude. They are a sort of *Swiss,* hired to be the Guards of their proud Master's Fame, and to applaud and vindicate all his Wickedness, Wildness, Usurpations, Prodigalities, and Follies. This therefore is the worst of all Prostitutions, the most immoral of all sort of Slavery; as it is supporting Servitude with the Breath of Liberty, and assaulting and mangling Liberty with her own Weapons. A Creature that lets out his Genius to hire, may sometimes have a very good one; but he must have a vile and beggarly Soul, and his Performances are at best but the basest Way of petitioning for Alms. . . .

G   *I am, &c.*

SATURDAY, APRIL 21, 1722.

A *Display of Tyranny, its destructive Nature, and Tendency to dispeople the Earth.*

SIR,

I Intend to finish in this Paper, what I have so largely handled in so many others, the Subject of Liberty and Tyranny; a noble Subject, superior to all others, and to the greatest Genius, but fit for the Consideration of every Genius, and of every Rank of Men. It concerns the whole Earth, and Children ought to be instructed in it as soon as they are capable of Instruction. Why should not the Knowledge and Love of God be joined to the Knowledge and Love of Liberty, his best Gift, which is the certain Source of all the civil Blessings of this Life? And I have shewn that Religion cannot subsist without it. And why should not the Dread and Hatred of *Satan* be accompanied with the Dread and Hatred of Tyrants, who are his Instruments, and the Instruments of all the civil Miseries in this Life? I have often thought that the *Barbarians,* who worship the Devil, must have borrowed their Idea of him from the Character and Behaviour of their own Princes. One might indeed defy any Thing out of Hell, or even in it, and all that are in it, to do half the Mischief upon this Earth that Tyrants do.

They reduce Mankind to the Condition of Brutes, and make that Reason, which God gave them, useless to them: They deprive them even of the Blessings of Nature, starve them in the midst of Plenty, and frustrate the natural Bounty of the Earth to Men; so that Nature smiles in vain where Tyranny frowns: The very Hands of Men, given them by Nature for their Support, are turned by Tyrants into the Instruments of their Misery, by being employed in vile Drudgeries or destructive Wars, to gratify the Lust and Vanity of their execrable Lords, who suffer neither Religion, nor Virtue, nor Knowledge, nor Plenty, nor any Kind of Happiness, to dwell within the Extent of their Power.

Nothing that is good or desirable can subsist under Tyrants, nor within their Reach; and they themselves subsist upon nothing but what is detestable and wicked. They are supported by general Ruin; they live by the Destruction of Mankind; And as Fraud and Villainy, and every Species of Violence and Cruelty, are the Props of their Throne; so they measure their own Happiness, and Security, and Strength, by the Misery and Weakness of their People; and continued Oppression and Rapine are their studied and necessary Arts of Reigning, as is every Art by which they can render their People poor, abject, and wretched; though by such Methods they do in effect render themselves so, and consequently become easy Preys to the next Invader. That Wealth, which dispersed amongst their Subjects, and circulated in Trade and Commerce, would employ, increase, and inrich them, and return often again with Interest into their Coffers, is barbarously robbed from the People, and engrossed by these their Oppressors, and generally laid out by them to adorn their Palaces, to cover their Horses or Elephants, or to embellish their own Persons, and those of their Concubines and Attendants, or else locked up in dark Caverns far from human Sight and Use.

Whilst it is yet in the Mine, it is within the Reach of Pickaxes and Shovels; and by the Labour and Industry of Men, may be made useful and beneficial to Men: But in the Den of a Tyrant, it is more securely, more irretrieveably buried and guarded from the Use of Men. Here are literally *Pluto*'s Brass Walls, and Adamantine Gates; here are Thousands of real *Cerberus's*, who never sleep; all to encompass and secure this dead Treasure, and to restrain a general Gift of God from the Use of his Creatures: From thence it is rarely fetched, even upon the greatest Emergencies, or for any Purposes but ill ones, 'till at last it becomes the Prize and Booty of a conquering Enemy. *Alexander* found more Riches in the *Persian* Treasures, than in the Hands of Freemen would have conquered the World; and 'tis thought that there are more at this Day in that of the Great *Mogul*, than would purchase the greatest and wealthiest Kingdom in *Europe;* and it has been computed that there are Thirty Millions of Wealth buried in the secret Vaults of the *Turkish* Seraglio, the Plunder of the People, or of those who plundered them; yet they are still plundered and miserably oppressed, to increase this dead, useless, and pernicious Store.

By these and the like inhuman Means, the Countries of Tyrants are come to be in the Condition which I have else-where described, desolate and uncultivated, and proper Receptacles for such savage Monsters, and ravening Beasts of Prey, who rather choose to live in barren Fields, unhospitable Deserts, and in dispeopled and empty Towns, than amongst Freemen in happy Climates, filled with rich and numerous Cities, abounding in Inhabitants who are possessed of Liberty, and will be bold to defend it.

Now where can all this dismal Ruin, this growing Depopulation end? If a continued Decay in the natural Body certainly ends in the Extinction of Life; in what can a continued and hasty Decay of Mankind end, but in the Extinction of Men? So that if the World last many Centuries more in its present wasting and mournful Situation, there must be a Dissolution of human Race, before the World is dissolved.

Several new Tyrannies have sprung up, like so many new Plagues, within the Memory of Man, and like them have laid waste, but with a more regular and continued Ruin, Countries once strong in Liberty and People: And as Tyranny, like every other full-grown Mischief, becomes more and more insupportable every Day, the Condition of Mankind under it must necessar[il]y, and does actually, grow every Day worse and worse, and they themselves fewer. And even when their Numbers and their Substances are lessened, or rather exhausted, the Demands of the Tyrant upon them are not lessened, nor his Rapine abated, nor his Expences and Exactions restrained.

When a Tyrant has reduced a Million of People to half that Number by his Cruelty and Extortions, he madly expects from the remaining Half the same Revenue and Assistance of Men, which he had from the Whole; and like the rest, they must perish to make good his Expectations; and he often encreases his Troops as fast as his People decrease. So that his Expence is enlarged as there becomes less to support it; but he will be supported, and his poor perishing People must do it, though they destroy themselves.

Such is the pestilent, savage, and unsatiable Nature of this Sort of Monster, whose Figure, Throne and Authority is established upon the Ruins of Reason, Humanity, and Nature: He takes all that his Subjects have, and destroys them to get more. . . .

Alas! Power encroaches daily upon Liberty, with a Success too evident; and the Balance between them is almost lost. Tyranny has engrossed almost the whole Earth, and striking at Mankind Root and Branch, makes the World a Slaughterhouse; and will certainly go on to destroy, till it is either destroyed itself, or, which is most likely, has left nothing else to destroy.

The Bulk of the Earth being evidently almost a Desert already, made so by Tyrants; it is Demonstration that the Whole must be so, and must soon be entirely so, if the Growth of Tyranny be not restrained; else if the general and wide Waste goes on, Men will become too few for the Management of Societies, and for Cultivation and Commerce; all which are supported by Numbers; and then degenerating into absolute Savages, they will live straggling and naked in the Woods and Wildernesses, like wild Beasts, and be devoured by them; or, like them, devour one another, or perish with Hunger. And thus there will be an End of Men; unless those States that are yet free, preserve, in the midst of this general Waste, their own Liberties and People, and, like the antient *Egyptians* and *Greeks,* fill the World again, in Process of Time, with Colonies of Freemen.

That there is such a terrible Waste of People in the World, cannot be denied; and it is as evident, that Tyrants, are the constant, regular, and necessary Cause of it. They are indeed so manifestly the Authors of all that is ruinous and wicked, that if God Almighty had left it to Satan to invent an Engine for the destroying of the World, and for defacing every Thing beautiful, good, or desirable in it, that Minister of Vengeance, and Enemy to God and Man, would doubtless have invented Tyrants, who by their wonderful Success in such Ministration, have ever shewn, and do still shew, their eminent Fitness for it. They shew every-where such a constant and strong Antipathy to the Happiness of Mankind, that if there be but one free City within their Ken, they are restless in their Designs and Snares against it, and never defend it but against one another, and practise the vilest and the meanest Rogueries to become Masters of it. There are Instances in this Age of free Cities falling into the Claws of Tyrants, and of the miserable Difference between their former Opulency, and their present Poorness: They have never since put off their Mourning, which grows daily more black and dismal.

The Breath of a Tyrant blasts and poisons every Thing, changes Blessings and Plenty into Curses and Misery, great Cities into gloomy Solitudes, and their rich Citizens into Beggars and Vagabonds: I could name Cities, which, while they governed themselves, could maintain Armies, and now enslaved can scarce maintain the poor proud Rogues who govern them. It is certain, that whatever Country or Place is subdued by a Prince who governs by his Will, is ruined by his Government.

It is confessed, that the arbitrary Princes in *Europe* have not yet, like those in *Asia,* declared themselves Masters of the Soil; and their People have a sort of Property. How long this will continue, I know not precisely. This is certain, that the Condition of their Subjects, which was always bad, grows hourly worse; and their Nobility, which were once rich and powerful, are now reduced very low, and greatly impoverished. These, who were the Supports of Royalty, having created Jealousy as if they had eclipsed it, have felt the terrible Effects of arbitrary Power as well as others, though not so much. Besides, when the common People, already wholly exhausted, and starving under Oppression, can supply the exorbitant Demands of their Prince no longer, the Estates of the Nobility will be the next Resource; and, like the Mastiff Dog at the Bee-hive, when he has sucked up all the Honey, he will swallow the Comb: And then most of *Europe* will be in the Condition of *Turky,* as many Parts of it are at present not much better; and, like the Great *Turk,* most of its Princes will be sole Proprietors of the Land, as they now make themselves of its Product, which very near answers the same End. When Tenants, exhausted by Taxes, are unable to pay Rent, the Land yielding no Profit, is as bad as none; and in some Instances worse than none, as we are particularly told by the noble Author of the *Account of Denmark,*[1] where some Landlords have begged the King upon their Knees to ease them of their Land, by taking it from them for good and all; for that it was taxed more than it was worth.

Most of the Princes of *Europe* have been long introducing the *Turkish* Government into *Europe;* and have succeeded so well, that I would rather live under the *Turk* than under many of them. They practise the Cruelties and Oppressions of the *Turks,* and want the tolerating Spirit of the *Turk;* and if some unforeseen Check be not thrown in their Way, the whole Polity of savage *Turky* will be established by them in all its Parts and Barbarity; as if the Depopulation which is already so quick, and taking such dreadful Strides, were still too slow. It is not

---

[1] Robert Molesworth was the author of *An Account of Denmark.* See *Letter* 24, note 2, p. 65.

enough for Tyrants to have consumed Mankind so fast, that out of Twenty Parts, they have within these Two Thousand Years destroyed perhaps Nineteen, (for so much at least I take to be the Disproportion) but fresh Machines of Cruelty are still sought after, besides never laying aside any of the Old, till the Destruction be fully completed. They seem to think, that they shall have Enemies as long as any Men remain; which indeed is a reasonable Apprehension: But it is astonishing at first View, that Mankind should have so long borne these unrelenting Slaughterers of Mankind.—But, alas! who knows not the Force of Corruption, Delusion, and standing Armies!

Oh Liberty! Oh Servitude! how amiable, how detestable, are the different Sounds! Liberty is Salvation in Politicks, as Slavery is Reprobation; neither is there any other Distinction but that of Saint and Devil, between the Champions of the one and of the other.

And here I conclude this noble Subject of Liberty; having made some weak Attempts to shew its glorious Advantages, and to set off the opposite Mischiefs of raging, relentless, and consuming Tyranny:—A Task to which no human Mind is equal. For neither the sublimest Wits of Antiquity, nor the brightest Genius's of late or modern Time, assisted with all the Powers of Rhetorick, and all the Stimulations of poetick Fire, with the warmest and boldest Figures in Language, ever did, or ever could, or ever can, describe and heighten sufficiently the Beauty of the one, or the Deformity of the other: Language fails in it, and Words are too weak.

Those who do not groan under the Yoke of heavy and pointed Vassalage, cannot possibly have Images equal to a Calamity which they do not feel: And those who feel it are stupefied by it, and their Minds depressed; nor can they have Conceptions large, bright, and comprehensive enough, to be fully sensible of their own wretched Condition; and much less can they paint it in proper Colours to others. We, who enjoy the precious, lovely, and invaluable Blessing of Liberty, know that nothing can be paid too dear to purchase and preserve it. Without it the World is a Wilderness, and Life precarious and a Burthen: Death is a Tribute which we all owe to Nature, and must pay; and it is infinitely preferable, in any Shape, to an ignominious Life: Nor can we restore our Beings back again into the Hands of our great Creator, with more Glory to him, more Honour to ourselves, or more Advantage to Mankind, than in Defence of all that is valuable, religious, and praise-worthy upon Earth, or includes whatever is so.

How execrable then and infamous are the Wretches, who, for a few precarious, momentary, and perhaps imaginary Advantages, would rob their Country, their happy Country, for ever, of every Thing that can render human Life desireable; and for a little Tinsel Pageantry, and false and servile Homage, unworthy of honest Men, and hated by wise Men, would involve Millions of their Fellow-Creatures in lasting Misery, Bondage, and Woe, and charge themselves with their just Hatred and bitter Curses! Such unnatural Parricides, unworthy of the human Shape and Name, would fill up the Measure of their Barbarity, by entailing Poverty, Chains, and Sorrow, upon their own Posterity. And often it has happened, that such Men have, unpitied, suffered in their own Persons, the sad Effects of those cruel Counsels and Schemes, which they intended for the Ruin of all but themselves; and have justly fallen into that Pit, which they had traiterously digged for others.

> ————*Nec lex est justior ulla,*
> *Quam necis artifices arte perire sua.*[2]

G _____   *I am, &c.*

_____

[2] The quotation is a corruption of Ovid, *Art of Love* I, 655–656:
   Lustus uterque fuit neque enim lex aequior ulla est,
   Quam necis artifices arte perire sua.
("Both were just; for there is no juster law than that the contrivers of death should die by their own contrivances.")

SATURDAY, MAY 5, 1722.

Of the Restraints which ought to be laid upon publick Rulers.

SIR,

After all that has been said of arbitrary Power, and of its hideous Nature and Effects, it will fall properly in, to say something here of the Restraints which all wise and fortunate Nations ought to put, and have ever put, upon their Magistrates. This is what I promised nine Months ago to do; and this is what I propose to do in this Letter and the following.

No wise Nation in the World ever trusted to the sole Management, mere Mercy, and absolute Discretion of its own Magistrates, when it could help doing it; and no Series of Magistrates ever had absolute Power over any Nation, but they turned the same to its Ruin, and their own wild Gratifications and ill-judged Profit. As long as the Passions of Men govern them, they will always govern by their Passions, and their Passions will always increase with their Power. And therefore, whenever a whole People, or any Part of them, cross the Passions of any Man that governs them, he will turn his Passions against a whole People, or any Number of them that offend him, and will destroy a whole People, rather than stifle his Passions. This is evident in Ten Thousand Instances; and the Publick will ever, and certainly, be sacrificed to private Lust, when private Lust governs the Publick. Nothing but Fear and selfish Considerations can keep Men within any reasonable Bounds; and nothing but the Absence of Fear can set Men at Defiance with Society, and prompt them to oppress it. It was therefore well judged of the *Spartan Ephori*,[1] when they erected an Altar to *Fear,* as the most proper Divinity to restrain the wild Ambition of Men, and to keep their Kings within the Confines of their Duty.

A nation has but two Sorts of Usurpation to fear; one from their Neighbours, and another from their own Magistrates: Nor is a foreign Usurpation more formidable than a domestick, which is the most dangerous of the Two, by being hardest to remove; and generally stealing upon the People by Degrees, is fixed before it is scarce felt or apprehended: Like wild Beasts in a Wood, beset with Toils as yet unseen by them, they think themselves free; but striving to escape, find themselves caught in the Chains, which had long been preparing for them, and stealing upon them. Besides, for One People undone by foreign Invaders, Ten have been undone by their own native Rogues, who were intrusted to defend them; but instead of it, either betrayed them to these Invaders, or seized traiterously for themselves those Rights which they were sworn to preserve for others; and then, by Oppression and Cruelty, and the other Consequences of their Treachery, reduced them to an utter Disability of defending themselves against any Invasion whatsoever. . . .

There is not upon Earth a Nation, which having had unaccountable Magistrates, has not felt them to have been crying and consuming Mischiefs. In truth, where they are most limited, it has been often as much as a whole People could do to restrain them to their Trust, and to keep them from Violence; and such frequently has been their Propensity to be lawless, that nothing but Violence, and sometimes nothing but a violent Death, could cure them of their Violence. This Evil has its Root in human Nature; Men will never think they have enough,

---

[1] The five ephors were the elected magistrates of Sparta, who shared considerable executive, judicial, and disciplinary power. They exercised a general supervisory power over Sparta's two kings and thus came to dominate the entire structure of the state.

whilst they can take more; nor be content with a Part, when they can seize the Whole. We are, indeed told of some absolute Princes, who have been very good Men and no Oppressors. But the Nature of their Power rendered their good Qualities almost useless, and gave to others an Opportunity of doing in their Name, and by their Authority, Mischiefs which perhaps they themselves abhorred. Besides, in any Series of arbitrary Princes upon Earth, scarce out of Ten can one be named who was tolerable, and who either did not himself prove an inhuman Tyrant, or suffered his Ministers to be so: And when an absolute Prince has had great Parts, they generally went to his Grave with him, and scarce ever proved hereditary. In truth, the Children of great Princes have almost always proved very unlike them. . . .

An unrestrained Power in one Man, or in a few, over all, is such an extravagant Deviation from Reason and Nature, that neither *Briareus,* with his many Hands, nor the *Hydra* with its numerous Heads, nor the *Centaurs,* half Man and half Beast, were Things more unshapen, monstrous, and frightful: Nor would these Fictions appear more fabulous and improbable, than such Power would be to a free People, who never had heard of it before. What could seem to common Sense a wilder *Chimera,* than that one Man, not created with Features and Endowments different from other Men, should have a lasting Right from his Blood, or his Pride, or his Madness, to domineer over all Men, and to rule, kill, starve, famish, banish, and imprison, as many as he pleased?

This Power is indeed so monstrous, that it turns Men that have it into Monsters; and therefore the most amiable and unexceptionable Man upon Earth is not to be trusted with it. Men change with their Stations, and Power of any sort rarely alters them for the better; but, on the contrary, has often turned a very good Man into a very bad. This shews that Men forbear Evil, chiefly to avoid the ill Consequence of it to themselves, and for want of Opportunity and Protection; and finding both in Power, they prove, by making use of them, that their Virtue was only Self-love, and Fear of Punishment. Thus Men of the best and brightest Characters have often done most Mischief, and by well serving their Country, have been enabled to destroy it: And they were good and evil from one and the same Motive; a Passion for themselves, and their own Security or Glory. . . .

Now all these Great Men derived, from the Good which they did, a Capacity to do much more Evil: So that as a Power to do great Good, does naturally include in it an Opportunity of doing much Evil; so those who are in the Possession of Power, as all Magistrates are, ought, above all other Men, to be narrowly watched, and checked with Restraints stronger than their Temptations to break them; and every Crime of theirs ought to be more penal, as it is evidently more pernicious, than the same Crime in any other sort of Men. For, besides that *quales in republica principis essent, tales reliquos solere esse cives;*[2] that is, that People are generally virtuous or corrupt as their Magistrates are; there is something exceeding solemn and important in the Nature of this great Trust; and accordingly as it is observed or betrayed, a Country is happy or miserable: And when any one Breach of it passes once off with Impunity, another will soon follow it; and in Time it will be considered no longer as a Trust, but an Estate.

So dangerous a Thing is an ill Precedent, which is often an Inlet to an endless Train of Mischiefs; and so depraved is the Nature of Man, that we justify ourselves in Wickedness by Examples that cannot be justified. An Action at first reckoned dishonest, by being practised once or twice, becomes unblameable; and that which was at first accounted an Extortion, grows by Use to be thought but a Perquisite. Thus Evil is mitigated, nay, cancelled, by Repetition, which is a real Aggravation of

---

[2] "As the rulers are in the state [*res publica*], so the remainder [of the people] are wont to be [as] citizens."

Evil; and there are certain Rogueries in Office, which being long practised, and by many, are at last reckoned as sacred as the Trust against which they are committed:—A sufficient Reason for providing, by great and certain Penalties, that none be committed.

G   *I am, &c.*

SATURDAY, MAY 12, 1722.

The same Subject continued.

SIR,

How cautiously and partially Men in Power are to be trusted, and how much to be restrained, appears from hence, that almost every civil Evil begins from Courts, and the Redress of every civil Evil from an Opposition to the Pretensions and Excesses of Courts.[1] This is so universally true, that no Nation ever continued happy, whose chief Magistrate was its absolute Master; and no Nation miserable, whose supreme Power was properly checked and divided. Nations are then free, when their Magistrates are their Servants; and then Slaves, when their Magistrates are their Masters: The Commonwealth does not belong to them, but they belong to the Commonwealth. *Tacitus* says with great Truth, *Nec unquam satis fida potentia ubi nimis est:* "Power without Controul is never to be trusted."[2] Every Nation has most to fear from its own Magis-

---

[1] Obviously, the word "Court" is used in the sense of "a sovereign and his retinue" or "a prince and his officials as a political body."

[2] The line comes from Tacitus, *Histories* II. 92. 9: "*Nec umquam satis fida potentia, ubi nimia est.*" ("When a man has excessive power, he never can have complete trust.")

trates; because almost all Nations have suffered most from their own Magistrates.

Cicero, mentioning the Condition of *Cilicia*, of which he was Proconsul, in a Letter to *Appius Pulcher*, says, that he was "moved by Pity, as well as Justice, to relieve from their Miseries the undone provincial Cities; undone chiefly by their own Magistrates."[3] It seems *Cicero* was that sort of whimsical Man, that he had really at Heart to do Good to the People whom he governed:—An odd and impracticable Character; which, had he lived since, would have rendered him utterly unfit for any manner of Preferment. He did not so much as know that he was to make the most of his Place and his Power, let what would become of the People. —A Lesson which other Governors have amply learned.

Aristotle makes it the great Argument and Proof of Liberty, that they who command do also obey; and indeed all legal and just Power being but a Trust, whoever executes the same, does an Act of Obedience as well as Command: And every Trust is best executed, where those who have it are answerable for it, else it never will be executed; but, where it is great and publick, is much more likely to be abused, violated, and turned to the Destruction of those, who, for their own Preservation, gave it. Nor is a People to be told, that such as want to be trusted with extraordinary Power of any kind, have always been Enemies to arbitrary Power; for so are all Men when they have it not, and expect no Advantage from it. Who was a greater Patriot than Sir *Thomas Wentworth?*[4] And who was a more arbitrary Minister than *Thomas Wentworth*, Earl of *Strafford?* All Men are for confining Power when it is over them; and for extending it when they are in it. *Oliver Cromwell* was once heartily in the Principles of Liberty, and afterwards more

---

[3] The passage is a rough rendering from a letter of Cicero to Appius Pulcher, his predecessor in Cilicia, written in October, 51 B.C., and to be found in the *Epistulae ad Familiares* III. 8. 5.

[4] See note 5, *Letter* 15, p. 41.

heartily in those of Tyranny: And I could name Two great Parties in *England*, who, when they were out of Power, seemed to place the Sum of Publick Spirit, in intrenching upon the Royal Authority; and when they were in Power, to know no other Law but the Prerogative Royal. So unlike is the same Man to himself in different Situations; and yet still very consistent with the Genius of human Nature!

Men sometimes do actually Good, in order to do Evil, *Sejanus, incipiente adhuc potestate, bonis consiliis notescere volebat:* "Sejanus, in the Beginning of his Administration, would found the Reputation of a good Minister in laudable Measures."[5] But there never proved a worse Minister than *Sejanus. Solyman,* the *Turkish* Emperor, used to say, that a Prince, to be well served by any Minister, must never use any Minister above once: And this Saying is thus far true generally, that Men, the longer they grow in Power, the worse they grow. I think it is *Tacitus* who says, *Superbire homines etiam annua designatione; quid si honorem per quinquennium agitent?* "If an annual Election to Power make Men insolent; what must be their Pitch of Insolence, if they hold it Five or Seven Years?"[6] *Aristotle* finds great fault with the Senate of *Sparta,* for being perpetual; and I think he says, that an unchanged or an hereditary Senate falls into Dotage.

Many of the Ecclesiasticks have been for trusting their favourite Princes (and no other) with unlimited Power over

---

[5] See note 8, *Letter* 15, p. 43. The line, "Sejanus, yet in the infancy of his power, desired to win a name by good advice," may be found in Tacitus, *Annals* IV. 7.

[6] Tacitus, in the *Annals* II. 36, puts the following speech in the mouth of the Emperor Tiberius when he voiced opposition to a proposal which, by fixing the course of elections of magistrates for five years, would have considerably lessened his control over them: "Men grew arrogant enough even in the twelve months after nomination: what if they had a whole quinquennium in which to play the official?" Tacitus notes what Gordon did not mention; the argument of Tiberius had a popular appearance only "outwardly."

others: But in every Thing that regarded themselves and their Interest, they have never failed to stipulate for the strictest Limitations upon all Princes, even upon those whom over the rest of the World they wished arbitrary, and endeavoured by every Means to make so. Nor did ever any Man give up the Freedom of his Country, but he meant to preserve his own; and hoped to continue a Freeman, as a Reward of his helping to make other People Slaves; and no Man ever set up a Tyrant, but in hopes of going Shares in his Tyranny: And upon these Terms and Expectations alone it is, that any Body of Men, or indeed any Army, is brought to aid and establish any Usurper. Passive Obedience was always intended for other People than those who preached it. Interest cannot lye; though he does, who says that he will submit to Servitude, when he can avoid it.

Who would establish a Bank in an arbitrary Country, or trust his Money constantly there? In *Denmark*, the Ministers and Minions of the Prince, think their Money safest out of his Dominions, and generally transmit the same to *Hamburgh*, and other free Cities, where the Magistrates have no divine Right to lay violent Hands upon what is none of theirs. Even what we gain by Rapine in a Land of Oppression, we are willing to save by the just Laws of Liberty, in a Country of Liberty. In *England* itself, and in our own free Constitution; if the Bank of *England* were put under the absolute Direction and Power of the Court, I doubt Stock would soon grow very cheap, and Sellers multiply very fast. Or if the Government of the Bank, which is purely Republican, were improved into Monarchical; I fancy our highest Monarchy-Men would rail at the Change, and hasten to sell out, notwithstanding their inviolable Attachment to the divine Right of Monarchy: —Unless perhaps they think that absolute Monarchy does best protect their Power, but a free State their Money. I am indeed of Opinion, that upon such a Change, the Bank would be broke, and shut up in three Days.

All this shews, that even Men who are against Liberty in General, contend for it in Particulars, and in all Particulars which affect themselves. Even *Lauderdale,* a *Tyrconnel,* or a *Jefferies,*[7] who were all for making the Crown absolute, as long as they could be as they were, the absolute Ministers of Oppression under it, would none of them, I dare say, have encouraged the Maxim of the Prince's rewarding his Ministers and faithful Oppressors with the Bow-string; as well as they themselves were entitled to that Reward, and as much as the *Turkish* Genius of Government did in other Instances suit their own!

When we hear any Sort of Men complain, as some Sort of Men do frequently complain, That the Crown wants Power; we should ask them, Whether they mean over Themselves? And if they answer, *No;* as certainly they will, if they speak Truth; we may further ask them, Why should they judge for themselves any more than others; or claim to themselves a Liberty and an Exemption which they will not allow to others? The Truth is, they who complain thus, only want to increase the Power of the Crown, because by it their own would be encreased, and other Advantages acquired.

The Fox in the Fable, wanting to rob a Hen-roost, or do some such Prank, humbly besought Admittance and House-room only for his Head; but when he got in his Head, his whole Body presently followed: And Courts, more crafty, as well as more craving, than that designing Animal, have scarce ever gained an Inch of Power, but they have stretched it to an

---

[7] John Maitland, First Duke of Lauderdale (1616–1682), Richard Talbot, Earl of Tyrconnel (1630–1691), and George Jeffreys (1648–1689) were all strong Stuart supporters. Lauderdale dominated Scotland through much of the reign of Charles II, until his fall from favor and death; Tyrconnel attempted to build an army in Ireland for James II, an armed force which would give the King greater independence in English politics; Jeffreys presided at the famed "Bloody Assizes" at the end of Monmouth's rebellion and himself died while imprisoned in the Tower after the flight of James II.

Ell; and when they have got in but a Finger, their whole Train has followed. *Pisistratus,*[8] having procured from the City of *Athens* Fifty Fellows armed only with Cudgels, for the Security of his Person from false and lying Dangers, improved them into an Army, and by it enslaved that free State. And I have read somewhere, of the States of a Country, who having wildly granted to their Prince a Power of raising Money by his own Authority, in Cases of great Necessity; every Case, ever afterwards, was a Case of great Necessity; and his Necessities multiplied so fast, that the whole Wealth of the Country was swallowed up to supply them: As it always will be in every Country, where those who ask are suffered to judge what ought to be given. —A Practice contrary to common Sense, and which renders Liberty and Property perfectly precarious; and where it is continued, will end in taking without asking. . . .

G   *I am, &c.*

Number 84.

SATURDAY, JULY 7, 1722.

Property the first Principle of Power.—The Errors of our Princes who attended not to this.

SIR,
      The Subjects which Men understand least are generally what they talk of most, and none so much as of Government; which almost every Man thinks he has Talents to direct,

---

[8] Pisistratus was tyrant of Athens from 560 to 527 B.C. He gained power with the support of a bodyguard granted him by the Athenian people and ruled intermittently thereafter with the help of mercenaries and through alliances with other cities. For Trenchard and Gordon, his story provided an obvious proof of the dangers of even small armed forces to the liberty of the people.

and, like *Sancha Pancha,* believes he can make a very good Viceroy: He thinks nothing is necessary, but to get at the Helm, where his Business is, to command, and that of others, to obey; and then, as the aforesaid *Sancha* (Viceroy-like) says, *Who but I?* But to govern a State well, is the most difficult Science in the World; and few Men, who have ever been in the Possession of Power, have known what to do with it, or ever understood the Principles upon which all Power is founded; and their Mistakes have made endless Havock amongst Mankind.

Government is political, as a human Body is natural, Mechanism: both have proper Springs, Wheels, and a peculiar Organization to qualify them for suitable Motions, and can have no other than that Organization enables them to perform; and when those Springs or Principles are destroyed by Accident or Violence, or are worn out by Time, they must suffer a natural or political Demise, and be buried, or else smell above Ground; and though neither of them ought to be murdered, yet, when they are dead, they ought to be interred.

Now it is most certain, that the first Principle of all Power is Property; and every Man will have his Share of it in Proportion as he enjoys Property, and makes use of that Property, where Violence does not interpose. Men will ever govern or influence those whom they employ, feed, and clothe, and who cannot get the same necessary Means of Subsistence upon as advantageous Terms elsewhere. This is natural Power, and will govern and constitute the political, and certainly draw the latter after it, if Force be absent; and Force cannot subsist long without altering Property; so that both must unite together, first or last, and Property will either get the Power, or Power will seize the Property in its own Defence: for, it is foolish to think, that Men of Fortunes will be governed by those who have none, and be plundered to make such whom they despise, and have every Day new Reasons to hate, rich and insolent: And, on the other Hand, Men will contentedly submit to be governed by those who have large Possessions, and from whom they receive Protection and Support, whilst they will yet always emulate their Equals. Though the People of *Rome* extorted a Law from the Senate, that Commoners might be admitted into the chief Offices of the State jointly with the Nobles; yet all the Address and Power of the Tribunes could not for a long Time make them choose one of their own Body into those Offices, till Commoners had got Estates equal to the Nobility; and then the Balance of Property turning to the People, they carried all before them.

The only true despotick Governments now in the World, are those where the whole Property is in the Prince; as in the Eastern Monarchies, that of *Morocco*, &c. where every Man enjoying what he has by the Bounty of his Sovereign, has no Motive or Means to contend with him, but looks upon him as his Benefactor; and such as have no Property, do not think themselves to be injured: But when Men are in Possession of any Thing which they call their own, and think they have a. Right to enjoy it, they will ever contend for it, when they have the Means to do so, and will always take Advantage of every Exigence in their Prince's Affairs to attain that Right. Other Princes, who have a mind to be as arbitrary as the former, and who want either the Capacity or the Power to acquire his natural Dominion, seize by Violence the Productions of their Subjects Estates and Industry; which is a constant State of Force on one Side, and Oppression on the other: It perpetually provokes the People, and yet leaves them often the Means of revenging the Injustice done them, and must end in restoring the old Government, or in setting up some new Form by the Extinction of the present Usurpation; whereas in States truly despotick, though the Monarchs be often destroyed, yet the Monarchy is preserved entire, there being no Interest in the State capable of shaking it.

But both these Sovereignties have one Mischief in common, and inseparable from them; *viz*. as they ever subsist by standing

Armies, so they must ever be subject to the Caprices and Disgusts of the military Men, who often depose and murder their Sovereigns; but in the latter much oftener than in the former: for whilst the People have the Name, and, as they think, a Right to Property, they will always have some Power, and will expect to be considered by their Princes, and the Soldiers will expect to have Leave to oppress them, which will make continual Struggles; and the Prince, finding himself obliged to take Part with one of them, often falls in the Struggle; which was the Case of the *Roman* Emperors, most of whom were slaughtered either by the People, or their own Soldiers: whereas in a natural absolute Government, there is no Danger but from the latter alone; and if he can please them, all is well, and he is safe.

But neither of these ought to be called by the Name of Government: Both indeed are only Violence and Rapine, and the Subjection of many Millions of miserable Wretches to the wild and wanton Will of often the worst Man among them: They deface human Nature, and render the bountiful Gifts of indulgent Providence useless to the World; and the best which can be said of them is, that they make the grand Tyrant and his inferior Oppressors as miserable and unsafe as the poor Wretches whom they oppress; nor should I have mentioned them as Governments, but to make what I have further to say the better understood.

All other Dominions are either limited Monarchies, simple Aristocracies, Democracies, or Mixtures of them; and the Actions and Operations in those Governments, or the Continuance of those Governments, depend upon the Distribution and Alteration of the Balance of Property; and the not observing the Variation and the frequent Changes of the *Primum Mobile*, causes all the Combustions that we see and feel in States. Men who fancy themselves in the same Situation, as to outward Appearances, stare about them and wonder what is become of the Power which their Predecessors enjoyed, without being able to judge how they lost it by the floating of Property: They think they have a Right to enjoy the same still; and so, in spite of Nature, use Fraud and Violence to attain what they cannot hold, if it were attained: However, they will struggle for it; and this Struggle produces Contentions and Civil Wars, which most commonly end in the Destruction of one of the Parties, and sometimes of both.

Now it seems to me, that the great Secret in Politicks is, nicely to watch and observe this Fluctuation and Change of natural Power, and to adjust the political to it by prudent Precautions and timely Remedies, and not put Nature to the Expence of Throws and Convulsions to do her own Work: I do not mean by altering the Form of Government, which is rarely to be done without Violence and Danger; and therefore ought not to be attempted when any Thing else can be done, but by gentle and insensible Methods. Suppose, for Example, a limited Monarchy, which cannot subsist without a Nobility: If the Nobles have not Power enough to balance the great Weight of the People, and support the Crown and themselves, it is necessary to take some of the richest of the Commoners into that Order; if they have more Power than is consistent with the Dependence upon their Monarch, it is right to create no more, but to let those already created expire and waste by Degrees, till they become a proper Balance: If the People by Trade and Industry grow so fast, that neither the Crown nor Nobles, nor both together, can keep Pace with them; then there is no Way left, but either, by using Violence, to hazard, by an unequal Contest, what the two latter are already in Possession of, or, by using Moderation and a beneficent Conduct, to let the former enjoy all they can hope to get by a Struggle, and voluntarily to give up all odious Powers of doing Mischief, though miscalled Prerogative; which must ever be understood to be a Power of doing Good, when ordinary Provisions fail and are insufficient. . . .

I shall only observe, before I conclude this Letter, that there is no need of the caballing of different Interests, the uniting in joint Councils, and concerting regular Measures, to bring about some of the greatest Events in human Affairs; and consequently in great publick Exigences, Oppressors will find no Security in the appearing Opposition of Parties, who, like a Pair of Sheers, will cut only what is between them, when they seem most to threaten one another. When Nature has prepared the Way, all Things will tend to their proper Center; and though Men for some Time will dally and play with their lesser Interests, yet at last they will mechanically fall into their great ones, and often without intending or knowing it: Men will always feel their Strength, when they cannot reason upon it, or are afraid to do so. I could name a Party that for above thirty Years together have acted in the Interests of Liberty, and for the greatest Part of the Time could not bear the Sound of Liberty, till at last great Numbers of them are caught by the Principles which they most detested; which I intend as a seasonable Caution to all those who have the Honour to sit at the Helm of States, or to advise Princes, who may at any Time hereafter want such a *Memento*. . . .

T   *I am, &c.*

Number 94.

SATURDAY, SEPTEMBER 15, 1722.

Against Standing Armies.

SIR,
When, in King *William*'s Reign, the Question was in Debate, Whether *England* should be ruled by Standing Armies? the Argument commonly used by some, who had the Presumption to call themselves *Whigs*, and owned in the *Bal-*

ancing Letter, (supposed to be written by one who gave the Word to all the rest) was, That all Governments must have their Periods one Time or other, and when that Time came, all Endeavours to preserve Liberty were fruitless; and shrewd Hints were given in that Letter, that *England* was reduced to such a Condition; that our Corruptions were so great, and the Dissatisfaction of the People was so general, that the publick Safety could not be preserved, but by encreasing the Power of the Crown: And this Argument was used by those shameless Men, who had caused all that Corruption, and all that Dissatisfaction.

But that Gentleman and his Followers were soon taught to speak other Language: They were removed from the Capacity of perplexing publick Affairs any more: The Nation shewed a Spirit that would not submit to Slavery; and their unhappy and betrayed Master, from being the most popular Prince who ever sat upon the *English* Throne, became, through the Treachery of his Servants, suspected by many of his best Subjects, and was rendered unable by their Jealousies, to defend himself and them; and so considerable a Faction was formed against his Administration, that no good Man can recollect, without Concern and Horror, on the Difficulties which that Great and Good King was reduced to grapple with during the Remainder of his troublesome Reign.

I have lately met with some Creatures and Tools of Power, who speak the same Language now: They tell us that Matters are come to that Pass, that we must either receive the *Pretender,* or keep him out with Bribes and Standing Armies; that the Nation is so corrupt, that there is no governing it by any others Means; and, in short, that we must submit to this great Evil, to prevent a greater: As if any Mischief could be more terrible than the highest and most terrible of all Mischiefs, universal Corruption, and a military Government. It is indeed impossible for the Subtilty of Traitors, the Malice of Devils, or for the Cunning and Cruelty of our most implacable Enemies, to suggest stronger Motives for the Undermining and Overthrow of our Excellent Establishment, which is built upon the Destruction of Tyranny, and can stand upon no other Bottom. It is Madness in Extremity, to hope that a Government founded upon Liberty, and the free Choice of the Assertors of it, can be supported by other Principles; and whoever would maintain it by contrary ones, intends to blow it up, let him alledge what he will. This gives me every Day new Reasons to believe what I have long suspected; for if ever a Question should arise, Whether a Nation shall submit to certain Rules, or struggle for a Remedy? these Gentlemen well know which Side they will choose, and certainly intend that which they must choose.

I am willing to think, that these impotent Babblers speak not the Sense of their Superiors, but would make servile Court to them from Topicks which they abhor. Their Superiors must know, that it is Raving and Frenzy to affirm, that a free People can be long governed by impotent Terrors; that Millions will consent to be ruined by the Corruptions of a few; or that those few will join in their Ruin any longer than the Corruption lasts: That every Day new and greater Demands will rise upon the Corrupters; that no Revenue, how great soever, will feed the Voraciousness of the Corrupted; and that every Disappointment will make them turn upon the Oppressors of their Country, and fall into its true Interest and their own: That there is no Way in Nature to preserve a Revolution in Government, but by making the People easy under it, and shewing them their Interest in it, and that Corruption, Bribery, and Terrors, will make no lasting Friends, but infinite and implacable Enemies; and that the best Security of a Prince amongst a free People, is the Affections of his People; which he can always gain, by making their Interest his own, and by shewing that all his Views tend to their Good. They will then, as they love themselves, love him, and defend him who defends them. Upon this faithful Basis his Safety will be better established than upon the ambitions and variable

Leaders of a few Legions, who may be corrupted, disobliged, or surprised, and often have been so; and hence great Revolutions have been brought about, and great Nations undone, only by the Revolt of single Regiments.

Shew a Nation their Interest, and they will certainly fall into it: A whole People can have no Ambition but to be governed justly; and when they are so, the Intrigues and Dissatisfactions of Particulars will fall upon their own Heads. What has any of our former Courts ever got by Corruption, but to disaffect the People, and weaken themselves? Let us now think of other Methods, if it be only for the Sake of the Experiment. The Ways of Corruption have been tried long enough in past Administrations: Let us try in this what publick Honesty will do; and not condemn it before we have fully proved it, and found it ineffectual; and it will be time enough to try other Methods when this fails.

That we must either receive the *Pretender,* or keep up great Armies to keep him out, is frightful and unnatural Language to *English* Ears. It is an odd Way of dealing with us, that of offering us, or forcing upon us, an Alternative, where the Side which they would recommend is full as formidable as the Side from which they would terrify us. If we be to be governed by Armies, it is all one to us, whether they be Protestant or Popish Armies; the Distinction is ridiculous, like that between a good and a bad Tyranny. We see, in effect, that it is the Power and Arms of a Country that form and direct the Religion of a Country; and I have before shewn, that true Religion cannot subsist where true Liberty does not. It was chiefly, if not wholly, King *James*'s usurped Power, and his many Forces, and not his being a Papist, that rendered him dreadful to his People. Military Governments are all alike; nor does the Liberty and Property of the Subject fare a bit the better or the worse for the Faith and Opinion of the Soldiery. Nor does an arbitrary Protestant Prince use his People better than an arbitrary Popish Prince; and we have seen both Sorts of them changing the Religion of their Country according to their Lust.

They are therefore stupid Politicians, who would derive Advantages from a Distinction which is manifestly without a Difference: It is like, however, that they may improve in their Subtilties, and come, in time, to distinguish between corrupt Corruption and uncorrupt Corruption, between a good ill Administration and an ill good Administration, between oppressive Oppression and unoppressive Oppression, and between *French* Dragooning, and *English* Dragooning; for there is scarce any other new Pitch of Nonsense and Contradiction left to such Men in their Reasonings upon publick Affairs, and in the Part which they act in them.

Of a piece with the rest is the stupid Cunning of some Sort of Statesmen, and practised by most foreign Courts, to blame the poor People for the Misery which they bring upon them. They say, that they are extremely corrupt; and so keep them starving and enslaved by way of Protection. They corrupt them by all manner of Ways and Inventions, and then reproach them for being corrupt. A whole Nation cannot be bribed; and if its Representatives are, it is not the Fault, but the Misfortune, of the Nation: And if the Corrupt save themselves by corrupting others, the People, who suffer by the Corruptions of both, are to be pitied, and not abused. Nothing can be more shameless and provoking, than to bring a Nation, by execrable Frauds and Extortions, against its daily Protestations and Remonstrances, into a miserable Pass, and then father all those Villainies upon the People, who would have gladly hanged the Authors of them. At *Rome* the whole People could be entertained, feasted, and bribed; but it is not so elsewhere, where the People are too numerous, and too far spread, to be debauched, cajoled, and purchased; and if any of their Leaders are, it is without the People's Consent.

There is scarce such a Thing under the Sun as a corrupt People, where the Government is uncorrupt: it is that, and that alone, which makes them so; and to calumniate them for what they do not seek, but suffer by, is a great Impudence as it would be to knock a Man down and then rail at him for hurting himself. In what Instances do the People of any Country in the World throw away their Money by Millions, unless by trusting it to those who do so? Where do the People send great Fleets, at a great Charge, to be frozen up in one Climate, or to be eaten out by Worms in another, unless for their Trade and Advantage? Where do the People enter into mad Wars against their Interest, or, after victorious ones, make Peace without stipulating for one new Advantage for themselves; but, on the contrary, pay the Enemy for having beaten them? Where do the People plant Colonies, or purchase Provinces, at a vast Expence, without reaping, or expecting to reap, one Farthing from them; and yet still defend them at a farther Expence? Where do the People make distracted Bargains, to get imaginary Millions; and, after having lost by such Bargains almost all the real Millions which they had, yet give more Millions to get rid of them? What wise or dutiful People consent to be without the Influence of the Presence of their Prince, and of his Virtues; or of those of his Family, who are to come after him? No,—these Things are never done by any People; but where-ever they are done, they are done without their Consent; and yet all these Things have been done in former Ages, and in neighbouring Kingdoms.

For such guilty and corrupt Men, therefore, to charge the People with Corruption, whom either they have corrupted, or cannot corrupt, and, having brought great Misery upon them, to threaten them with more; is in effect, to tell them plainly, "Gentlemen, we have used you very ill, for which you, who are innocent of it, are to blame; we therefore find it necessary, for your Good, to use you no better, or rather worse: And, if you will not accept of this our Kindness, which, however[,] we will force upon you, if we can, we will give you up into the terrible Hands of Raw-head and Bloody-bones; who, being your Enemy, may do you as much Mischief as we, who are your Friends, have done you." I appeal to common Sense, whether this be not the Sum of such Threats and Reasonings in their native Colours.

The Partizans of *Oliver Cromwell,* when he was meditating Tyranny over the three Nations, gave out, that it was the only Expedient to balance Factions, and to keep out *Charles Stuart;* and so they did worse Things to keep him out, than he could have done if they had let him in. And, after the King's Restoration, when there was an Attempt made to make him absolute, by enabling him to raise Money without Parliament, (an Attempt which every Courtier, except Lord *Clarendon,* came into) it was alledged to be the only Expedient to keep the Nation from falling back into a Commonwealth: as if any Commonwealth upon Earth were not better than any absolute Monarchy. His Courtiers foresaw, that by their mad and extravagant Measures they should make the Nation mad, and were willing to save themselves by the final Destruction of the Nation: They therefore employed their Creatures to whisper abroad stupid and villainous Reasons, why People should be content to be finally undone, lest something not near so bad should befal them.

Those who have, by abusing a Nation, forfeited its Affections, will never be for trusting a People, who, they know, justly detest them; but, having procured their Aversion and Enmity, will be for fortifying themselves against it by all proper Ways: and the Ways of Corruption, Depredation, and Force, being the only proper ones, they will not fail to be practised; and those who practise them, when they can no longer deny them, will be finding Reasons to justify them; and, because they dare not avow the true Reasons, they must find such false ones as are most likely to amuse and terrify. And hence so much Nonsense and Improbability uttered in that Reign, and sometimes since, to vindicate guilty Men, and vilify an innocent People, who were so extravagantly fond of that Prince, that their Liberties were almost gone, before they would believe them in Danger.

It is as certain, that King *James* II. wanted no Army to help him to preserve the Constitution, nor to reconcile the People to their own Interest: But, as he intended to invade and destroy both, nothing but Corruption and a Standing Army could enable him to do it; and (thank God) even his Army failed him, when he brought in *Irish* Troops to help them. This therefore was his true Design, but his Pretences were very different: He pleaded the Necessity of his Affairs, nay, of publick Affairs; and of keeping up a good Standing Force to preserve his Kingdoms, forsooth, from Insults at Home and from Abroad. This was the Bait; but his People, who had no longer any Faith in him, and to whom the Hook appeared threatening and bare, would not believe him, nor swallow it; and if they were jealous of him, restless under him, and ready to rise against him, he gave them sufficient Cause. He was under no Hardship nor Necessity, but what he created to himself; nor did his People withdraw their Affections from him, till he had withdrawn his Right to those Affections. Those who have used you ill will never forgive you; and it is no new Thing wantonly to make an Enemy, and then calumniate and destroy him for being so.

When People, through continual ill Usage, grow weary with their present ill Condition, they will be so far from being frightened with a Change, that they will wish for one; and, instead of terrifying them, by threatening them with one, you do but please them, even in Instances where they have no Reason to be pleased. Make them happy, and they will dread any Change; but while they are ill used, they will not fear the worst. The Authors of publick Misery and Plunder may seek their own Safety in general Desolation; but to the People nothing can be worse than Ruin, from what Hand soever it comes: A Protestant Musket kills as sure as a Popish one; and an

Oppressor is an Oppressor, to whatever Church he belongs: The Sword and the Gun are of every Church, and so are the Instruments of Oppression. The late Directors were all staunch Protestants; and *Cromwell* had a violent Aversion to Popery.

We are, doubtless, under great Necessities in our present Circumstances; but to encrease them, in order to cure them, would be a preposterous Remedy, worthy only of them who brought them upon us; and who, if they had common Shame in them, would conceal, as far as they could, under Silence, the heavy Evils, which, though they lie upon every Man's Shoulders, yet lie only at the Doors of a few. The Plea of Necessity, if it can be taken, will justify any Mischief, and the worst Mischiefs. Private Necessity makes Men Thieves and Robbers; but publick Necessity requires that Robbers of all Sizes should be hanged. Publick Necessity therefore, and the Necessity of such pedant Politicians, are different and opposite Things. There is no Doubt, but Men guilty of great Crimes would be glad of an enormous Power to protect them in the greatest; and then tell us that there is a Necessity for it. Those against whom Justice is armed will ever talk thus, and ever think it necessary to disarm her. But whatever sincere Services they may mean to themselves by it, they can mean none to his Majesty, who would be undone with his Subjects by such treacherous and ruinous Services: And therefore it is fit that Mankind should know, and they themselves should know, that his Majesty can and will be defended against them and their *Pretender*, without Standing Armies; which would make him formidable only to his People, and contemptible to his Foes, who take justly the Measure of his Power from his Credit with his Subjects.

But I shall consider what present Occasion there is of keeping up more Troops than the usual Guards and Garisons; and shall a little further animadvert upon the Arts and frivolous Pretences made use of, in former Reigns, to reduce this Government to the Condition and Model of the pretended *Jure*

Divino Monarchies, where Millions must be miserable and undone, to make One and a few of his Creatures lawless, rampant, and unsafe.

T and G   *I am, &c.*

SATURDAY, SEPTEMBER 22, 1722.

Further Reasonings against Standing Armies.

SIR,

It is certain, that Liberty is never so much in Danger, as upon a Deliverance from Slavery. The remaining Dread of the Mischiefs escaped, generally drives or decoys men into the same or greater: for then the Passions and Expectations of some run high; the Fears of others make them submit to any Misfortunes, to avoid an Evil that is over; and both Sides concur in giving a Deliverer all that they are delivered from. In the Transports of a Restoration, or Victory, or upon a Plot discovered, or a Rebellion quelled, nothing is thought too much for the Benefactor, nor any Power too great to be left to his Discretion, though there can never be less Reason for giving it him than at those Times; because, for the most part, the Danger is past, his Enemies are defeated and intimidated, and consequently that is a proper Juncture for the People to settle themselves, and to secure their Liberties, since no one is likely to disturb them in doing so. . . .

Almost all Men desire Power, and few lose any Opportunity to get it; and all who are like to suffer under it ought to be strictly upon their Guard, in such Conjunctures as are most likely to encrease and make it uncontroulable. There are but two Ways in Nature to enslave a People, and to continue that Slavery over them; the first is Superstition, and the last is Force:

By the one we are persuaded that it is our Duty to be undone; and the other undoes us whether we will or no. I take it, that we are pretty much out of Danger of the first, at present, and, I think, we cannot be too much upon our Guard against the other: for, though we have nothing to fear from the best Prince in the World; yet we have every thing to fear from those who would give him a Power inconsistent with Liberty, and with a Constitution which has lasted almost a Thousand Years without such a Power, which will never be asked with an Intention to make no Use of it. . . .

I should be glad to know in what Situation of our Affairs it can be safe to reduce our Troops to the usual Guards and Garisons, if it cannot be done now. There is no Power in *Europe* considerable enough to threaten us, who can have any Motives to do so, if we pursue the old Maxims and natural Interest of *Great Britain;* which is, *To meddle no farther with Foreign Squabbles, than to keep the Balance even between* France *and* Spain. And this is less necessary too for us to do now than formerly; because the Emperor[1] and *Holland* are able to do it, and must and will do it, without us, or at least with but little of our Assistance; but if we unnecessarily engage against the Interests of either, we must thank ourselves, if they endeavour to prevent the Effects of it, by finding us Work at Home. . . .

I presume, no Man will be audacious enough to propose, that we should make a Standing Army Part of our Constitution; and if not, When can we reduce them to a competent Number better than at this Time? Shall we wait till *France* has recovered its present Difficulties; till its King[2] is grown to full Age

---

[1] The Emperor Charles VI ruled the Holy Roman Empire from 1711 to 1740. He had been an ally of Great Britain in the War of the Spanish Succession.

[2] Louis XV (1710–1774) became King in 1714, and his government was run by a succession of regent-ministers. In 1722, when Trenchard and Gordon were writing this passage, France was still recovering from the aftereffects of Louis XIV's wars and the financial schemes of John Law.

and Ripeness of Judgment; till he has dissipated all Factions and Discontents at Home, and is fallen into the natural Interests of his Kingdom, or perhaps aspires to Empire again? Or, shall we wait till the Emperor and King of *Spain* have divided the Bear's Skin, and possibly become good Friends, as their Predecessors have been for the greatest Part of two Centuries;[3] and perhaps cement that Friendship, by uniting for the common Interests of their Religion? Or, till Madam *Sobiesky's* Heir[4] is at Age, who may have Wit enough to think, that the Popish Religion is dearly bought at the Price of Three Kingdoms? Or, are we never to disband, till *Europe* is settled according to some modern Schemes? Or, till there are no Malecontents in *England*, and no People out of Employments who desire to be in them?

It is certain, that all Parts of *Europe* which are enslaved, have been enslaved by Armies; and it is absolutely impossible, that any Nation which keeps them amongst themselves can

---

[3] From the reign of King Charles I of Spain (1516–1556), who was also Holy Roman Emperor (1519–1556), to 1700, the rulers of Spain and the Empire were members of two branches of the Hapsburg family. However, Philip V of the house of Bourbon became King of Spain in 1700. Once his claim to the throne had been generally recognized in the Treaties of Utrecht (1713) and Rastatt (1714), Philip attempted to regain Spanish possessions in Italy and to assign them to his children. His policy involved him in a succession of diplomatic controversies and wars; at one time or another, his country was fighting with Austria, with Great Britain, or with France. The term "Bear's Skin" was probably derived from the expression "to sell the bear's skin before one has caught the bear," that is, to be careless of the future. Philip, by trying to claim territories which were not recognized as his, had involved his country in a series of international complications. However, there was always the possibility, as Trenchard and Gordon imply, that he might reach agreement with the Austrian Emperor on dividing the "Bear's Skin." In fact, Austria and Spain did conclude a pact in 1725 and became involved in a war with England and France in the years 1727–1729.

[4] Madam Sobieski's heir was the son of the "Old Pretender," James Edward Stuart, the heir to James II's claim to the throne. The "Young Pretender," Charles Edward, was born in 1720, and would, after James Edward's death, carry on the claim of the Catholic Stuarts to the crowns of the three kingdoms of England, Ireland, and Scotland.

long preserve their Liberties; nor can any Nation perfectly lose their Liberties who are without such Guests: And yet, though all Men see this, and at Times confess it, yet all have joined in their Turns, to bring this heavy Evil upon themselves and their Country. *Charles* II. formed his Guards into a little Army, and his Successor encreased them to three or four times their Number; and without doubt these Kingdoms had been enslaved, if known Events had not prevented it. We had no sooner escaped these Dangers, than King *William*'s Ministry formed Designs for an Army again, and neglected *Ireland* (which might have been reduced by a Message) till the Enemy was so strong, that a great Army was necessary to recover it; and when all was done Abroad that an Army was wanted for, they thought it convenient to find some Employment for them at Home. However, the Nation happened not to be of their Mind, and disbanded the greatest Part of them, without finding any of these Dangers which they were threatened with from their Disbanding. A new Army was raised again when it became necessary, and disbanded again when there was no more need of them; and his present Majesty came peaceably to his Crown, by the Laws alone, notwithstanding all his Endeavours to keep him out, by long Measures concerted to that Purpose. . . .[5]

But I desire to know of these sagacious Gentlemen [proponents of a standing army], in what Respect shall we be in a worse State of Defence than we are now, if the Army were reduced to the same Number as in King *William*'s Time, and in the latter End of the Queen's Reign; and that it consisted of the same Proportion of Horse and Foot, that every Regiment had its complete Number of Troops and Companies, and every Troop and Company had its Complement of private Men. It

---

[5] Under King William and during the War of the League of Augsburg (1688–1697), England raised a large army which reached a maximum size of 90,000 in 1694. This was reduced to 19,000 men (including 12,000 in Ireland) in 1698. Thus, at the start of the War of the Spanish Succession in 1702, a new army had to be raised.

is certain, that, upon any sudden Exigency, his Majesty would have as many Men at Command as he has now, and, I presume, more common Soldiers, who are most difficult to be got upon such Occasions; for Officers will never be wanting, and all that are now regimented will be in Half-pay, and ready at Call to beat up and raise new Regiments, as fast as the others could be filled up, and they may change any of the old Men into them, which reduces it to the same Thing. By this we shall save the Charge of double or treble Officering our Troops, and the Terror of keeping up the Corps of Thirty or Forty Thousand Men, though they are called only Thirteen or Fourteen; and sure it is high time to save all which can be saved, and, by removing all Causes of Jealousy, to unite all, who, for the Cause of Liberty, are zealous for the present Establishment, in order to oppose effectually those who would destroy it.

I will suppose, for once, what I will not grant, that those called Whigs are the only Men amongst us who are heartily attached to his Majesty's Interest; for I believe the greatest Part of the Tories, and the Clergy too, would tremble at the Thought of Popery and arbitrary Power, which must come in with the *Pretender:* But taking it to be otherwise, it is certain that the Body of the Whigs, and indeed I may say almost all, except the Possessors and Candidates for Employments or Pensions, have as terrible Apprehensions of a Standing Army, as the Tories themselves. And dare any Man lay his Hand upon his Heart, and say, That his Majesty will find greater Security in a few Thousand more Men already regimented, than in the steady Affections of so many Hundred Thousands who will be always ready to be regimented? When the People are easy and satisfied, the whole Kingdom is his Army; and King *James* found what Dependence there was upon his Troops, when his People deserted him. Would not any wise and honest Minister desire, during his Administration, that the publick Affairs should run glibly, and find the hearty Concurrence of the States of the Kingdom, rather than to carry their Measures by perpetual Struggles and Intrigues, to waste the Civil List by constant and needless Pensions and Gratuities, be always asking for new Supplies, and rendering themselves, and all who assist them, odious to their Countrymen?

In short, there can be but two Ways in Nature to govern a Nation: One is by their own Consent; the other by Force: One gains their Hearts; the other holds their Hands. The first is always chosen by those who design to govern the People for the People's Interest; the other by those who design to oppress them for their own: for, whoever desires only to protect them, will covet no useless Power to injure them. There is no Fear of a People's acting against their own Interest, when they know what it is; and when, through ill Conduct, or unfortunate Accidents, they become dissatisfied with their present Condition, the only effectual Way to avoid the threatening Evil is, to remove their Grievances.

When *Charles* Duke of *Burgundy*, with most of the Princes of *France*, at the Head of an Hundred Thousand Men, took up Arms against *Lewis* XI.[6] this Prince sent an Embassy to *Sforza*, Duke of *Milan*, desiring that he would lend him some of his veteran Troops; and the Duke returned him for Answer, That he could not be content to have them cut to pieces (as they would assuredly have been) but told him at the same time, that he would send him some Advice which would be worth Ten times as many Troops as he had; namely, That he should give Satisfaction to the Princes, and then they would disperse of course. The King improved so well upon the Advice, that he diverted the Storm, by giving but little Satisfaction to the Princes, and none at all to those who followed them. The Body of the People in all Countries are so desirous to live in Quiet, that a few good Words, and a little good Usage from their

---

[6] On Charles the Bold of Burgundy and Louis XI, see *Letter* 65, note 2, p. 154. Charles co-operated with the French nobility in a lengthy war with their nominal feudal superior, the King of France. Charles's death in 1477 brought the collapse of Burgundian resistance to the French.

Governors, will at any time pacify them, and make them very often turn upon those Benefactors, who, by their Pains, Expence, and Hazard, have obtained those Advantages for them. Indeed, when they are not outrageously oppressed and starved, they are almost as ready to part with their Liberties as others are to ask for them.

By what I have before said I would not be understood to declare absolutely against continuing our present Forces, or encreasing them, if the Importance of the Occasion requires either, and the Evils threatened be not yet dissipated: But I could wish, that if such an Occasion appear, those who think them at this Time necessary, would declare effectually, and in the fullest Manner, that they design to keep them no longer than during the present Emergency; and that, when it is over, they will be as ready to break them, as I believe the Nation will be to give them, when just Reasons offer themselves for doing so.

T   *I am, &c.*

SATURDAY, OCTOBER 27, 1722.

Discourse upon Libels.

SIR,

I Intend in this, and my next Letter, to write a Dissertation upon Libels, which are Liberties assumed by private Men, to judge of and censure the Actions of their Superiors, or such as have Possession of Power and Dignities. When Persons, formerly of no superior Merit to the rest of their Fellow-Subjects, came to be possessed of Advantages, by Means which, for the most part, they condemned in another Situation of Fortune, they often have grown, on a sudden, to think themselves a different Species of Mankind; they took it into their Heads to call themselves the Government, and thought that others had nothing to do but to sit still, to act as they bade them, and to follow their Motions; were unwilling to be interrupted in the Progress of their Ambition, and of making their private Fortunes by such Ways as they could best and soonest make them; and consequently have called every Opposition to their wild and ravenous Schemes, and every Attempt to preserve the People's Right, by the odious Names of Sedition and Faction, and charged them with Principles and Practices inconsistent with the Safety of all Government.

This Liberty has been approved or condemned by all Men, and all Parties, in proportion as they were advantaged or annoyed by it. When they were in Power, they were unwilling to have their Actions scanned and censured, and cried out, that such Licence ought not to be borne and tolerated in any well-constituted Commonwealth; and when they suffered under the Weight of Power, they thought it very hard not to be allowed the Liberty to utter their Groans, and to alleviate their Pain, by venting some Part of it in Complaints; and it is certain, that there are Benefits and Mischiefs on both Sides the Question.

What are usually called Libels, undoubtedly keep Great Men in Awe, and are some Check upon their Behaviour, by shewing them the Deformity of their Actions, as well as warning other People to be upon their Guard against Oppression; and if there were no further Harm in them, than in personally attacking those who too often deserve it, I think the Advantages which such Persons receive will fully atone for the Mischiefs which they suffer. But I confess, that Libels may sometimes, though very rarely, foment popular and perhaps causeless Discontents, blast and obstruct the best Measures, and now and then promote Insurrections and Rebellions; but these latter Mischiefs are much seldomer produced than the former Benefits; for Power has so many Advantages, so many

Gifts and Allurements to bribe those who bow to it, and so many Terrors to frighten those who oppose it; besides the constant Reverence and Superstition ever paid to Greatness, Splendor, Equipage, and the S¹ ᵌw of Wisdom, as well as the natural Desire which all or most Men have to live in Quiet, and the Dread which they have of publick Disturbances, that I think I may safely affirm, that much more is to be feared from flattering Great Men, than detracting from them.

However, it is to be wished, that both could be prevented; but since that is not in the Nature of Things, whilst Men have Desires or Resentments, we are next to consider how to prevent the great Abuse of it, and, as far as human Prudence can direct, preserve the Advantages of Liberty of Speech, and Liberty of Writing (which secures all other Liberties) without giving more Indulgence to Detraction than is necessary to secure the other: For it is certainly of much less Consequence to Mankind, that an innocent Man should be now and then aspersed, than that all Men should be enslaved.

Many Methods have been tried to remedy this Evil: In *Turky,* and in the Eastern Monarchies, all Printing is forbidden; which does it with a Witness: for if there can be no Printing at all, there can be no Libels printed; and by the same Reason there ought to be no Talking, lest People should talk Treason, Blasphemy, or Nonsense; and, for a stronger Reason yet, no Preaching ought to be allowed, because the Orator has an Opportunity of haranguing often to a larger Auditory than he can persuade to read his Lucubrations: but I desire it may be remembered, that there is neither Liberty, Property, true Religion, Art, Sciences, Learning, or Knowledge, in these Countries.

But another Method has been thought on, in these Western Parts of the World, much less effectual, yet more mischievous, than the former; namely, to put the Press under the Direction of the prevailing Party; to authorize Libels to one Side only, and to deny the other Side the Opportunity of defending themselves. Whilst all Opinions are equally indulged, and all Parties equally allowed to speak their Minds, the Truth will come out; and even, if they be all restrained, common Sense will often get the better: but to give one Side Liberty to say what they will, and not suffer the other to say any thing, even in their own Defence, is comprehensive of all the Evils that any Nation can groan under, and must soon extinguish every Seed of Religion, Liberty, Virtue, or Knowledge.

It is ridiculous to argue from the Abuse of a Thing to the Destruction of it. Great Mischiefs have happened to Nations from their Kings and their Magistrates; ought therefore all Kings and Magistrates to be extinguished? A thousand enthusiastick Sects have pretended to deduce themselves from Scripture; ought therefore the Holy Writings to be destroyed? Are Mens Hands to be cut off, because they may and sometimes do steal and murder with them? Or their Tongues to be pulled out, because they may tell Lyes, swear, or talk Sedition?

There is scarce a Virtue but borders upon a Vice, and, carried beyond a certain Degree, becomes one. Corruption is the next State to Perfection: Courage soon grows into Rashness; Generosity into Extravagancy; Frugality into Avarice; Justice into Severity; Religion into Superstition; Zeal into Bigotry and Censoriousness; and the Desire of Esteem into Vainglory. Nor is there a Convenience or Advantage to be proposed in human Affairs, but what has some Inconvenience attending it. The most flaming State of Health is nearest to a Plethory: There can be no Protection, without hazarding Oppression; no going to Sea, without some Danger of being drowned; no engaging in the most necessary Battle, without venturing the Loss of it, or being killed; nor purchasing an Estate, going to Law, or taking Physick, without hazarding ill Titles, spending your Money, and perhaps losing your Suit, or being poisoned. Since therefore every Good is, for the most part, if not always, accompanied by some Evil, and cannot be separated from it, we are to consider which does predominate; and accordingly determine our Choice by taking both, or leaving both.

To apply this to Libels: If Men be suffered to preach or reason publickly and freely upon certain Subjects, as for Instance, upon Philosophy, Religion, or Government, they may reason wrongly, irreligiously, or seditiously, and sometimes will do so; and by such Means may possibly now and then pervert and mislead an ignorant and unwary Person; and if they be suffered to write their Thoughts, the Mischief may be still more diffusive; but if they be not permitted, by any or all these Ways, to communicate their Opinions or Improvements to one another, the World must soon be over-run with Barbarism, Superstition, Injustice, Tyranny, and the most stupid Ignorance. They will know nothing of the Nature of Government beyond a servile Submission to Power; nor of Religion, more than a blind Adherence to unintelligible Speculations, and a furious and implacable Animosity to all whose Mouths are not formed to the same Sounds; nor will they have the Liberty or Means to search Nature, and investigate her Works; which Employment may break in upon received and gainful Opinions, and discover hidden and darling Secrets. Particular Societies shall be established and endowed to teach them backwards, and to share in their Plunder; which Societies, by degrees, from the want of Opposition, shall grow as ignorant as themselves: Armed Bands shall rivet their Chains, and their haughty Governors assume to be Gods, and be treated as such in proportion as they cease to have human Compassion, Knowledge, and Virtue. In short, their Capacities will not be beyond the Beasts in the Field, and their Condition worse; which is universally true in those Governments where they lie under those Restraints.

On the other Side, what Mischief is done by Libels to balance all these Evils? They seldom or never annoy an innocent Man, or promote any considerable Error. Wise and honest Men laugh at them, and despise them, and such Arrows always fly over their Heads, or fall at their Feet. If King *James* had acted according to his Coronation Oath, and kept to the Law, *Lilly-*

Bulero might have been tuned long enough before he had been sung out of his Kingdoms.[1] And if there had been no *South-Sea* Scheme, or if it had been justly executed, there had been no Libels upon that Head, or very harmless ones.[2] Most of the World take part with a virtuous Man, and punish Calumny by the Detestation of it. The best Way to prevent Libels, is not to deserve them, and to despise them, and then they always lose their Force; for certain Experience shews us, that the more Notice is taken of them, the more they are published. Guilty Men alone fear them, or are hurt by them, whose Actions will not bear Examination, and therefore must not be examined. It is Fact alone which annoys them; for if you will tell no Truth, I dare say you may have their Leave to tell as many Lyes as you please.

The same is true in speculative Opinions. You may write Nonsense and Folly as long as you think fit, and no one complains of it but the Bookseller: But if a bold, honest, and wise Book sallies forth, and attacks those who think themselves secure in their Trenches, then their Camp is in Danger, they call out all Hands to Arms, and their Enemy is to be destroyed by Fire, Sword, or Fraud. But it is senseless to think that any Truth can suffer by being thoroughly searched, or examined into; or that the Discovery of it can prejudice true Religion, equal Government, or the Happiness of Society, in any respect: Truth has so many Advantages above Error, that she wants only to be shewn, to gain Admiration and Esteem; and we see

---

[1] The song "Lilliburlero," its title derived from this nonsense word, was extraordinarily effective politically. In appearance the song was a dialogue between two Catholic Irishmen who were anticipating their triumph over the Protestant and English causes. In fact, it was a very potent bit of anti-Stuart and pro-Whig propaganda.

[2] In 1720, the South Sea Company proposed a funding of the British national debt. The acceptance of this proposal, the bribery which accompanied it, and the eventual and predictable collapse of the scheme provided the text for many sermons on contemporary corruption. See also *Letter* 15, note 6, p. 41.

every Day that she breaks the Bonds of Tyranny and Fraud, and shines through the Mists of Superstition and Ignorance: and what then would she do, if these Barriers were removed, and her Fetters taken off?

Notwithstanding all this, I would not be understood, by what I have said, to argue, that Men should have an uncontrouled Liberty to calumniate their Superiors, or one another; Decency, good Manners, and the Peace of Society, forbid it: But I would not destroy this Liberty by Methods which will inevitably destroy all Liberty. We have very good Laws to punish any Abuses of this kind already, and I well approve them, whilst they are prudently and honestly executed, which I really believe they have for the most part been since the Revolution:[3] But as it cannot be denied, that they have been formerly made the Stales of Ambition and Tyranny, to oppress any Man who durst assert the Laws of his Country, or the true Christian Religion; so I hope that the Gentlemen skilled in the Profession of the Law will forgive me, if I entrench a little upon their Province, and endeavour to fix stated Bounds for the Interpretation and Execution of them; which shall be the Subject of my next Letter.

T   *I am, &c.*

Number 101.

Saturday, November 3, 1722.

Second Discourse upon Libels.

SIR,

I Have been told that in some former Reigns, when the Attorney General took it in his Head to make innocent or doubtful Expressions criminal by the Help of forced Innuendo's, the Method of Proceeding was as follows: If the Counsel for the

Prisoner insisted, that the Words carried no seditious Meaning, but might and ought to be understood in a reasonable Sense; he was answered, that his Exception would be saved to him upon Arrest of Judgment; in the mean time the Information was tried, and the malign Intention of the Words was aggravated and left to a willing Jury; and then, upon a Motion in behalf of the Prisoner, to arrest Judgment, because the Words were not criminal in Law, he was told, that the Jury were Judges of the Intention; and having found it an ill one, it was too late to take the Exception. Whether this was ever the Truth, I have not lived long enough to affirm from my own Knowledge; or, whether this Method of Proceeding be Law now, I have not Skill enough in that Science to determine: But I think I may justly say, that if it be Law, it is worth the Consideration of our Legislature whether it ought to continue so.

It is certain, that there is no Middle in Nature, between judging by fixed and steady Rules, and judging according to Discretion, which is another Word for Fancy, Avarice, Resentment, or Ambition, when supported by Power, or freed from Fear. And I have said in my former Letter, that as there can be no Convenience but has an Inconvenience attending it, so both these Methods of judging are liable to Objections. There is a constant War between the Legislature and the Pleader; and no Law was ever enacted with so much Circumspection, but Flaws were found out afterwards in it, and it did not answer all the Purposes intended by the Law-makers; nor can any positive law be framed with so much Contrivance, but artful Men will slip out of it, and particularly in relation to Libels. There are so many Equivoques in Language, so many Sneers in Expression, which naturally carry one Meaning, and yet may intend another, that it is impossible by any fixed and stated Rules to determine the Intention, and punish all who deserve to be punished. But to get rid of this Inconvenience at the Expence of giving any Man, or Number of Men, a discretionary Power to judge another's Intentions to be criminal, when his

Words do not plainly denote them to be so, is subverting all Liberty, and subjecting all Men to the Caprices, to the arbitrary and wild Will, of those in Power. A Text in Scripture cannot be quoted, without being said to reflect on those who break it; nor the Ten Commandments read, without abuseing all Princes and great Men, who often act against them all.

I must therefore beg Leave to think, that it is a strange Assertion, which, as I have heard, has been advanced by Lawyers in *Westminster-Hall; viz.* That it is an Absurdity to affirm, That a Judge and Jury are the only People in *England* who are not to understand an Author's meaning; which, I think, may be true in many Instances, when they act judicially, and the Words which he uses, candidly construed, do not import that Meaning. *Tiberius* put many Senators to Death, for looking melancholy or dissatisfied, or enviously at his Power; and *Nero* many others, for not laughing at his Play, or laughing in the wrong Place, or sneering instead of laughing; and very probably both judged right in their Intentions; but sure no body will think amongst us, that such Examples ought to be copied. A Man, by not pulling off his Hat, or not low enough, by a Turn upon his Heel, by a frowning Countenance, or an over-pleasant one, may induce his Spectators to believe that he intends a Disrespect to one to whom it is criminal to own it; yet it would be a strange Act of Power to punish him for this Unobservance. So Words may be certainly chosen with such Art, or Want of it, that they may naturally carry a Compliment, and perhaps may mean it; and yet other People, by knowing that the Person intended does not deserve one, may think him abused. And if this Way of judging may be indulged in *Westminster-Hall,* the Lord have Mercy upon Poets, and the Writers of Dedications, and of the Epitaphs too upon Great Men. Surely it is of less Consequence to Mankind, that a witty Author should now and then escape unpunished, than that all Men should hold their Tongues, or not learn to write, or cease writing.

I do agree, when the natural and genuine Meaning and

Purport of Words and Expressions in libellous Writings carry
a criminal Intention, that the Writer ought not to escape Punishment by Subterfuge or Evasion, or by a sly Interpretation
hid in a Corner, and intended only for a Court of Justice, nor
by annexing new Names to known Things, or by using Cir-
cumlocutions instead of single Sounds and Expressions; for
Words are only arbitrary Signs of Ideas; and if any Man will
coin new Words to old Ideas, or annex new Ideas to Old Words,
and let this Meaning be fully understood, without doubt he is
answerable for it. But when Words used in their true and
proper Sense, and understood in their literal and natu[r]al
Meaning, import nothing that is criminal; then to strain their
genuine Signification to make them intend Sedition (which
possibly the Author might intend too) is such a Stretch of discretionary Power, as must subvert all the Principles of free
Government, and overturn every Species of Liberty. I own,
that with[out] such a Power, some Men may escape Censure
who deserve Censure, but with it no Man can be safe; and it
is certain, that few Men or States will be aggrieved by this
Indulgence, but such as deserve much worse Usage.

It is a Maxim of Politicks in despotick Governments, That
Twenty innocent Persons ought to be punished, rather than
One guilty Man escape; but the Reverse of this is true in free
States, in the ordinary Course of Justice: For since no Law
can be invented which can give Power enough to their Magis-
trates to reach every Criminal, without giving them, by the
Abuse of the same Law, a Power to punish Innocence and
Virtue, the greater Evil ought to be avoided: And therefore
when an innocent or criminal Sense can be put upon Words or
Actions, the Meaning of which is not fully determined by other
Words or Actions, the most beneficent Construction ought to
be made in favour of the Person accused. The Cause of Liberty,
and the Good of the Whole, ought to prevail, and to get the
better of the just Resentment otherwise due to the Impertinence
of a factious Scribbler, or the impotent Malice of a turbulent
Babbler.

This Truth every Man acknowledges, when it becomes his own Case, or the Case of his Friends or Party; and almost every Man complains of it when he suffers by it: So great is the Difference of Mens having Power in their Hands or upon their Shoulders! But at present, I think that no Party amongst us can find their Account either in the Suppression or in the Restraint of the Press, or in being very severe in their Animadversion upon the Liberties taken by it. The Independent *Whigs*[1] think all Liberty to depend upon Freedom of Speech, and Freedom of Writing, within the Bounds of Manners and Discretion, as conceiving that there is often no other Way left to be heard by their Superiors, nor to apprize their Countrymen of Designs and Conspiracies against their Safety; which they think ought to be done boldly, though in respect to Authority, as modestly as can be consistent with the making themselves understood; and such among them as have lately quitted their Independence, think themselves obliged to handle a Subject tenderly, upon which they have exerted themselves very strenuously in another Circumstance of Fortune.

Very many of the *Tories*, who may be at present ranked amongst the former Sort of Men, and who every Day see more and more the Advantages of Liberty, and forget their former Prejudices, will not be contented hereafter to receive their Religion and Politicks from an ignorant Licenser, under the Direction of those who have often neither Religion nor Politicks. And even the *Jacobites* themselves are so charmed with their own doughty Performances, that they would not lose the Pleasure of scolding at or abusing those whóm they cannot

---

[1] The phrase, obviously taken from the title of Trenchard and Gordon's own *Independent Whig,* here connotes men who have not attached themselves unswervingly to the ministry and implies the extent to which such independence was being lost because of the offices at the disposal of the government. The allegation that some "have lately quitted their Independence" might be regarded by the reader as a somewhat peculiar comment in view of Gordon's own later supposed loss of independence and his attachment to the cause of Sir Robert Walpole.

hurt.[2] Many of our spiritual Guides will not be deprived of doing Honour to themselves, and Advantage to their Flocks, from informing the World what they ought to believe by their particular Systems; and the Dissenting Preachers are willing to keep their own Flocks, and would not have the Reasonableness of their Separation judged of alone by those who differ from them, and have an Interest in suppressing them. And I believe that all our World would be willing to have some other News besides what they find in the *Gazette;* and I hope that I may venture to say, that there is no Number of Men amongst us so very popular, as by their single Credit and Authority to get the better of all these Interests.

But, besides the Reasons that I have already given, there is another left behind, which is worth them all; namely, That all the Methods hitherto taken to prevent real Libels have proved ineffectual; and probably any Method which can be taken, will only prevent the World from being informed of what they ought to know, and will increase the others. The subjecting the Press to the Regulation and Inspection of any Man whatsoever, can only hinder the Publication of such Books, as Authors are willing to own, and are ready to defend; but can never restrain such as they apprehend to be criminal, which always come out by stealth. There is no hindering Printers from having Presses, unless all Printing is forbidden, and scarce then: And dangerous and forbidden Libels are more effectually dispersed, enquired after, and do more Mischief, than Libels openly published; which generally raise Indignation against the Author and his Party. It is certain, that there were more published in King *Charles* II's and King *James*'s Times, when they were severely punished, and the Press was restrained, than have ever been since. The Beginning of *Augustus*'s Reign swarmed with Libels, and continued to do

---

[2] The Jacobites were the persistent supporters of the pretensions of the Stuart family to the throne. They took part in the uprising of 1715 and, well after the date of the original version of *Cato's Letters,* in that of 1745.

so, whilst Informers were encouraged; but when that Prince despised them, they lost their Force, and soon after died. And, I dare say, when the Governors of any Country give no Occasion to just Reflexions upon their ill Conduct, they have nothing to fear but Calumny and Falshood.

Whilst *Tiberius*, in the Beginning of his Reign, would preserve the Appearance of governing the *Romans* worthily, he answered a Parasite, who informed him in the Senate, of Libels published against his Person and Authority, in these Words; *Si quidem locutus aliter fuerit, dabo operam ut rationem factorum meorum dictorumque reddam; si perseveraverit, invicem eum odero:* "If any Man reflect upon my Words or Actions, I will let him know my Motives and Reasons for them; but if he still go on to asperse and hate me, I will hate him again."[3] But afterwards, when that Emperor became a bloody Tyrant, Words, Silence, and even Looks, were capital.

T   *I am, &c.*

Number 106.

SATURDAY, DECEMBER 8, 1722.

Of Plantations and Colonies.

SIR,
     I Intend, in this Letter, to give my Opinion about Plantations; a Subject which seems to me to be understood but by few, and little Use is made of it where it is. It is most certain, that the Riches of a Nation consist in the Number of its Inhabitants, when those Inhabitants are usually employed, and

---

[3] The quotation is from Suetonius, *Lives of the Caesars* III. 28. Suetonius reported upon the regime of Tiberius in a generally critical way. However, he lacked the depth of criticism and philosophical judgment to be found in Tacitus.

no more of them live upon the Industry of others (like Drones in a Hive) than are necessary to preserve the Economy of the Whole: For the rest, such as Gamesters, Cheats, Thieves, Sharpers, and Abbey-Lubbers, with some of their Betters, waste and destroy the publick Wealth, without adding any thing to it. Therefore, if any Nation drive either by Violence, or by ill Usage and Distress, any of its Subjects out of their Country, or send any of them out in foolish Wars, or useless Expeditions, or for any other Causes, which do not return more Advantage than bring Loss, they so far enervate their State, and let out Part of their best Heart's Blood.

Now, in many Instances, Men add more to the publick Stock by being out of their Country, than in it; as Ambassadors, publick Ministers, and their Retinues, who transact the Affairs of a Nation; Merchants and Tradesmen, who carry on its Traffick; Soldiers, in necessary Wars; and sometimes Travellers, who teach us the Customs, Manners and Policies, of distant Countries, whereby we may regulate and improve our own. All, or most of these, return to us again with Advantage. But, in other Instances, a Man leaves his Country, never, or very rarely to return again; and then the State will suffer Loss, if the Person so leaving it be not employed Abroad in such Industry, in raising such Commodities, or in performing such Services, as will return more Benefit to his native Country, than they suffer Prejudice by losing an useful Member.

This is often done by planting Colonies, which are of Two Sorts: One to keep conquered Countries in Subjection, and to prevent the Necessity of constant Standing Armies: a Policy which the *Romans* practised, till their Conquests grew too numerous, the conquered Countries too distant, and their Empire too unweildy to be managed by their native Force only; and then they became the Slaves of those whom they conquered. This Policy for many Ages, we ourselves used in *Ireland*, till the Fashion of our Neighbours, and the Wisdom of modern Ages, taught us the Use of Armies: And I wish that those who come after us may never learn all their Uses. I must confess, that I am not wise enough to enter into all the Policy made use of formerly in governing that Country; and shall in proper Time communicate my Doubts, in hopes to receive better Information. In the mean time, I cannot but persuade myself, that when our Superiors are at leisure from greater Affairs, it may be possible to offer them a Proposition more honourable to the Crown, more advantageous to each Kingdom, and to the particular Members of them, and vastly more conducive to the Power of the whole *British* Empire, than the doubtful State which they are now in. But as this is not the Purpose of my present Letter, I shall proceed to consider the Nature of the other Sort of Colonies.

The other Sort of Colonies are for Trade, and intended to encrease the Wealth and Power of the native Kingdom; which they will abundantly do if managed prudently, and put and kept under a proper Regulation. No Nation has, or ever had, all the Materials of Commerce within itself: No Climate produces all Commodities; and yet it is the Interest, Pleasure, or Convenience, of every People, to use or trade in most or all of them; and rather to raise them themselves, than to purchase them from others, unless in some Instances, when they change their own Commodities for them, and employ as many or more People at Home in that Exchange, such as would lose their Employment by purchasing them from Abroad. Now, Colonies planted in proper Climates, and kept to their proper Business, undoubtedly do this; and particularly many of our own Colonies in the *West Indies* employ ten times their own Number in *Old England,* by sending them from hence Provisions, Manufactures, Utensils for themselves and their Slaves, by Navigation, working up the Commodities that they send us, by retaining and exporting them afterwards, and in returning again to us Silver and Gold, and Materials for new Manufactures; and our Northern Colonies do, or may if encouraged, supply us with Timber, Hemp, Iron, and other Metals, and indeed with most or all the Materials of Navigation, and our Neighbours too, through our Hands; and by that Means settle a solid Naval Power in *Great Britain,* not precarious, and subject to Disappointments, and the Caprices of our Neighbours; which Management would make us soon Masters of most of the Trade of the World.

I would not suggest so distant a Thought, as that any of our Colonies, when they grow stronger, should ever attempt to wean themselves from us; however, I think too much Care cannot be taken to prevent it, and to preserve their Dependences upon their Mother-Country. It is not to be hoped, in the corrupt State of human Nature, that any Nation will be subject to another any longer than it finds its own Account in it, and cannot help itself. Every Man's first Thought will be for himself, and his own Interest; and he will not be long to seek for Arguments to justify his being so, when he knows how to attain what he proposes. Men will think it hard to work, toil, and run Hazards, for the Advantage of others, any longer than they find their own Interest in it, and especially for those who use them ill: All Nature points out that Course. No Creatures suck the Teats of their Dams longer than they can draw Milk from thence, or can provide themselves with better Food: Nor will any Country continue their Subjection to another, only because their Great-Grandmothers were acquainted.

This is the Course of human Affairs; and all wise States will always have it before their Eyes. They will well consider therefore how to preserve the Advantages arising from Colonies, and avoid the Evils. And I conceive, that there can be but two Ways in Nature to hinder them from throwing off their Dependence; one to keep it out of their Power, and the other out of their Will. The first must be by Force; and the latter by using them well, and keeping them employed in such Productions, and making such Manufactures, as will support themselves and Families comfortably, and procure them Wealth too, or at least not prejudice their Mother-Country.

Force can never be used effectually to answer the End, without destroying the Colonies themselves. Liberty and Encouragement are necessary to carry People thither, and to keep them together when they were there; and Violence will hinder both. Any Body of Troops considerable enough to awe them, and keep them in Subjection, under the Direction too of a needy Governor, often sent thither to make his Fortune, and at such a Distance from any Application for Redress, will soon put an end to all Planting, and leave the Country to the Soldiers alone; and if it did not, would eat up all the Profit of the Colony. For this Reason, arbitrary Countries have not been equally successful in planting Colonies with free ones; and what they have done in that kind has, either been by Force, at a vast Expence, or by departing from the Nature of their Government, and giving such Privileges to Planters as were denied to their other Subjects. And I dare say, that a few prudent Laws, and a little prudent Conduct, would soon give us far the greatest Share of the Riches of all *America*, perhaps drive many of other Nations out of it, or into our Colonies, for Shelter.

If Violence, or Methods tending to Violence, be not used to prevent it, our Northern Colonies must constantly encrease in People, Wealth, and Power. Men living in healthy Climates, paying easy or no Taxes, not molested with Wars, must vastly encrease by natural Generation; besides that vast Numbers every Day flow thither from our own Dominions, and from other Parts of *Europe*, because they have there ready Employment, and Lands given to them for Tilling; insomuch that I am told they have doubled their Inhabitants since the Revolution, and in less than a Century must become powerful States; and the more powerful they grow, still the more People will flock thither. And there are so many Exigences in all States, so many foreign Wars, and domestick Disturbances, that these Colonies can never want Opportunities, if they watch for them, to do what they shall find their Interest to do; and therefore we ought to take all the Precautions in our Power, that it shall never be their Interest to act against that of their native Country; an Evil which can no otherwise be averted than by keeping them fully employed in such Trades as will encrease their own, as well as our Wealth; for it is much to be feared, if we do not find Employment for them, they may find it for us.

No two Nations, no two Bodies of Men, or scarce two single Men, can long continue in Friendship, without having some Cement of their Union; and where Relation, Acquaintance, or mutual Pleasures are wanting, mutual Interests alone can bind it: But when those Interests separate, each Side must assuredly pursue their own. The Interest of Colonies is often to gain Independency; and is always so when they no longer want Protection, and when they can employ themselves more advantageously than in supplying Materials of Traffick to others: And the Interest of the Mother-Country is always to keep them dependent, and so employed; and it requires all their Address to do it; and it is certainly more easily and effectually done by gentle and insensible Methods than by Power alone.

Men will always think that they have a Right to Air, Earth, and Water, a Right to employ themselves for their own Support, to live by their own Labours, to apply the Gifts of God to their own Benefit; and, in order to it, to make the best of their Soil, and to work up their own Product: And when this cannot be done without Detriment to their Mother-Country, there can be but one fair, honest, and indeed effectual Way to prevent it; which is, to divert them upon other Employments as advantageous to themselves, and more so to their Employers; that is, in raising such Growth, and making such Manufactures, as will not prejudice their own, or at least in no Degree equal to the Advantage which they bring: And when such Commodities are raised or made, they ought to be taken off their Hands, and the People ought not to be forced to find out other Markets by Stealth, or to throw themselves upon new Protectors. Whilst People have full Employment, and can maintain themselves comfortably in a Way which they have been used to, they will never seek after a new one, especially when they meet Encouragement in one, and are discountenanced in the other.

As without this Conduct Colonies must be mischievous to their Mother-Country, for the Reasons before given, so with it the greatest Part of the Wealth which they acquire centers there; for all their Productions are so many Augmentations of our Power and Riches, as they are Returns of the People's Labour, the Rewards of Merchants, or Increase of Navigation; without which all who are sent Abroad are a dead Loss to their Country, and as useless as if really dead; and worse than so, if they become Enemies: for we can send no Commodities to them, unless they have others to exchange for them, and such as we find our Interest in taking.

As to our Southern Plantations, we are in this respect upon a tolerable Foot already; for the Productions there are of so different a Nature from our own, that they can never interfere with us; and the Climates are so unhealthy, that no more People will go or continue there than are necessary to raise the Commodities which we want; and consequently they can never be dangerous to us: But our Northern Colonies are healthy Climates, and can raise all or most of the Commodities, which our own Country produces. They constantly encrease in People, and will constantly encrease; and, without the former Precautions, must, by the natural Course of human Affairs, interfere with most Branches of our Trade, work up our best Manufactures, and at last grow too powerful and unruly to be governed for our Interest only: And therefore, since the Way lies open to us to prevent so much Mischief, to do so much Good, and add so much Wealth and Power to *Great Britain,* by making those Countries the Magazines of our naval Stores, I hope we shall not lose all these Advantages, in Compliment to the Interests of a few private Gentlemen, or even to a few Countries.

We have had a Specimen of this wise Conduct in prohibiting the *Irish* Cattle, which were formerly brought to *England* lean, in Exchange for our Commodities, and fatted here; but are now killed and sent Abroad directly from *Ireland:* And so we lose the whole Carriage and Merchants Advantage, and the Vent of the Commodities sent to purchase them.[1] And lately we have made such another prudent Law, to prevent the importing their Woollen Manufacture; which has put them upon wearing none of ours, making all or most of their own Cloth themselves; exporting great Quantities of all Sorts by stealth, and the greater Part of their Wool to rival Nations; and, by such Means it is that we are beholden to the Plague in *France*, to their *Mississippi* Company, and their total Loss of Credit, that we have not lost a great Part of that Manufacture. It is true, we have made some notable Provision to hedge in the Cuckoo, and to make all the People of that Kingdom execute a Law, which it is every Man's Interest there not to execute; and it is executed accordingly.

I shall sometime hereafter consider that Kingdom in relation to the Interest of *Great Britain;* and shall say at present only, that it is too powerful to be treated only as a Colony; and that if we design to continue them Friends, the best Way to do it is, to imitate the Example of Merchants and Shopkeepers; that is, when their Apprentices are acquainted with their Trade and their Customers, and are out of their Time, to take them into Partnership, rather than let them set up for themselves in their Neighbourhood.

T   *I am, &c.*

---

[1] Parliament used its power over Ireland's trade to restrain competition between that country's products and those of England. In 1667 and 1681, Ireland was forbidden to export certain pastoral products, including cattle, either to England or to the colonies. The restriction on cattle lasted until 1758.

[Not all the numbers of *Cato's Letters* were concerned directly with political matters. Occasionally, the two authors would venture onto other issues, though usually they would manage to give their subjects some political significance. Thus, the *Letters* discussed flattery, loyalty, and eloquence "considered politically," and "the vulgar Absurdities about Ghosts and Witches." The following number is reprinted as an example of Trenchard and Gordon's varied interests, in this case, their concern with the problem of the origins of good and evil.]

Number 109.

SATURDAY, DECEMBER 29, 1722.

Inquiry into the Origin of Good and Evil.

SIR,

We have been long confounded about the Origin of Good and Evil, or, in other Words, of Virtue and Vice. The Opinion of some is, that Virtue is a sort of real Being, and subsists in its own Nature. Others make it to consist in Rules and Cautions, given us by the supreme Being for our Conduct here on Earth and either implanted in our Natures, or conveyed to us by Revelation. A late Philosopher fetches it from the Will and Commands of the civil Magistrate. But, for my own Part, I must conceive it only as a Compound of the two last; namely, a Relation of Mens Actions to one another, either dictated by Reason, by the Precepts of Heaven, or the Commands of the Sovereign, acting according to his Duty.

It is the Misfortune of those publick-spirited and acute Gentlemen, who have obliged the World with Systems, that they always make common Sense truckle to them; and when they are bewildered, and entangled amongst Briars and Thorns, never go back the Way that they got in, but resolve to scramble through the Brake, leap over Hedge and Ditch, to get into their old Road, and so for the most part scratch themselves from Head to Foot, and sometimes break their Necks into the Bargain. They never look back, and examine whether their System be true or false, but set themselves to work to prove it at all Adventures: They are determined to solve all Contradictions, and grow very angry with all who are not so clearsighted as themselves.

This seems to me to be the Case in the present Question. The common Light of Reason has told all Mankind, that there cannot be an Effect without a Cause; and that every Cause must be an Effect of some superior Cause; till they come to the last of all, which can be no otherwise than self-existent, that is, must have existed from all Eternity. Some Sects of Philosophers have thought this first Cause to be only pure Matter, not being able to conceive that any thing can be made out of nothing, or can be annihilated again afterwards; and they suppose that Matter has been in eternal Motion, and has the Seeds of Animals, Vegetables, and of every thing else within itself, and by its constant Motion and Revolutions gives them Life, Duration, and at last Death; and throws them into the Womb of Nature again to rise up in new Shapes.

But others, by far the greatest Part of Mankind, are not able by this dark System to account for the exquisite Contrivance and comsummate Wisdom shewn in the Formation of Animals and Vegetables, in the regular and stupendous Structure and Circulation of the heavenly Bodies, and of the Earth, no more than for the Operations of our own Minds. They therefore most reasonably judged, that when so much Contrivance is necessary to bring about our own little Designs; the great Machine of Heaven and Earth, and the infinite and admirable Systems in it, could not be the spontaneous or necessary Productions of blind Matter. Thence they determine, that the first Being must have suitable Wisdom to contrive and execute these great and amazing Works.

But these latter are not so well agreed amongst themselves about the Manner of Acting, or the Operations of this Being. For some think that he must act from the Necessity of his own Nature: For, since his Being is necessary, they think that his Will and Attributes (which are Parts of his Being, essential to it, and inseparable from it) and consequently his Actions, which are Results of that Will, and of those Attributes, must be necessary too. They cannot conceive how a Being, who has the Principles and Causes of all Things within itself, could exist without having seen every thing intuitively from all Eternity; a Consideration which must exclude from his Actions all Choice and Preference, as these imply Doubt and Deliberation.

They cannot apprehend how Reason and Wisdom can be analagous in Him to what are called by the same Names in Men: For Judgment in them, as far as it regards their own voluntary Operations, is only the Balance of the Conveniences or Inconveniences which will result from their own or others Thoughts or Actions, as they have relation to Beings or Events out of their Power, and which depend upon other Causes: But if a Being can have no Causes without itself, but produces every Thing by its own Energy and Power, sees all things at once, and cannot err, as Men may, nor consequently deliberate and debate with itself, they think that it must act singly, and in one Way only; and where there is no Choice, or, which is the same thing, but one Choice, they conceive that there is always Necessity.

But the contrary is much the more orthodox and religious Opinion, and has been held by far the greatest and best Part of Mankin[d] in all Ages, before and without Revelation: They have thought that this last Opinion bordered too much upon the material System, as being able to see but little Difference in the Operations of a Being acting necessarily, and the Productions of blind Matter constantly in Action, and acting mechanically; since the Effect is supposed to be the same, though Wisdom and Contrivance, or what we are forced to call by those Names for want of another, be the first Spring, or chief Wheel of the Machine, or one Link of the Chain of Causes: And therefore Men have condemned this Opinion as impious and atheistical.

Indeed the other Speculations have been only the wild and babbling Notions of Fairy Philosophers, or of enthusiastick and visionary Madmen; for all prudent and modest Men pretend to know no more of this Being, without Revelation, than that he is wise, good, and powerful, and made all Things; and do not presume farther to enquire into the *Modus* of his Existence and Operations. However, their own Interest and Curiosity were so much concerned to guess at his Designs and Motives in placing them here, that it was impossible they could be otherwise than sollicitous and inquisitive about it; and finding, or fancying themselves to be the most valuable Part of the Whole, it was very natural for them to believe, that all was made for their Sakes; and that their Happiness was the only or chief View of the supreme Being.

With these Thoughts about him, every Man knowing what he had a Mind to have himself, and what he believed would constitute his own Happiness, and not being able to attain it without making the same Allowance to other People; Men agreed upon equal Rules of mutual Convenience and Protection, and finding these Rules dictated to them by impartial Reason, they justly believed that they were implanted within them by the Deity; and as they expected themselves Returns of Gratitude or Applause for Benefits conferred by them upon others, they thought the same were due to the original Being who gave them Life, and every thing else which they enjoyed: And this is called Natural Religion.

But as the Motive which Men had to enter into this equal Agreement, was their own Pleasure and Security, which most or all Men prefer before the Advantage of others, so they often found themselves in a Condition, by superior Power, Will, and Abilities, to circumvent those who had less than themselves, and either by artful Confederacies, Impostures, or by downright Force, to oppress them; and in order to it, have invented Systems or partial Schemes of separate Advantage, and have annexed suitable Promises or Menace to them: All which they have pretended to receive from this Divine Being. They assumed to have Communication with him, and to know his Will, and denounced his Anger against all who would not take their Word, and let them do by his Authority what they would never have been permitted to do by any other; and the Herd not daring to oppose them, or not knowing how, have acquiesced to their Tales, and come in Time to believe them. From hence sprang all the Follies and Roguery of the Heathen and Jewish Priests, and all the false Religions in the World; with all the Persecutions, Devastations, and Massacres caused by them; which were all heterogeneous Engraftments upon Natural Religion.

Almighty God thought it proper therefore at last to communicate himself again to Man, and by immediate Revelation to confirm what he at first implanted in all Mens Minds, and what was eradicated thence by Delusion and Imposture; but though he thought it not necessary to tell us more than we were concerned to know, namely, to do our Duty to himself and to one another, yet we will still be prying into his Secrets, and sifting into the Causes of his original and eternal Decrees, which are certainly just and reasonable, though we neither know his Reasons, nor could judge of them, if we did.

From hence arises this Dispute concerning the Origin of Good and Evil, amongst a thousand others. For, our Vanity inducing us to fancy ourselves the sole Objects of his Providence, and being sure that we receive our Beings from him, and consequently our Sensations, Affections, and Appetites, which are Parts of them, and which evidently depend either mediately or immediately, upon Causes without us, and seeing at the same Time, that many Things happen in the World seemingly against his revealed Will, which he could prevent if he thought fit; we either recur to the Intrigues of a contrary Being, whose Business is to thwart his Designs, and disappoint his Providence, or else account for it by a Malignity in human Nature, more prone to do Evil than Good, without considering from whence we had that Nature; for if the Malignity in it be greater than Precepts, Examples, or Exhortations can remove, the Heavier Scale must weigh down.

How much more modest and reasonable would it be to argue, that moral Good and Evil in this World, are only Relations of our Actions to the supreme Being, and to one another, and would be nothing here below, if there were no Men? That no Event can happen in the Universe but what must have Causes strong enough to produce it? That all Causes must first or last center in the supreme Cause; who, from the Existence of his own Nature, must always do what is best, and all his Actions must be instantaneous Emanations of himself? He sees all Things at one View, and nothing can happen without his Leave and Permission, and without his giving Power enough to have it effected: When therefore we see any thing which seems to contradict the Images which we have presumed to form about his Essence, or the Attributes which we bestow upon him (which Images and Attributes are, for the most part, borrowed from what we think most valuable amongst ourselves,) we ought to suspect our own Ignorance, to know that we want Appetites to fathom Wisdom, and to rest assured that all Things conduce to the Ends and Designs of his Providence, who always chuses the best Means to bring them about.

T   *I am, &c.*

Number 115.

SATURDAY, FEBRUARY 9, 1722.

The encroaching Nature of Power, ever to be watched and checked.

SIR,

Only the Checks put upon Magistrates make Nations free; and only the Want of such Checks makes them Slaves. They are free, where their Magistrates are confined within certain Bounds set them by the People, and act by Rules prescribed them by the People: And they are Slaves, where their Magistrates choose their own Rules, and follow their Lust and Humours; than which a more dreadful Curse can befal no People; nor did ever any Magistrate do what he pleased, but the People were undone by his Pleasure; and therefore most Nations in the World are undone, and those Nations only who bridle their Governors do not wear Chains.

Unlimited Power is so wild and monstrous a Thing, that however natural it be to desire it, it is as natural to oppose it; nor ought it to be trusted with any mortal Man, be his Intentions ever so upright: For, besides that he will never care to part with it, he will rarely dare. In spight of himself he will make many Enemies, against whom he will be protected only by his Power, or at least think himself best protected by it. The frequent and unforeseen Necessities of his Affairs, and frequent Difficulties and Opposition, will force him for his own Preservation, or for the Preservation of his Power, to try Expedients, to tempt Dangers, and to do Things which he did not foresee, nor intend, and perhaps, in the Beginning, abhorred.

We know, by infinite Examples and Experience, that Men possessed of Power, rather than part with it, will do any thing, even the worst and the blackest, to keep it; and scarce ever any Man upon Earth went out of it as long as he could carry every thing his own Way in it; and when he could not, he resigned. I doubt that there is not one Exception in the World to this Rule; and that *Dioclesian, Charles* the Fifth, and even *Sylla,* laid down their Power out of Pique and Discontent, and from Opposition and Disappointment.[1] This seems certain, That the Good of the World, or of their People, was not one of their Motives either for continuing in Power, or for quitting it.

It is the Nature of Power to be ever encroaching, and converting every extraordinary Power, granted at particular Times, and upon particular Occasions, into an ordinary Power, to be used at all Times, and when there is no Occasion; nor does it ever part willingly with any Advantage. From this Spirit it is, that occasional Commissions have grown sometimes perpetual; that Three Years have been improved into seven, and One into Twenty; and that when the People have done with their Magistrates, their Magistrates will not have done with the People.

The *Romans,* who knew this Evil, having suffered by it, provided wise Remedies against it; and when one ordinary Power grew too great, checked it with another. Thus the Office and

---

[1] The three absolute rulers here were among the most famous, the Roman Emperor Diocletian, the Hapsburg Emperor Charles V, and the Roman Dictator Sulla. Gaius Aurelius Valerius Diocletianus rose from an obscure background through military success to rule the remnants of the Roman Empire in 284. Nominally, he retired in 305, eight years before his death. Charles V was frustrated in his efforts to dominate Europe through his control of all the Hapsburg dominions and divided his Spanish and German possessions among his heirs. He spent his closing years in a Spanish monastery. Lucius Cornelius Sulla (138–78 B.C.) was triumphant dictator of Rome, infamous for the bloody proscriptions of his opponents. He helped set the pattern for forcible violation of the Republican constitution. While the actual events may not have supported the judgments of Trenchard and Gordon, the two authors viewed Diocletian as the bloody persecutor of early Christians, Sulla as an equally vindictive and tyrannical ruler, and Charles as the chief agent of the effort to end the Reformation and re-establish Catholicism throughout Europe.

Power of the Tribunes was set up to balance that of the Consuls, and to protect the Populace against the Insolence, Pride, and Intrenchments of the Nobility: And when the Authority of the Tribunes grew too formidable, a good Expedient was found out to restrain it; for in any turbulent or factious Design of the Tribunes, the Protest or Dissent of any one of them made void the Purposes and Proceedings of all the rest. And both the Consuls and the Tribunes were chosen only for a Year.

Thus the *Romans* preserved their Liberty by limiting the Time and Power of their Magistrates, and by making them answerable afterwards for their Behaviour in it: And besides all this, there lay from the Magistrates an Appeal to the People; a Power which, however great, they generally used with eminent Modesty and Mercy; and, like the People of other Nations, sinned much seldomer than their Governors. Indeed, in any publick Disorder, or Misfortune, the People are scarce ever in the Fault; but far on the other Side, suffer often, with a criminal Patience, the sore Evils brought wantonly or foolishly upon them by others, whom they pay dear to prevent them. . . .

And because the being frequently chosen into Power, might have Effects as bad as the long Continuance in it, *Cicero,* in his Book *De Legibus,* tells us, that there was an express Law, *Eundem Magistratum, ni interfuerint decem Anni, ni quis capito;* "That no Man should bear the same Magistracy which he had borne before, but after an Interval of ten Years."[2] This Law was afterwards strengthened with severe Penalties. Hence *Rutilius Censorius* blamed the People in a publick Speech for creating him twice *Censor:* And *Fabius Maximus* would have hindered them from chusing his Son *Consul,* though possessed

___

[2] Cicero wrote his *Laws* as a sequel to his *Republic.* The *Laws* were the rules to be followed in this ideal government and were not, in many cases, literal statements of Roman practice. The quotation comes from Book III. iii. 9.

of every Virtue proper for one, because the chief Magistracies had been too long and too often in the *Fabian* Family.[3] And there are many Instances in the *Roman* History, of Magistrates, Chief Magistrates, being degraded for their Pride, Avarice, and Male-Administration; and those who were thus degraded, were by Law disabled, like our late Directors,[4] from ever enjoying again any Post or Power. Nor were the *Romans* less careful to oblige their Magistrates as soon as they came out of their Offices and Governments, to make up their Accounts, and to give a strict Account of their good Behaviour; and for an ill one they were often condemned, and their Estates confiscated. Besides all which, to be a Senator, or a Magistrate, a certain Qualification in point of Fortune was required; and those who had run through their Fortunes were degraded from the Dignity of Senators. —A reasonable Precaution, that they who were entrusted with the Interest of their Country, should have some Interest of their own in it.

In this Manner did the *Roman* People check Power, and those who had it; and when any Power was grown quite ungovernable, they abolished it. Thus they expelled *Tarquin*,[5] and the Kingly Government, having first suffered much of it; and they prospered as eminently without it. That Government too had been extremely limited: The first *Roman* Kings were little more than Generals for Life: They had no negative Vote in the Senate, and could neither make War nor Peace; and even in the Execution of Justice, an Appeal lay from them to the People, as is manifest in the Case of the surviving *Hora-*

---

[3] Fabius Maximus (d. 203 B.C.), Roman consul and dictator, was the architect of the policy of gradually exhausting the forces of Carthage and of avoiding pitched battles with them. His relatively inexperienced son was made consul in 213.

[4] This is another reference to the directors of the South Sea Company.

[5] By traditional accounts, Tarquinius Superbus was the last king of Rome and was overthrown by a popular uprising in 510 B.C.

tius,[6] who slew his Sister. *Servius Tullius*[7] made Laws, says *Tacitus, which even the Kings were to obey.* By confining the Power of the Crown within proper Bounds, he gained Power without Bounds in the Affections of the People. But the insolent *Tarquin* broke through all Bounds, and acted so openly against Law, and the People of *Rome,* that they had no Remedy left but to expel him and his Race; which they did with glorious Success.

The Dictatorial Power was afterwards given occasionally, and found of great Use; but still it was limited to so many Months; and there are Instances where even the Dictator could not do what he pleased, but was over-ruled by the Judgment of the People. Besides, when the *Romans* came to have great and distant Territories, and great Armies, they thought the Dictatorial Power too great and too dangerous to be trusted with any Subject, and laid it quite aside; nor was it ever afterwards used, till it was violently usurped, first by *Sylla,* afterwards by *Caesar,* and then *Rome* lost its Liberty.

T   *I am, &c.*

[The following selection, *Inquiry into the Doctrine of Hereditary Right,* includes a good example of Trenchard and Gordon's use of irony. The two authors consider the various meanings given to hereditary right in various countries and at different times in history. To them, it seems that those who

---

[6] The "surviving Horatius" was one of three brothers of popular legend. Convicted of the murder of his sister, he was acquitted on appeal. The mention of Horatius provides another example of Trenchard and Gordon's use of popular Roman traditions or legends about the factually obscure early years of that Republic.

[7] Servius Tullius was the sixth king of Rome and, thus, by tradition, the predecessor of Tarquinius, mentioned in note 5 above. The story of his lawgiving and establishment of a constitution for Rome is probably fiction, the invention of a later generation desiring a precedent for its own actions.

uphold the doctrine of "divine, unalterable, indefeasible Right" have a remarkable ability to subject it to changes, conditions, and widely varying interpretations in practice.]

Number 132.

SATURDAY, JUNE 8, 1723.

Inquiry into the Doctrine of Hereditary Right.

SIR,

We have had a World of Talk both in our Pulpits and our Addresses, about Hereditary Right, and I think that no one has yet fully explained what it means; I will therefore try whether I can unfold or cut asunder the Gordian Knot. It is a divine, unalterable, indefeasible Right to Sovereignty, dictated or modified by the positive Laws, and human Constitutions of national Governments. In *France, Turkey,* and the large Eastern Monarchies, it descends wholly upon the Males. In the Kingdom, or rather Queendom of *Achem,*[1] it falls only upon Females. In *Russia* formerly it descended upon all the Males jointly, and it would not operate upon the Females at all. In *Poland* the Nobility have an human Right to confer Part of this Divine Right, but not all of it, upon whom they please; and in *Old Rome* the Soldiery often make bold to confer it: But in *England* and other Countries, all of it falls upon the Male who chances to be born first; and so on to the next, according to Priority of Birth; and for want of Males to the eldest Female, contrary to other Inheritances, which descend upon Females equally. However, though this same Right be

---

[1] Achem, variously spelled as Achin or Atchien, was a Moslem kingdom of northern Sumatra which rose to power in the late sixteenth and early seventeenth centuries. From 1641 to 1699 it was ruled by a succession of queens.

absolute and unalterable, yet it is often limited and circumscribed by human Laws, which ought not to be transgressed,
yet may be transgressed with Impunity, unless it interfere with
another Divine Right, which is the Divine Right of the High
Clergy. In all other Cases, it is boundless and unconditioned,
though given and accepted upon Conditions.

There is one Circumstance particularly remarkable in the
Exercise of this Divine Right; namely, that it may make as bold
as it thinks fit with other Divine Right (except as before ex-
cepted,) of which we have a late and very pregnant Instance,
approved by very good Churchmen, and all our able Divines,
who thanked God, publickly for thus exercising it; that is, when
the Queen made that honourable Peace which executed itself.[2]
Then the unalterable Divine Right of the Dauphin to the
Kingdom of *Spain* was given to his younger Son, and the indefeasible Divine Right of the present King of *Spain,* to the
Monarchy of *France,* was assigned over to a younger Branch
of the House of Bourbon; and sometime before, the Divine
Right of the last Emperor to the *Spanish* Dominions, was given
to the present Emperor. Nay, it seems that this alienable, unalienable, indivisible Right, is divisible too. The Divine Right
to *Sardinia,* is given to the Duke of Savoy; that of *Naples,
Sicily,* and *Flanders,* to the Emperor; and that of *Gibraltar* and
Port-Mahon to us, as long as we can keep it; which I hope we
are now in a fair Way to do. All the rest of this Divine Right,
besides what is thus disposed of, remains where it was before,
and where it should be.

But there are certain human Ingredients, Experiments, and
Operations, which are necessary to attain to this Divine Right.

---

[2] Queen Anne accepted the Peace of Utrecht, which ended the War of
the Spanish Succession, insofar as Great Britain was concerned, in 1713.
The remainder of the paragraph refers to the complicated territorial ar-
rangements which were part of the peace settlement. Great Britain left the
war by deserting its allies, while the French and Spanish left it by sur-
rendering some of their "indefeasible" claims.

In most Countries, and particularly in our own, the Priests must have a Finger in modelling the same; nor will it come down from above, and settle here below upon any Prince whatsoever, unless they say certain Words over the married Couple, which they alone have the Right to say: But in *Turkey, India,* and other Mahometan and Pagan Countries, (*heu Pudor!*)³ this same Divine Right is to be got without the Benefit of their Clergy, and will make its Conveyance through the Channel of a Strumpet; yet in most Nations all is not well, unless the Clergy say Grace over it; but then it is of no Consequence who it is that gets the Divine Babe, so he be but born in Wedlock; and in a late Instance it appeared no ways necessary whether he were born in Wedlock or not, or of whom he was born, so he were but born at all. Now, Sir, you must know, that this is a Mystery, and like some other Mysteries, wholly inexplicable, yet may be explained by the *Jacobite* Clergy; but then you are not to understand the Explication, but are to take their Words for it; and we all know that they are Men of Probity, and will not deceive you. From this Divine Right all other Rights are derived, except their own, which comes down from above too; and if the Possessors of these two Divine Rights can agree together, all is as it should be; otherwise, you are to take Notice, that God is to be obeyed before Man, and the Regale is to bow down, like the Sheaves in *Joseph*'s Dream, before the Pontificate.⁴

But this is not all: There are some Circumstances very particular and whimsical in this Divine Right. Though, as has

---

³ "Alas, the shame."

⁴ In Genesis 37:7-8 may be found the following passages describing how Joseph reported a dream to his brothers:

For behold, we were binding sheaves in the field, and, lo, my sheaf arose, and also stood upright; and, behold your sheaves stood around about, and made obeisance to my sheaf.

And his brethren said to him, Shalt thou indeed reign over us? Or shalt thou indeed have dominion over us? And they hated him yet the more for his dreams, and for his words.

been said, it may be conveyed away, yet nothing passes by the Conveyance in many Cases: Part of it may be granted and conceded to its Subjects, and yet they have no Right to keep what is so given, always excepting the High-Clergy, who may take it without being given. I had almost forgot another Conveyance of this Right, which is Conquest, or, in other Words, the Divine Right of Plunder, Rapine, Massacre: But the Right is never the worse for the Wickedness of Men; for howsoever they get Possession of Sovereign Power, the Right is that Moment annexed to the Possession, unless in special Cases, still preserving a Right to the *Jacobite* Clergy, to give a Right to whomsoever they else please. This same Right is of so odd and bizarre a Nature, that it receives no Addition or Diminution from the Consent of Men, or the Want of that Consent. It is lawful to swear to it, when there is an Interest in doing so; yet it is no ways necessary to believe what you swear, or to keep your Oath. It is not to be resisted; yet in particular Cases it may be opposed. It is limited, and yet unlimitable. You may make Laws to bind it, yet it is Treason and Damnation to defend those Laws, unless you have the *Verbum Sacerdotis*[5] on your Side.

What Contradictions, Absurdities, and Wickedness, are Men capable of! We have a Set of abandoned Wretches amongst ourselves, who seem to have a Design to destroy human Race, as they would human Reason! Every Doctrine, every Opinion, which they advance, is levelled against the Happiness of all Mankind. Nothing conduces to Virtue, to true Religion, to the present or future Interests of Men, but is represented as destructive to Piety. We are to be the Vassals of Tyrants, the Dupes of Impostors, the Zanies of Mountebanks, or else are in a State of Damnation. Men, for whose Sakes Government was instituted, have no Right to be protected by Government. Religion which was given by Almighty God to make Men vir-

---

5 "Priest's word," that is, the approval of the clergy.

tuous here, and happy hereafter; has been made use of to destroy their Happiness both here, and hereafter. Scarce any thing is discovered to be true in Nature and Philosophy, but is proved to be false in Orthodoxy: What is found to be beneficial to Mankind in their present State is represented hurtful to their future; nay, some are risen up amongst us, who are such implacable Enemies to their Species, that they make it Sin to take proper Precautions against the Danger of the Small-Pox, even when they are advised by the most able Physicians, and when these Physicians are most disinterested.

What can be more cruel, wicked and detrimental to human Society, or greater Blasphemy against the good God; than to make Government, which was designed by him to render Men numerous, industrious, and useful to one another, designed to improve Arts, Sciences, Learning, Virtue, Magnanimity and true Religion, an unnatural Engine to destroy the greatest Part of the World? to make the rest poor, ignorant, superstitious and wicked; to subject them like Cattle, to be the Property of their Oppressors; to be the tame Slaves of haughty and domineering Masters, and the low Homagers of gloomy Pedants; to work for, to fight for, and to adore those who are neither better nor wiser than themselves; and to be wretched by Millions, to make one or a few proud and insolent? And yet we are told, that this is the Condition which God has placed us in, and that it is Damnation to strive to make it better.

All these Mischiefs, and many more, are the inseparable Consequences of an indefeasible hereditary Right in any Man, or Family whatsoever; if it can never be alienated or forfeited: For if this be true, then the Property of all Mankind may be taken away, their Religion overturned, and their Persons butchered by Thousands, and no Remedy attempted: They must not mutter and complain; for Complaints are Sedition, and tend to Rebellion: They must not stand upon their Defence, for that is resisting the Lord's Anointed: They must not revile the Ministers and Instruments of his Power; for Woe be to the Man who speaketh ill of him whom the King honoureth. And all this has been told us by those who have never shewn any Regard to Authority, either human or divine, when it interfered with their own Interests. What shall I say; what Words use to express this monstrous Wickedness, this utter Absence of all Virtue, Religion, or Tenderness to the human Species: What Colours can paint it, what Pen can describe it!

Certainly, if Government was designed by God for the Good, Happiness, and Protection of Men, Men have a Right to be protected by Government; and every Man must have a Right to defend what no Man has a Right to take away. There is not now a Government subsisting in the World, but took its Rise from the Institution of Men; and we know from History when, and how it was instituted: It was either owing to the express or tacit Consent of the People, or of the Soldiers, who first erected it; it could have no more Power than what they gave it; and what Persons soever were invested with that Power, must have accepted it upon the Conditions upon which it was given; and when they renounced those Conditions, they renounced their Government. In some Countries it was hereditary; in others elective; in some discretionary; in others limited: But in all, the Government must have derived their Authority from the Consent of Men, and could exercise it no farther than that Consent gave them Leave. Where positive Conditions were annexed to their Power, they were certainly bound by those Conditions; and one Condition must be annexed to all Governments, even the most absolute, That they act for the Good of the People; for whose Sake alone there is any Government in the World. In this Regard there can be no Difference between hereditary and elective Monarchies; for the Heir cannot inherit more than his Ancestor enjoyed, or had a Right to enjoy, any more than a Successor can succeed to it.

Then the wise Question will arise, What if any Man, who has no natural Right, nor any Right over his Fellow Creatures, accept great Powers, immense Honours and Revenue, and other personal Advantages to himself and his Posterity, upon Conditions either express, as in all limited Constitutions, or implied, as in all Constitutions whatsoever; and yet either by deliberate Declarations, or deliberate Actions, publickly proclaim, that he will no longer be bound by those Conditions, that he will no longer abide by his legal Title, but will assume another that was never given him, and to which he can have no Right at all; that he will govern his People by despotick Authority; that instead of protecting them, he will destroy them; that he will overturn their Religion to introduce one of his own; and instead of being a Terror to evil Works, will be a Terror to good: I ask, in such a Case, Whether his Subjects will be bound by the Conditions, which he has renounced? Do the Obligations subsist on their Part, when he has destroyed them on his? And are they not at Liberty to save themselves, and to look out for Protection elsewhere, when it is denied where they have a Right to expect and demand it, and to get it as they can, though at the Expence of him and his Family, when no other Method or Recourse is left?

And now, O ye gloomy Impostors! O ye merciless Advocates for Superstition and Tyranny! Produce all your texts, all your knotty Distinctions! Here exert all your quaint Eloquence, your *Quiddities*, your *Aliquo modo sit, Aliquo modo non;*[6] appear in solemn Dump, with your reverential Robes, and your horizontal Hats, with whole Legions of Phantoms and Chimera's, and Cart-loads of Theology, broken Oaths, and seditious Harangues, and try whether you can maintain the Battle, and defend the Field against one single Adversary, who undertakes to put all your numerous and fairy Battalions to Flight.

Let us hear what you can say for your abdicated Idol.[7] Distinguish, if you can, his Case from that which I have repre-

---

[6] "Sometimes some are, sometimes not." A bit of legal quibbling.

[7] The idol of the Jacobites, the late James II, who had fled from England at the beginning of the Glorious Revolution of 1688–1689. The following passage concerns the various Whig charges against the overthrown monarch.

sented: Shew that Almighty God gave him a Divine Right to
play the Devil; or, if he had no such Right, that his Subjects
had none to hinder him: Prove that Kings are not instituted
for the Good of the People, but for their own and the Clergy's
Pride and Luxury: But if they be instituted for the Good of the
People, then shew that they are left at Liberty to act for their
Destruction, and that their Subjects must submit to inevitable
Ruin, yet kiss the Iron Rod whenever his Majesty pleases:
Shew that it was possible for the Kingdom to trust themselves
again to the Faith and Oaths of a Popish Prince, who, during
his whole Reign, did nothing else but break his Faith and his
Oaths, and whose Religion obliged him to do so; or that it was
possible for them to place his Son upon the Throne which he
had abdicated, (if they had believed him to be his Son,)[8] when
he was in Possession of the most implacable Enemy of their
Country, or of *Europe,* or of the Protestant Religion; and that
it would not have been direct Madness to have sent for him
afterwards from *France* or *Rome,* inraged by his Expulsion,
educated, animated, and armed with *French* and Popish Principles; and shew too, that the poor oppressed People had any
Recourse, but to throw themselves under the Protection of their
great Deliverer, who was next Heir to their Crown.

If you cannot do this, there is nothing left for you to do, but
to shew, That the late King *James* did not violate and break
the fundamental Laws and Statutes of this Realm, which were
the original Contract between him and his People; and that
he did not make their Allegiance to him incompatible with
their own Safety, for the Preservation of which he was entitled
to their Allegiance: Shew that he did not claim and exercise a
Power to dispense with their Laws; that he did not levy the
Customs without the Authority of Parliament; or that he called
Parliaments according to the Constitution which he had sworn

---

[8] The Whigs charged that the boy proclaimed as the son of James II in
1688 was in reality not his or his wife's. The boy became the "Old Pretender," called by his supporters James III.

to; and that when he intended to call one, he did not resolve
to pack it, and closeted many of the Gentlemen of *England*,
and with Promises and Menaces endeavoured to make them
practicable to his Designs: Shew that he did not disarm Protestants, and arm Papists; set up exorbitant and unlawful Courts;
cause excessive Bail to be required, excessive Fines to be imposed, and excessive Punishments to be inflicted; that he did
not prosecute Members in the *King's-Bench* for what they did
in Parliament; and discharge others committed by Parliament;
that he did not grant Fines and Forfeitures of Persons to be
tried, before their Conviction; that he did not erect an Ecclesiastical Commission directly against an Act of Parliament, and
suspended, by Virtue of it, Clergymen, for not reading in their
Churches a Proclamation, which he issued by his own Authority, to give Liberty of Conscience to Papists and Protestant
Dissenters: Shew that he did not imprison and try seven Bishops for their humble Petition against it, which Petition they
were impowered by Law to make; that he did not combine
with *France* and *Rome* to overthrow the established Church,
which he was bound to defend, and to introduce another in the
Room of it, which was worse than none; that, in order to it,
he brought not professed Papists into Offices, both Civil and
Military; sent not, nor received Ambassadors to and from *Rome,*
who were guilty of High Treason by the Laws of the Land,
and brought not from thence swarms of Locusts, to devour and
pollute every Thing that it produced; turned not out the Masters and Fellows of *Magdalen-College* against Law, for not
doing what they were sworn not to do, nor substituted in their
room, those who were not qualified by Law to be there: And
to make good all these Breaches upon our Liberties, that he did
not raise a Popish Army in *Ireland,* and another in *England,*
which had many Papists in it, without Authority of Parliament.

Shew, if you can, that he ever discovered the least Inclination
to reform these Abuses; but on the contrary, when he could
continue them no longer, that he did not desert his People:

That he dared to trust himself to a free Parliament, after he had called it, and dissolved it not again, and did not foolishly throw his great Seal into the *Thames,* that no other might be called; and when he resolved to leave his People, that he would suffer his Pretended Son to remain amongst us. Shew that you yourselves did not help to expel him; that you have not taken Oaths, repeated Oaths to this Government, and Abjurations of every other; and that you have adhered to either one or the other. When you have done this, I will allow you to be honest Men, good *Englishmen,* and true Protestants.

T   *I am, &c.*

SATURDAY, JULY 27, 1723.

Cato's Farewell

SIR,

As I have with a Success which no Man has yet met with (if I regard the Number of my Readers, and the Sale of these Papers) carried on a Weekly Performance, under this and another Title*, for near four Years; in doing which, it was impossible that I could have any other View but the Good of my Country and of Mankind; by shewing them the Advantage and the Beauty of Civil and Ecclesiastical Liberty, and the odious Deformity of Priestcraft and Tyranny: As I have vindicated Almighty God, and the Religion which he has taught us, from the Superstition, Follies, and Wickedness of Men, who would prostitute it to Ambition and Avarice, and build a visionary Empire upon the plain and simple Precepts of Christianity; and have endeavoured to remove all the Rubbish,

* *The Independent Whig.*

Grimace, and Pageantry, with which it has been long stifled and oppressed, by shewing to the World, and I think proving, that true Piety consists only in honouring the Diety, and in doing Good to Men, and not in Postures, Cringes, and canting Terms, and in barren and useless Speculations: As I think I have unanswerably shewn that Civil Governments were instituted by Men, and for the Sake of Men, and not for the Pride and Lust of Governors; and consequently that Men have a Right to expect from them Protection and Liberty, and to oppose Rapine and Tyranny wherever they are exercised; and have thereby vindicated our present Establishment, which can pretend to no other Title:

As I have done all this openly, and in the Face of the World, and have defied and called upon all the merciless and detestable Advocates for Superstition and Slavery, to shew that I have transgressed the Rules of Morality or Religion, or the Peace and Happiness of Society in any Respect; and no one has yet dared to enter the Lists against me; from whence I may reasonably hope that I have removed many of the Prejudices imbibed by Education and Custom, and set many of my Countrymen free from the wild, wicked, and servile Notions, strongly infused and planted in their Minds by Craft and Delusion:——
I shall now with Cheerfulness lay down this Paper, which I am well informed will be continued by an able Hand, under another Name, and upon various Subjects; and it is probable that I may so far join in the Undertaking, as to give my Assistance now and then, when proper Occasions require it; at least, I am not determined not to do so.[1]

There are some Papers, especially those signed *Diogenes*, which have given an undesigned Offence to some, whose Per-

---

[1] Trenchard and Gordon's plans for further literary activities were, as Gordon later explained, curtailed by the illness of Trenchard. Gordon himself did write additional pieces on political and religious subjects. The six additional numbers on politics were included by Gordon as an appendix in later editions of *Cato's Letters*.

sons I honour, and whose Opinions I reverence. For I have no
Regard to the Persons, and narrow Notions of Bigots, who will
renounce any Opinion as soon as it appears to be rational, and
would rather make Nonsense of it, than not make it a Mystery.
It is a Principle become constitutional to me, that God gave
us our Understandings to use them, and that we cannot offend
him in carrying them as far as they will carry us. However, as
the principal Question handled in those Papers is a Matter of
mere Speculation, understood but by few, and to be understood
but by few, the Belief or Disbelief of it can no way affect
human Society; and whether it be true or not, the Actions of
Men will be the same, and Men will be alike actuated by the
Motives that operate upon them, and equally pursue what they
take to be their Advantage upon the whole, at the Time, and
in the Circumstances which they are then in, whether they be
obliged to do so, or chuse to do so without being necessitated
to that Choice.

What led me into this Thought, is the Observation which
runs almost through the World, that the Bulk of Mankind in
all Ages, and in all Countries, are violently attached to the
Opinions, Customs, and even Habits, which they have been
used to; that Sounds, Shews, Prejudices, vain and idle Terrors,
Phantoms, Delusions, and sometimes Diet and Physick, are
more prevalent with them, and operate more upon them than
true and strong Reasons; and that all Animals of the same
Species act in the same Manner, and have the same Passions,
Sensations and Affections, with very little Alterations: All
which I could not account for, but by supposing those Operations to be mechanical, and the Results of their several Constitutions, as they were altered and modified by Habit, and by
different Occasions or Motives of making Use of them, such
as acted upon them.

For the rest, I saw with a sensible Concern, the many
Mischiefs, which the Leaders and Deceivers of Parties and
Factions in Religion did to the World, by throwing God's

Judgments at one another, and impiously confining his Providence and Mercies to themselves; and by applying the common Phaenomena and Events of Nature to their own Advantage, and interpreting the same as Denunciations of his Wrath against their Enemies; by which unhallowed Presumption they have raised up and inflamed implacable Hatred, Animosities and Uncharitableness amongst Men of the same Nation, who are all Brethren. I have therefore shewn, that the Almighty dispenses his Favours to all his Creatures; that his Sun shines upon the Just and the Unjust; and that it is the highest and most daring Boldness in any sort of Men to search into, and to pretend to unriddle the secret Dispensations of his Providence; to know his Mind before he unfolds it; to throw about such Balls of Contention and Wrath; and to make the Condition of Men, already too miserable by the Lot of Nature, still more miserable.

I saw the many Evils and barbarous Consequences arising from the idle and foolish Stories of Witches, Spirits, and Apparitions, first infused into our tender Minds by Nurses, Chamber-Maids, and old Women, and afterwards continued and improved by Tutors and Priests; which Impressions and Stories the wisest and bravest Men often carry about them to their Graves, and which make them always uneasy till they go thither; insomuch, that Numbers of People dare not be alone, nor go about their necessary Affairs, in the Night-time; but are kept in constant Dread of Phantoms and Non-entities; and Multitudes of Innocents have been murdered under the Appearance of Justice upon Satan's Confederates. I have therefore shewn, that there is no Foundation in Nature, in Reason or in Religion, for these Fairy Tales; that they are inconsistent with the Mercies, and even with the Being, of the great and good God; and that the telling or believing these Tales, is endeavouring to give an Empire to the Devil at the Expence of the Almighty.

It is certain, that the Capacities of Men would carry them

much farther than they are suffered to go, if they were not cramped by Custom and narrow Education, and by narrow Principles taken from those who design and derive Advantages from this their Ignorance. I have therefore lamented to see Men of large and extensive Genius, such as seemed designed by Nature to carry human Knowledge many Degrees further than it has yet gone, seemed designed to manumit their Country and Mankind from the servile and wicked Notions infused into them by prating Pedants, and babling Impostors; I say, I have lamented to see such extensive Capacities employed and conversant only about Whims, idle Speculations, empty Notions, Fairy-Dreams, and Party-Distinctions, all tending to contract and imbitter the Mind, to stifle and oppress the Faculties, and to render Men Dupes and Machines to the Ambition, Pride, and Avarice of selfish and haughty Ecclesiasticks, or of corrupt Statesmen. Nor can I see how this great Evil can ever be cured, til we change the Education of our Youth; and let Gentlemen be bred by Gentlemen, and not by Monks and Pedants; whom yet I would suffer to dream on with their Bellies full of College-Ale, and their Heads full of College-Distinctions; but think that they ought not to be trusted with the Education of our Nobility and Gentry, till they have some themselves.

And now I beg Leave again to repeat, that it was impossible I could engage in this Undertaking so troublesome to myself, and I hope of some Benefit to my Countrymen, with any View to my own personal Advantage. I hope that no one will think so meanly of my Understanding, to believe that I intended to make my Court to any of the Powers of this World, by attacking Vice, Corruption and Folly wheresoever and in whomsoever they were found. I knew that I was to walk over burning Plough-Shares; that I must provoke numerous and powerful Societies and Parties; that I must disturb Nests of Hornets, and sometimes venture too near the Lion's Den, and perhaps within the reach of *Jove's* Thunder; that Men in Possession of Reverence would not bear being told, that they did not deserve it; that those who rioted in Power, and upon the pub-lick Misfortune, would very unwillingly hear that they were trusted with that Power for the publick Advantage, and not for their own; that they were obliged by all the Motives of Honour, Virtue, and Religion, to serve and protect the People out of whose Industry and Wealth they were so highly re-warded; and that they deserved the severest Punishment if they did otherwise. I had all this before my Eyes: But armed with Innocence, and animated by Love to God and Mankind, I resolved to brave the Danger, in defiance of the worst that could happen to myself, in the Service of my Country; and I have braved it. I have now the Pleasure to see great Numbers of my Fellow-Subjects approve my Endeavours, and embrace my Opinions. I therefore here lay down this Paper, and with it the most virtuous and noble Subject that can employ the human Soul; the Subject of Religion and Government.

I am, &c.

T and G   *CATO.*

Index

THE AMERICAN HERITAGE SERIES

TOPICAL VOLUMES

The Library of Liberal Arts

Below is a representative selection from The Library of Liberal Arts. This partial listing—taken from the more than 200 scholarly editions of the world's finest literature and philosophy—indicates the scope, nature, and concept of this distinguished series.

HOBBES, T., Leviathan, I and II

HORACE, The Odes of Horace *and* The Centennial Hymn

HUME, D., Dialogues Concerning Natural Religion
Inquiry Concerning Human Understanding
Inquiry Concerning the Principles of Morals
Of the Standard of Taste, and Other Essays
Philosophical Historian
Political Essays

KANT, I., Analytic of the Beautiful
Critique of Practical Reason
First Introduction to the Critique of Judgment
Foundations of the Metaphysics of Morals
The Metaphysical Elements of Justice, Part I of *Metaphysik der Sitten*
The Metaphysical Principles of Virtue, Part II of *Metaphysik der Sitten*
On History
Perpetual Peace
Prolegomena to Any Future Metaphysics

LEIBNIZ, G., Monadology and Other Philosophical Essays

LUCIAN, Selected Works

LUCRETIUS, On Nature

MACHIAVELLI, N., The Art of War

MILL, J. S., Autobiography
On Liberty
On the Logic of the Moral Sciences
Utilitarianism

MOLIÈRE, Tartuffe

PAINE, T., The Age of Reason

PICO DELLA MIRANDOLA, On the Dignity of Man, On Being and the One, *and* Heptaplus

PLATO, Epistles
Euthydemus
Euthyphro, Apology, Crito
Gorgias
Meno
Phaedo
Phaedrus
Protagoras
Statesman
Symposium
Theatetus
Timaeus
Commentaries:
BLUCK, R., Plato's Phaedo
CORNFORD, F., Plato and Parmenides
Plato's Cosmology
Plato's Theory of Knowledge
HACKFORTH, R., Plato's Examination of Pleasure
Plato's Phaedo
Plato's Phaedrus

POPE, A., An Essay on Man

PLAUTUS, The Menaechmi

QUINTILIAN, On the Early Education of the Citizen-Orator

REYNOLDS, J., Discourses on Art

Roman Drama, Copley and Hadas trans.

RUSSELL, B., Philosophy of Science

Sappho, The Poems of

SCHLEGEL, J., On Imitation and Other Essays

SCHOPENHAUER, A., On the Basis of Morality

SHELLEY, P., A Defence of Poetry

Song of Roland, Terry, trans.

TERENCE, The Woman of Andros

VERGIL, Aeneid

VICO, G. B., On the Study Methods of Our Time

XENOPHON, Recollections of Socrates *and* Socrates' Defense Before the Jury

THE GREAT MISTAKE MYSTERIES

The Best Mistake Mystery
The Artsy Mistake Mystery
The Snake Mistake Mystery
The Diamond Mistake Mystery